Anthology of Non-Fiction

Barbara Bleiman, Kate Oliver,
Michael Simons and Lucy Webster

Edited by Barbara Bleiman, Kate Oliver, Michael Simons and Lucy Webster

Activities by Barbara Bleiman, Kate Oliver and Lucy Webster

Cover by Darrel Rees/Heart
Printed by Giunti

© The English and Media Centre 2002
18 Compton Terrace, London, N1 2UN

ISBN 0 907016 79 0

Based on *Klondyke Kate and Other Non Fiction Texts* (English and Media Centre, 1995), edited by Barbara Bleiman, Sabrina Broadbent and Michael Simons, with additional material by Jenny Grahame, and designed by Liz Earle.

Acknowledgements

Thanks to the following who have kindly given permission for the use of copyright material:

'Find it' is taken with permission from *The Rough Guide to the Internet* by Angus J. Kennedy, published 2002 by Rough Guides Ltd; an extract from *Bad Blood* is reprinted by permission of HarperCollins Publishers Ltd Copyright © Lorna Sage, 2000; 'A Prison Letter' originally published in *The Mail & Guardian*, May 1995. Copyright © 1995 Ken Saro-Wiwa. With permission of the author's estate; 'The Toughest Trip' by Don George Copyright © 2002 Lonely Planet Publications. All rights reserved. Used with permission. www.lonelyplanet.com; an extract from *McCarthy's Bar* by Pete McCarthy, 2000 reproduced by permission of Hodder and Stoughton Limited; 'Beyond Belief' Copyright © Ian McEwan 2001. First published in *The Guardian* newspaper. Reproduced by permission of the author c/o Rogers, Coleridge & White Ltd., 20 Powis Mews, London W11 1JN; an extract from *Don't Let's Go to the Dogs Tonight* by Alexandra Fuller, 2002, reproduced by kind permission of Macmillan, London, UK; an extract from *And When Did You Last See Your Father?* Copyright © Blake Morrison reproduced by permission of Granta Books; an extract from 'Arithmetic Town' by Copyright © Todd McEwen, first published in *Granta 55: Childhood* by permission of the author, c/o AP Watts Ltd; an extract from *How to be a Celebrity* by Rosemarie Jarski published by Ebury Press. Used by permission of The Random House Group Limited; 'Stud U-Like' © Diane Taylor, 'Tattoos' © Amalie Finlayson, 'It Was Not the Drug' © Fulton Gillespie, 'Night Cleaner at the Savoy' © Fran Abrams, 'How to ... Use Email' © Guy Browning, 'The Last Post' © Madeleine Reiss and 'The Secret Life of Chips' © William Leith, all reproduced by kind permission of *The Guardian/Observer;* 'Hating Football' © Andrew O'Hagan, first published in the *London Review of Books*, 27th June 2002, by kind permission of the author and *Review*; 'Big Brother – a Boring Showcase for Exhibitionists' © David Aaronovitch, 'My Beating by Refugees' © Robert Fisk and 'Klondyke Kate' © Liza Cody are published by kind permission of the authors and *The Independent* newspaper; Victor Gollancz for *Fever Pitch* by Nick Hornby; an extract from *The Great Railway Bazaar* by Paul Theroux (1975) reproduced by permission of the publishers Hamish Hamilton Ltd; extract from *The Bog People* by P.V. Glob and 'The Tollund Man' from *Wintering Out* both published by Faber and Faber Ltd; David Higham Associates for an extract from *Distant Voices* by John Pilger, published by Vintage; Reed Consumer Books for an extract from *The Lost Continent* by Bill Bryson published by William Heinemann Ltd; Random House UK Ltd. for extract from *If This is A Man* by Primo Levi; 'Interrogation; excerpted from *Just the Facts, Ma'am* Copyright © 1998 by Greg Fallis. Used with permission of Writer's Digest Books, an imprint of F&W Publications, Inc. All rights reserved; an extract from *Gather Together in My Name* Copyright © 1974 by Maya Angelou. Published by Virago Press, part of Time Warner Books UK by arrangement with Random House Inc; extract from *A Passage to Africa* Copyright © George Alagiah by permission of Time Warner Books UK; extract from *Down and Out in Paris and London* Copyright © George Orwell (1933) by permission of Bill Hamilton, Literary executor of the estate of the late Sonia Bronwell Orwell and Martin Secker and Warburg Ltd.; From *The Roving Mind* by Isaac Asimov, 'Black Holes', chapter 33, pp. 162-164 (Amherst, NY: Prometheus Books). Copyright ©1983 Isaac Asimov. Reprinted with permission.

We have made every effort to obtain copyright permission. We would be grateful to hear from anyone we have been unable to contact.

Contents

Argument

Autobiography

Reportage

Introduction

In recent years, with the introduction of the National Curriculum and the National Literacy Strategy, children going through primary and early secondary education have had an increasingly broad experience of non-fiction texts and genres. The revised National Curriculum places an emphasis on reading both literary and non-literary non-fiction. In addition, three of the four triplets in the *writing* objectives – writing to inform, explain, describe; writing to persuade, argue, advise and writing to analyse, review, comment – are predominantly non-fiction genres. To teach them effectively, teachers need to be able to offer students plenty of high quality models of such writing. Reading and writing go together hand in hand.

When *Klondyke Kate and Other Non-fiction Texts* was first published in 1995, the case had not yet been made for non-fiction being given such prominence in the English curriculum. The anthology broke new ground, winning the *TES* School Book Award and finding its way into thousands of schools and colleges. Most teachers of English now accept the importance of pupils' entitlement to experience a range of significant non-fiction texts during their time in school. However, finding such texts and making them accessible is still as time-consuming and demanding as ever. In this revised edition we have included many 'favourite' texts from the original publication, but we have also added 26 new texts, along with accompanying classroom activities. The selection represents a variety of genres, voices, times, cultures, attitudes and issues. The writing is vigorous, powerful and sustained and should be read aloud, just as one might a short story or a class novel. The activities at the end of each section aim to enhance pupils' ability to discuss, read and write about non-fiction as well as develop their own non-fiction writing repertoire. The underlying thinking behind both the selection of texts and the activities has been to make challenging texts accessible and enjoyable and to offer detailed suggestions for classroom work that will allow pupils to engage with the texts.

Most of the texts in this anthology are suitable for GCSE, GCSE Mature, A Level Language and Language and Literature. However, there are several texts which most Year 9 classes could tackle, possibly with a bit of extra teacher support.

Using the Anthology

The texts themselves appear without contextualising material, as in most short story collections. Where it is considered useful to provide background information, this appears in the activities at the end of each section.

It is important that teachers look at the activities section before embarking on work on individual texts, to see whether there are activities for pupils before reading or at a specified point during the reading.

It is essential that teachers read the texts thoroughly before using them with a class in order to be aware of the level of difficulty and the suitability of the subject matter and language for their pupils. Some of the texts contain strong language, or deal with controversial issues and teachers should use their discretion when selecting texts for reading aloud.

Klondyke Kate

The first time I saw Klondyke Kate in person was one dark rainy night at the Bath Pavilion. The MC introduced her as 'the official British Ladies Wrestling Champion', but she didn't come out. The crowd howled. She was balking because the management had got her music wrong. Someone in the back row yelled, 'Play 'Roll Out the Barrel'. She'll come out to that.' Everyone laughed, but eventually she appeared. The first thing I heard her say was, 'Shut yer mouth. Shut yer *dirty* mouth.' This was before she reached the ring. She snarled her way through an unruly mob of hissing, spitting people, already winding them up, already threatening and playing dirty. The Ladies Champion was *not* a lady.

Wrestling is basic entertainment, rude in the old sense of the word, and a wrestling crowd is not an opera crowd. The people who go to the fights are not there for subtlety or aesthetics. They want stories. They are a panto audience thirty years on, and they want to be part of the act. They need heroes and villains. In the ring, Klondyke Kate is a villain, but she is a heroine to me.

She breaks all the rules. She is fat and she shows it off in a black leotard, under bright lights, in front of hundreds of jeering, sneering men and women. Most overweight women hide. Klondyke Kate leans over the ropes and shouts, 'What are you looking at? Eh? Eh?'

She talks back. By no stretch of the imagination could she be called deferential. If you insult her, she insults you in return. 'My arse is prettier than your face,' a man screams. 'Come up and show us,' Kate screams back.

'Ignore them,' my mother used to say to me when I came home bleeding internally from some playground slight. 'Show them you're above it all.' I couldn't. I wasn't. I always made matters worse by fighting back. But like most little girls I wanted to be loved and approved of. So when I grew up I learned to control my temper. I taught myself to be nice. Most of the time. Women are supposed to look good, to behave well, to court love and approval.

Klondyke Kate doesn't. She glares across the ring at her little, perky opponent and shows no sympathy for her knee bandage. She will work mercilessly on that hurt knee later. She is not in the ring to show that women are the nurturing, caring sex. She is there to win by fair means or foul –

preferably foul. A villain is supposed to play dirty, and Kate takes the job seriously.

One thing that Channel 4's coverage of sumo has taught us is that fat people can be athletic. They can be very fast and very strong. Klondyke Kate is a fast, strong wrestler. She need not bite, choke, pull hair, stomp or gouge. She could win fairly, if she wanted to. She does not because it is her job to be the villain, and she is forced to be the villain because she is big and does not look pretty in a leotard. She does not look like what our culture demands of a heroine. She is not large-eyed, long-legged, glossy-haired, neat or petite.

Not many women have enough courage to be unpopular. It goes against our conditioning. We try hard to be acceptable. We try to look acceptable. If we are fat, we diet. If we're hairy, we depilate. If we are not pretty, we compensate with make-up and humour. If we are angry or ambitious, we hide it as far as we can. Kate does none of this. I don't know if she would rather be the popular heroine. If she would, it doesn't show, and in any case nature didn't give her much choice. She makes the best of a bad job by becoming a beautiful villain.

So there she is in the middle of the ring, a barrel in black tights. She smashes, mashes and crushes her opponent. The game little thing, pretty in pink, fights back. Kate becomes quite evil. She cheats blatantly. The crowd goes berserk. 'Dirty slag!' they scream.

A little old man is so furious that he bounds out of his seat and runs down the aisle to the ringside. The bouncers are waiting for him, but he stops short. He is beside himself with rage and probably hasn't moved this fast for forty years.

'You ...' he screams, 'you ...' Spittle flies from his mouth glittering like diamonds in the spotlights. He cannot think of anything bad enough to say. Finally it comes out: 'You ... you *bucket nut!*' he screeches.

'Come up here,' Kate sneers at the hysterical old man. 'We'll see who's got a bucket nut!' Kate's face – her bucket nut – says it all. It isn't a face to look at over the teacups.

Afterwards, when it was all over, I went to talk to Kate. She had been disqualified – there was no way her opponent could have won if she hadn't – and I was a little nervous. But the outrageous villain was calmly signing autographs at the back of the hall. She was watching the time, she said, because she had to get home to her little boy.

'What's your weak point?' I asked. 'As a fighter, I mean.' 'These,' she said, and she held out her hands. 'I keep breaking my fingers.' Her hands were tiny. 'I have to wear children's rings and gloves.'

Up there, behind the ropes, she had been so big and mean I'd never even noticed.

Liza Cody
Heroes & Villains, *The Independent*, 25 July 1992

Boring, Boring Arsenal

Arsenal v Newcastle 27.12.69

'All those terrible nil-nil draws against Newcastle,' my father would complain in years to come. 'All those freezing, boring Saturday afternoons.' In fact, there were only two terrible nil-nil draws against Newcastle, but they occurred in my first two seasons at Highbury, so I knew what he meant, and I felt personally responsible for them.

By now I felt guilty about what I had got my father into. He had developed no real affection for the club, and would rather, I think, have taken me to any other First Division ground. I was acutely aware of this, and so a new source of discomfort emerged: as Arsenal huffed and puffed their way towards 1-0 wins and nil-nil draws I wriggled with embarrassment, waiting for Dad to articulate his dissatisfaction. I had discovered after the Swindon game that loyalty, at least in football terms, was not a moral choice like bravery or kindness; it was more like a wart or a hump, something you were stuck with. Marriages are nowhere near as rigid – you won't catch any Arsenal fans slipping off to Tottenham for a bit of extra-marital slap and tickle, and though divorce is a possibility (you can just stop going if things get too bad), getting hitched again is out of the question. There have been many times over the last twenty-three years when I have pored over the small print of my contract looking for a way out, but there isn't one. Each humiliating defeat (Swindon, Tranmere, York, Walsall, Rotherham, Wrexham) must be borne with patience, fortitude and forbearance; there is simply nothing that can be done, and that is a realisation that can make you simply squirm with frustration.

Of course I hated the fact that Arsenal were boring (I had by now conceded that their reputation, particularly at this stage in their history, was largely deserved). Of course I wanted them to score zillions of goals and play with the verve and thrill of eleven George Bests, but it wasn't going to happen, certainly not in the foreseeable future. I was unable to defend my team's inadequacies to my father – I could see them for myself, and I hated them – and after each feeble attempt at goal and every misplaced pass I would brace myself for the sighs and groans from the seat next to me. I was chained to Arsenal and my dad was chained to me, and there was no way out for any of us.

3

Life after football
Arsenal v Valencia 14.5.80

Football teams are extraordinarily inventive in the ways they find to cause their supporters sorrow. They lead at Wembley and then throw it away; they go to the top of the First Division and then stop dead; they draw the difficult away game and lose the home replay; they beat Liverpool one week and lose to Scunthorpe the next; they seduce you, half-way through the season, into believing that they are promotion candidates and then go the other way ... always, when you think you have anticipated the worst that can happen, they come up with something new.

Four days after losing one cup final, Arsenal lost another, to Valencia in the European Cup-Winners Cup, and the seventy-game season came to nothing. We outplayed the Spanish team, but couldn't score, and the game went to penalties; Brady and Rix missed theirs (some say that Rix was never the same again after the trauma of that night, and certainly he never recaptured his form of the late seventies, even though he went on to play for England), and that was that.

As far as I am aware, there isn't another English club that has lost two finals in a week, although in the years to come, when losing in a final was the most that Arsenal supporters dared to hope, I wondered why I felt quite so stricken. But that week also had a beneficially purgative side effect: after six solid weeks of semi-finals and finals, of listening to the radio and looking for Wembley tickets, the football clutter was gone and there was nothing with which to replace it. Finally I had to think about what I was going to do, rather than what the Arsenal manager was going to do. So I applied for teacher training college back in London, and vowed, not for the last time, that I would never allow football to replace life completely, no matter how many games Arsenal played in a year.

Seats
Arsenal v Coventry 22.8.89

These are some of the things that have happened to me in my thirties: I have become a mortgage holder; I have stopped buying *New Musical Express* and *The Face,* and, inexplicably, I have started keeping back copies of *Q Magazine* under a shelf in my living room; I have become an uncle; I have bought a CD player; I have registered with an accountant; I have noticed that certain types of music – hip-hop, indie guitar pop, thrash metal – all sound the same, and have no tune; I have come to prefer restaurants to clubs, and dinners with friends to parties; I have developed an aversion to the feeling that a bellyful of beer gives you, even though I still enjoy a pint; I have started to covet items of furniture; I have bought one of those cork boards you put up in the kitchen; I have started to develop certain views – on the squatters who live in my street, for example, and about unreasonably loud parties – which are not altogether consistent with the attitudes I held when I was younger. And, in 1989, I bought a season-ticket for the seats, after standing on the North Bank for over fifteen years. These details do not tell the whole story of how I got old, but they tell some of it.

You just get tired. I got tired of the queues, and the squash, and tumbling half-way down the terrace every time Arsenal scored, and the fact that my view of the near goal was always partially obscured at big games, and it seemed to me that being able to arrive at the ground two minutes before kick-off without being disadvantaged in any way had much to recommend it. I didn't miss the terraces, really, and in fact I enjoyed them, the backdrop they provided, their noise and colour, more than I ever had when I stood on them. This Coventry game was our first in the seats, and Thomas and Marwood scored directly in front of us, at our end, and from our side.

There are five of us: Pete, of course, and my brother, and my girlfriend, although her place is usually taken by someone else nowadays, and me, and Andy, who used to be Rat when we were kids in the Schoolboys' Enclosure – I bumped into him on the North Bank in George's second season, a decade or so after I had lost touch with him, and he too was ready to leave the terraces behind.

What you're really doing, when you buy a seat season-ticket, is upping the belonging a notch. I'd had my own spot on the terraces, but I had no proprietorial rights over it and if some bloody big-game casual fan stood in it, all I could do was raise my eyebrows. Now I really do have my own home in the stadium, complete with flatmates, and neighbours with whom I am on cordial terms, and with whom I converse on topics of shared interest, namely the need for a new midfielder/striker/way of playing. So I correspond to the stereotype of the ageing football fan, but I don't regret it. After a while, you stop wanting to live from hand to mouth, day to day, game to game, and you begin wanting to ensure that the remainder of your days are secure.

Nick Hornby
Fever Pitch, 1992

Hating Football

I can tell you the exact moment when I decided to hate football for life. It was 11 June 1978 at 6.08pm. Scotland were playing Holland in the first stage of the World Cup Finals in Argentina. It happened to be the day of my tenth birthday party: my mother had to have the party after my actual birthday owing to a cock-up involving a cement-mixer and the police, but the party was called for that afternoon, and the cream of St Luke's Primary School turned up at 4pm, armed with Airfix battleships and enough £1 postal orders to keep me in sherbet dib-dabs for a month.

Things started to go badly the minute my father rolled into the square in a blue Bedford van. He came towards the house in the style of someone in no great mood for ice-cream and jelly, and within minutes, having scanned the television pages of the *Daily Record*, he threw the entire party out of the living room – Jaffa Cakes, Swizzle Sticks, cans of Tizer, the lot – all the better to settle down to a full 90 minutes with Ally's Tartan Army, now taking the field in Mendoza.

A full cast of Ayrshire Oompa-Loompas (myself at the head) was then marched upstairs to a requisitioned boxroom, where several rounds of pass-the-parcel proceeded without the aid of oxygen. I managed to eat an entire Swiss roll by myself and take part in several sorties of kiss, cuddle or torture before losing my temper and marching to the top of the stairs. From there, looking through the bars, I could see the television and my father's face. Archie Gemmill, at 6.08, wearing a Scotland shirt with the number 15 on the back, puffed past three Dutch defenders and chipped the ball right over the goalie's head. The television was so surprised it nearly paid its own licence fee, and my father, well, let's just say he stood on the armchair and forgot he was once nearly an altar-boy at St Mary's.

My school chums were soon carried out of the house on stretchers, showing all the signs of a good time not had, by which point my mother was mortified and my father was getting all musical. 'We're here to show the world that we're gonnae do or die,' he sang unprophetically, 'coz England cannae dae it coz they didnae qualify.' My birthday was spoiled, and I decided always to hate football and to make my father pay. I had a hidden stash of books in a former breadbin upstairs – the revenge of the English swot! – and I went out to the swingpark to read one and to fantasise about becoming the West of Scotland's first international male netball champion.

Hating football was a real task round our way. For a start, my brothers were really good at it; the fireplace had a line of gold and silver strikers perched mid-kick on alabaster bases, and they turned out to be the only part of the fireplace where my father wouldn't flick his cigarette ash. For another thing, I went to a school where Mr Knocker, the teacher, was football-daft, and he'd sooner you packed in Communion than afternoon football. But Mark McDonald – my fellow cissy – and I broke his spirit after he gave us new yellow strips to try on. We absconded from the training session and stretched the shirts over our knees, all the better to roll down Toad Hill in one round movement before dousing the shirts in the industrial swamp at the bottom. The destruction of footballing equipment was beyond the pale: we were too young for Barlinnie Prison, so we got banned to Home Economics instead and were soon the untouchable kings of eggs Mornay.

My father gave up on me. Mr Knocker put me down for a hairdresser and a Protestant. But there was always my Uncle Peter, a die-hard Celtic supporter – not like my brothers, but a real Celtic supporter, the sort who thought Rangers fans should be sent to Australia on coffin ships, or made to work the North Sea oilrigs for no pay – and Uncle Peter for a while appointed himself the very man who would, as he delicately put it, 'get all that poofy shite oot his heid before it really does him some damage'.

Game on. But not for long. Uncle Peter arranged to take me to see Celtic and Rangers play at Hampden Park. He was not unkind and had put some planning into the day out, but not as much planning as I had: for a whole week it had been my business to make sure that the only clothes available for me to wear to the treat were blue. For the uninitiated, I should say that Celtic fans tend not to wear blue, especially not to the football, and *never*, in all the rules of heaven and earth, to a Rangers game.

My uncle was distressed. He called me a Blue Nose to my face (strong words for a bishop) and when we arrived at the ground he made me walk behind him. He said that if Rangers scored and I made a noise he would throw me to the Animals (the stand in Celtic Park where men peed and drank Bovril was affectionately known as the Jungle). When Celtic lost the game 1-0 he called me a Jonah and said everything was lost with me and I should stick at school because I was bound to end up at university or worse.

Easier said than done. Academic distinction at our secondary school was mostly a matter for the birds, so the best a boy could do was to set his mind on surviving four years of PE [...] It was a wonderful education in the intricacies of human nature. I had pals, good pals, and as a resident smoker at the corner and a fearless talker-back to the nuns, I was in a position to feel confident about their loyalty when we came before Mr Scullion, the chief lion at the gym hall.

Not a bit of it. No sooner had Scullion given some Kenny Dalglish-in-the-making the chance of picking a football team than all affection and loyalty would fall away like snow off a dyke. First lesson: let nothing stand in the way of winning. My good-at-football erstwhile mate would choose one loon after another – a bandy-legged chaser here, a cross-eyed soap-dodger there – until the teams were nearly complete, except for me and Mark McDonald and some poor dwarf called Scobie left glistening with shame on the touchline. A new deputy headmaster came to the school; you could tell by looking at his hair that he was all brown rice and liberal experiment, so I wrote him a well-spelled note about reversing the method used for the picking of teams. I remember the day and the very hour.

'O'Hagan,' the PE assistant said, 'pick your team.'

I walked the few yards onto the field like General Patton contemplating the sweep of his 3rd Army over France. 'Scobie,' I said, 'McDonald.' And so it went on until every lousy player in the group had smilingly succumbed to an early invitation from the worst football picker in the history of St Michael's Academy. My hand-picked Rovers and I got beat 12-0.

When I was 12, I had nearly run out of juice on the football-hating front; it was an exhausting business not playing the game. But then I had an idea of quite intense perversity. Even my friend Mark had to shake his head sadly and note that in the arsenal of anti-football weaponry my new device was just too much: for a moment he pitied my trophy-winning brothers, he truly felt for my Scotland-deluded dad. I had gone nuclear: Jacqueline Thompson's School of Ballet.

Ah, the pleasures of disownment. Before setting off to Dancewear in Glasgow to buy my first set of pumps, however, I was dragooned by the seething Scullion to take part in a hateful five-a-side against Kilwinning Academy. What happened? With only two minutes to go I ran into the ball with the ferocity of a POW making a dash for the barbed wire. Reader, I broke my leg. As I fell to the ground in agony I was sure the *sylphides* were coming to fetch me *en point*, but – after even more delusion – I woke up in Kilmarnock Infirmary wearing a plaster cast the size of Siberia, and my father drove me home in perfect silence. The years have passed now, but I can still see him smiling in the audience many months later, the night of Jacqueline Thompson's Christmas Dance Display at the Civic Centre in Ayr, as his youngest son came onto the stage, football boots and socks pristine, whistle in mouth, to make his first appearance onstage in a dance number called – I swear to God – 'Match of the Day'.

Andrew O'Hagan
London Review of Books, 27 June 2002

Stud U-Like

Body-piercing is moving into the mainstream but is it safe?

Body piercing studios in the high street are now almost as familiar as a certain ubiquitous hamburger chain. Sporting jewellery through navel, nose or nipple has become a very mainstream fashion statement. So it is only when a rare case such as that of 39-year-old Lesley Hovvells of Llanelli, south Wales who died of septicaemia following 118 piercings, hits the headlines that we are reminded of the medical dimension.

A verdict of misadventure was recorded on Hovvells at an inquest last week. Coroner William Owen said: 'There is a considerable risk in body piercings unless hygiene is maintained. Miss Hovvells neglected these precautions and died as a direct result.'

The hygiene practices of both the piercer and the pierced are absolutely crucial to prevent potentially fatal septicaemia or other infections, but as long as sensible precautions are taken, complications are unlikely to arise. Risks exist because of inconsistencies in current legislation. Cowboy piercers outside London can operate legally without a local authority licence – only London boroughs can license piercing premises after carrying out checks to ensure that they use sterile equipment and give clients proper advice about aftercare.

Anna Kai was one of the first female body piercers to move into what was, in the early 90s, a very male-dominated scene closely linked to tattooing. Now she runs one of the biggest body-piercing operations in the UK, the Manchester and Leeds Bodypiercing Company. She is worried about under-16s who are dedicated followers of fashion but have little awareness of the dangers.

'We always turn children away but there's a piercing business I know of which makes between £800 to £1,000 a week out of business we refuse to take on.' Kai takes the medical aspect very seriously – she spent three years at medical school before gaining a qualification as a radiographer and paramedic.

'Apart from scrupulous hygiene there are two main things to be aware of – people fainting during or after a piercing, and bleeding,' she says. Her customers have to fill out a very detailed medical form and she urges them to

9

be frank about any medical condition, even if they don't consider it to be relevant.

'One person had psoriasis on her arm but didn't mention it when she came to have her navel pierced. She returned after the piercing saying she had developed psoriasis in her navel. She hadn't mentioned the condition because she'd never had it around the navel and didn't think the fact that she had it on her arm was relevant.'

Sometimes medical conditions can reveal themselves for the first time during a piercing. 'If someone faints we check their blood pressure for a while before letting them go. One man didn't recover very well and I suspected his blood sugar was low. We took him to hospital and he was diagnosed as having diabetes.'

People who seek out piercing will often not own up to having conditions like HIV or Hepatitis C. 'We treat everyone as if they have something very infectious, as that's the only way to be safe,' says Kai.

Health issues are not always uppermost in the minds of those who seek out piercings. According to James Glover, a north London piercer who has 24 piercings, aesthetics are a major consideration: 'For some people getting a new piercing is the same as getting a new outfit or a new hairdo. Having a piercing done can be slightly painful and there is a sense of having achieved something.'

After its cult beginnings, piercing has been propelled into the mainstream. So sanitised has it become that even Barbie was set to add a nose stud to her fluffy pink wardrobe – toymakers Mattel dropped the plans only when parents voiced opposition.

Social psychologist Dr Martin Skinner believes that it has always been a way of controlling how the body looks. 'Someone with a lot of body piercings takes the initiative in an encounter. A piercing is very in-your-face, it's almost like a wound. Someone with piercings does not look soft and sweet, you are forced to look at them on their terms.'

While piercing is often seen as an expression of individuality he believes there is also an element of belonging to a club. He also argues that even those who have scores of piercings are not addicted to the practice but rather demonstrate the qualities of a collector. 'It's a consumer thing, like acquiring a new car or a new pair of shoes.'

But for some trendsetters the buzz has begun to pall. Slicing the tongue down the middle to create a forked effect and placing small Teflon beads under the skin to create a scaly appearance are the newest crazes. Kai and others say they want to wait and see what the medical implications of these latest forms are before deciding whether to add them to their repertoire. So it may be a while before models sashay down the catwalk with chopped tongues and beads from their dresses sewn into their skin.

Diane Taylor
The Guardian, 3 October 2000

Tattoos

Skin Deep – a history of tattooing has just opened at the National Maritime Museum. Find out all you need to know about carving, slinging ink and pounding skin with this web guide.

1. The National Maritime Museum has a new exhibition opening today called Skin Deep – a history of tattooing, which traces the development and diversity of tattooing in Britain over the past 200 years.

2. Sailors were, of course, the first group in British society to ink their skins, after Captain Cook's voyage on the HMS Endeavour through the Pacific Islands in 1768 brought them in contact with often heavily tattooed islanders. The word tattoo also has its origins from this time: the Hawaiian, and Polynesian, word for tattoo being kakau, or tatau.

3. Tattooing started to take off in Britain in the late 1800s. It gained a royal sanction in 1862 when the Prince of Wales, in a visit to the Holy Land, had the Jerusalem Cross tattooed on his arm. Then, around 1870, D.W. Purdy opened a tattooing shop in north London, thought to be the first professional studio in Great Britain.

4. In 1891, Samuel O'Reilly invented the first tattoo machine, based on a piece of equipment originally designed by Thomas Edison for engraving hard surfaces. Ouch. But, of course, that took the hard graft out of the craft and, by 1900, it was estimated that 90% of the United States Navy were tattooed.

5. These days, though, it is not only bluejackets who like carving, slinging ink and pounding skin. Tattoos are everywhere, from your local bank clerk to your little sister – even your mum.

6. An eye-watering number of celebrities have tattoos. During the filming of the *Lord of the Rings* in New Zealand, the nine actors who formed the Fellowship of the Ring all got an Elvish tattoo, meaning 'the Nine'.

7. For many people, tattoos are a statement of highly personal significance and meaning. Prisoners' tattoos can read like books, telling the history of their past convictions, types of offence and level of authority within prison. They also use ink to commemorate their life outside prison walls, marking their bodies with the names of their loved ones and family members.

8. Having your lover's name indelibly marked on your skin can have its problems. One of Pamela Anderson's tattoos used to say Tommy, after her then-husband Tommy Lee, but had to be changed to Mommy after their break-up. According to Pammy, 'Tattoos are like stories – they're symbolic of the important moments in your life.' Presumably she has since changed her mind after reports that she contracted hepatitis C when she shared a tattoo needle with Mr Lee. And our very own David Beckham is famous for his body art: along with a pair of angel wings across his shoulder blades, he has his son's name, Brooklyn, writ large across his lower back. Another tattoo, intended to spell out his wife's name on his arm in Hindi, was said to be misspelt, reading 'Vihctoria' instead of 'Victoria'. A spokesperson for Mr Beckham denied the mistake, saying: 'The tattoo has been checked by a Hindu expert.'

9. Many celebrities, however, wary of forever staining their glowing hides, adorn themselves instead with temporary tattoos, or the henna-based mehndi tattoos that have been used for thousands of years in Africa, Asia, and the Middle East to decorate the hands and feet for weddings and other celebrations.

10. This seems sensible: after all a tattoo is forever, and it is estimated that more than 50% of people who get a tattoo later regret it. And removal of tattoos can often leave scars and skin discolouration – which means that unless you have a very good reason, don't give a brass monkey, or are three sheets to the wind and incapable of rational thought, it might be wise to think before you ink.

Amalie Finlayson
The Guardian, 22 March 2002

What is a Celebrity?

A celebrity is a person who is known for his well-knownness. **Daniel Boorstin**

A celebrity is one who is known to many persons he is glad he doesn't know. **H.L. Mencken**

A celebrity is a person whose name is in everything except the phone directory. **Fred Allen**

A celebrity is a person in the public eye as evidenced through substantial mainstream national and international media, awards and achievements. **The New York Celebrity Assistants Association**

A celebrity is anyone who spends more than two hours working on his hair. **Steve Martin**

As these varied definitions demonstrate, 'celebrity' is a slippery word that runs the gamut of meaning from the highest form of praise to the lowest form of insult. Perhaps 'celebrity' is best thought of as a generic term for the species, *homo celebritus*, of which there are many subspecies. From the top of the food chain to the bottom, the main varieties are as follows:

Celebrity Food Chain

Legend A dead celebrity whose reason for becoming famous has been forgotten e.g. Attila the Hun.

Living Legend A living celebrity whose reason for becoming famous has been forgotten e.g. Elizabeth Taylor.

National Treasure Like a living legend but held in more affection. Differs from country to country e.g. in the UK, Dame Judi Dench is a national treasure, like a cup of tea or *The Book of Common Prayer*. In the USA, Johnny Carson is a national treasure, like Coca-Cola or chewing gum.

Superstar A celebrity at the pinnacle of their fame.

Star A star that is not yet super.

Icon A celebrity who symbolizes something and who kids copy.

> **Cult** A celebrity 50 people have heard of.
>
> **Micro-celebrity** The celebrity equivalent of a micro-scooter i.e. a fad that will disappear as rapidly as it appeared.
>
> **'Celebrity'** A nonentity who thinks they're a celebrity.
>
> **Wannabe** Famous in their own imagination – so far.

Celebrity life cycle

There are five stages in the life of a celebrity: Who is Julia Roberts? Get me Julia Roberts. Get me a Julia Roberts type. Get me a young Julia Roberts. Who is Julia Roberts?

What do you actually do?

The word 'celebrity' means 'renowned' in Latin: that is, one who is celebrated.

Traditionally, a person had to have a special talent or achieve some distinction to become a celebrity. If you won a famous battle, or conquered a mountain, you'd be celebrated for that achievement. Modern celebrities don't have to do anything to be admired: they are celebrated simply for being. Like the lilies of the field, modern celebrities neither toil nor spin. At a red-carpet event, a reporter rushed up to Caprice Bourret, and demanded to know: 'What do you actually do?' Ask not what your celebrity can do for you. Ask what you can do for your celebrity.

What are celebrities *for*?

If celebrities don't do anything, what is the point of them?

Celebrities are pointless, that is the point of them. Celebrities are there to kill time for those who like it better dead. They're trivia for the train-ride home. The postmodern ironic take on fame treats celebrities as entertainment fluff to be mocked and ridiculed. 'All that money, and still no taste!' 'Another boyfriend? What a tart!' Celebrities are not to be taken seriously. But as Agatha Christie once said of celebrity: 'It is completely unimportant. That is why it is so interesting.'

After 9/11, the media declared celebrity dead. The diets and lifestyles of very rich and shallow people were no longer of interest to anybody apparently. Trivia had been swept away; we were entering a new era where serious issues and weighty concerns would take precedence.

But the death knell for celebrity proved premature. More resilient than a cockroach, the species survived. No thanks to the media, it has to be said. Long frustrated by the stranglehold of celebrity, the media would gladly have hammered the final nail in the coffin of celebrity.

Celebrities survived because people want them to survive. They may be trivial, but that is precisely why they are needed. Mankind, said T.S. Eliot, cannot stand too much reality. Celebrities are an escape from humdrum existence. They are a change from the shootings and starving and plane crashes. They add color to a drab world.

Celebrities are also central to people's emotional lives. They drive our dreams and reaffirm our deepest desires and fondest hopes. People identify with stories about celebrities – the love affairs, the break-ups, who's gay, who's pregnant – and connect on a personal, human level. The impersonal power games of politics or foreign affairs seem remote and incomprehensible in comparison.

People live vicariously through celebrities. They do all the things we would like to do: they behave outrageously and irresponsibly so we don't have to. 'People lead flat lives. They need some sort of peak. I like to be that peak,' declared Michael Hutchence who paid the ultimate price for a life lived at the peak.

St Augustine said that there is a God-shaped hole in the human spirit. Celebrities presently fill that spiritual vacuum. They haven't taken the place of God; rather, they have become profane saints and martyrs. They embody qualities people aspire to possess themselves: fame, sex, beauty and money.

In this fast-moving, uncertain world, celebrities bring people together. Marriages split, families fragment, people no longer know their neighbors, but celebrities are a common frame of reference, a social currency we can all share. Information technology has transformed the world into a virtual village to gossip in, but it also needs people to gossip about. Celebrities serve that purpose.

The future of celebrity

Some argue that the market is saturated; celebrity has gone as far as it can. Nothing could be further from the truth.

Everybody who's nobody wants to be somebody. Ask any kid what they want to be when they grow up and they no longer say 'train driver' or 'nurse', they just say, 'I wannabe famous.' The desire to become a celebrity is the ethic on which the world turns. The imprimatur of celebrity is on everything from news to entertainment to charity. Everything is a branch of showbiz. Celebrity is so integral to our culture that it surely can't be long before it is enshrined in the Constitution: life, liberty, the pursuit of happiness and fifteen minutes of fame.

Rosemarie Jarski
How to be a Celebrity, 2002

Style and Culture Activities

Klondyke Kate

1. The writer

This piece comes from the *The Independent Magazine* which used to run a column called 'Heroes and Villains' in which well known people were invited to write about someone they admire or detest. The editor of the column says that the choice of hero or villain should tell the readers as much about the writer as about the object of his or her attention. How much does this piece tell you about the writer Liza Cody?
• In pairs, look through 'Klondyke Kate' again and note down where and what information we get about the writer from the text on a chart like this one.

Quote or reference	What this tells us about Liza Cody
'Not many women have enough courage to be unpopular'	She admires women who break society's rules about female behaviour

2. My hero

• Working in small groups, draw up a list of people that you are interested in and think would be suitable as subjects for the 'Heroes and Villains' column in the magazine. Here are some suggestions to help you get started.

Emmeline Pankhurst
Will Smith
The Tweenies
Kylie Minogue
David Beckham

• Working in pairs or alone, choose one person that you want to write about. Draft a piece of writing about them called 'My Hero'.
• When you are happy with what you have written, try writing about the same person but as if you hate and detest them calling it 'My Villain'.

Boring, Boring Arsenal

1. Writing in the same style

• Share out the extracts. Help each other to think about Hornby's writing style by answering the following questions about your extract.

– Is this written using a lot of specialist football language that excludes non-football fans or does he manage to avoid that?
– Is this written in very formal language which makes the reader feel distanced or in a conversational style that draws the reader in (by using personal pronouns for example, like 'they', 'I' and 'you')?
– Does this writer take himself and his subject very seriously?
– Is this just about football?

• Now try writing a short paragraph about something you're keen on, in the same style as Nick Hornby.

2. Fans and fanatics – 'Seats'

• How accurate is Nick Hornby's description of the obsessed fan? Does such behaviour apply only to football?

• Talk for a few minutes about obsessions that you have had yourself.

• In small groups draw up a list of ten symptoms of the obsessive fan. It doesn't have to be about football, it could be about a singer, cheese and onion crisps or some other obsession.

3. Getting older

• Look again at the final section where Nick Hornby writes about getting older and describes some of the tell-tale signs.

• Write your own short piece about becoming a teenager in which you point out all the little changes in habits, attitudes, lifestyle, behaviour and possessions. You could begin like this:

'These are some of the things that have happened to me in my teens. I stopped collecting lollipop sticks ...'

Hating Football

1. Before reading
The first sentence of this piece is:
'I can tell you the exact moment when I decided to hate football for life.'
• With a partner come up with three possible explanations for the writer's hatred of football.

2. The first paragraph
• Now read the first paragraph. Discuss how the writer makes you want to read on.

3. Writing about memories
• Finish reading the piece.

• Talk about whether the writer convinces you that these are real memories and that he can remember how he thought and felt as a child.

• Find a quotation from the text to support your opinion and be prepared to explain to the class what it was about this extract that you found particularly convincing or unconvincing.

One of the techniques the writer uses is to include very specific details of his 70s childhood such as brand names, a football song and party games.
• Find two or three examples of childhood memories you share with Andrew O'Hagan and two or three examples of things which have changed or which you don't recognise.

• With a partner discuss these questions.

– Why do you think the writer uses these details?
– What would be the effect on a reader of a similar age to the writer?
– What is the effect on you?

4. Your own writing
• List some of the details (brand names, television programmes, songs, games, books, food) which you associate with your early childhood.

• Now write a short piece beginning:

I remember the exact moment when I decided to hate/love ...

Your memory can be real or imagined, but you should try to make it convincing by using some of the details you listed.

5. Conversations
• Brainstorm everything you know about persuasive techniques. You are going to role-play one of the conversations suggested on page 19.

1. The writer's father has one last attempt to persuade his son, now an adult, to like football.
2. Read 'Boring, Boring Arsenal' on pages 3-5. Imagine the conversation between the two writers, Nick Hornby and Andrew O'Hagan.

• Before you start, think about how you could use some persuasive techniques to argue your case. You may find the work on 'An Introduction to Argument' in the argument section on pages 74-75 useful.

Stud U-Like

1. Before reading
The title of the article you are going to read is 'Stud U-Like'.
• In pairs, talk about what sort of article this title leads you to expect.

2. The opening
The opening paragraph of 'Stud U-Like' is reprinted here, sentence by sentence.
• Read the opening, pausing after each sentence to share your responses. Is it the sort of opening the title led you to expect? What is the effect of opening in this way?

Body-piercing is moving into the mainstream but is it safe?

Body piercing studios in the high street are now almost as familiar as a certain ubiquitous hamburger chain.

Sporting jewellery through navel, nose or nipple has become a very mainstream fashion statement.

So it is only when a rare case such as that of 39-year-old Lesley Hovvells of Llanelli, south Wales who died of septicaemia following 118 piercings, hits the headlines that we are reminded of the medical dimension.

• Read the rest of the article.

3. A good read?

An article like 'Stud U-Like' has several different purposes, for example to raise awareness, provide information and challenge myths surrounding the trend. But at the same time it is an enjoyable – even entertaining – read. This is something you may already have spoken about when looking at the title.

• Look through the article again and pick out two or three sentences or phrases which stand out for you or amuse you. Make a note of how they add to your experience of reading the article. Take it in turns to explain your choices either to a partner or to the rest of the class.

4. Exploring the structure

Diane Taylor uses different forms and sources of information in 'Stud U-Like':
– facts (something that can be proven to the satisfaction of most people)
– opinions (a judgement not necessarily based on fact)
– quotations from interviews
– anecdotes.

• Go through the article labelling each paragraph to show the different sorts of information Diane Taylor makes use of.

• Now identify the sections that had the most impact on you. Was the writer using fact, opinion, quotation or anecdote in these sections? Does one technique seem to have more impact on you than the others?

5. An article for ...

• Re-read the article and pull out all the quotations taken from interviews (for example with Anna Kai, the piercer). Using these quotations, write your own article on body piercing for a different purpose or audience. You could use one of the ideas suggested here or come up with one of your own.

– An article for a teenage magazine.
–A Health Education leaflet for the doctor's surgery.

Use the work you did in Activity 4 to help you decide where it would be most appropriate for you to use the interview material and where it might be better to stick to straight facts.

Tattoos

1. Before reading

• Share what you know about tattoos, either in small groups or as a class.

• Read 'Tattoos', identifying and noting down everything which is new to you.

• Talk about the sort of article this seems to be. Who do you think it is written for? For what purpose? What is it about the layout and the style of writing which suggests this to you?

2. A guide to ...

'Tattoos' was first published on *The Guardian* newspaper's website. It is a 'web guide' with links to other sources of information on tattooing. This means that the writer of the guide only needs to provide the essential details for each point. The interested reader can click on a link to find out more.

• Choose a subject you are interested in and write a ten point list of facts, stories, rumours or celebrity gossip connected with it.

• If possible, research your subject on the internet and include links to where your reader can find out more.

What is a Celebrity?

1. Before reading – defining celebrity

The Oxford Compact English Dictionary defines 'celebrity' as:

Celebrity – noun; 1. a famous person 2. the state of being famous

The dictionary definition is neutral, in other words it is neither positive nor negative.

• Look at these definitions from the text you are about to read and decide whether they are positive, negative or neutral. Explain your decisions.

A celebrity is a person who is known for his well-knownness.

A celebrity is one who is known to many persons he is glad he doesn't know.

A celebrity is anyone who spends more than two hours working on his hair.

21

A celebrity is a person in the public eye as evidenced through substantial mainstream national and international media, awards and achievements.

2. Before reading – introductions
• Write a short definition that explains the purposes and features of an introduction and the type of information it should include.

• Now read 'What is a Celebrity?' It is the introduction to a book called *How to be a Celebrity*.

3. After reading – introductions
• Compare this introduction with your definition: does this text fit your definition (what is the purpose and content)? Does it use any features or techniques you hadn't thought of (such as headings, quotations, bullet points)?

4. Predictions
• Talk about what you would expect from the rest of the book now that you have read the introduction. What clues did you use from the text? Find a quotation to support your predictions using these headings and suggestions to help you:
– tone: serious; humorous
– content: real advice; information about celebrities; satire (the use of humour and exaggeration to make fun of and criticize people's faults)
– audience: 'wannabes'; people who are already celebrities; people who like reading gossip about celebrities
– purpose: to entertain; to advise; to inform.

5. Humour
The text uses several types of humour. Here are some examples:

Amusing comparisons
'More resilient than a cockroach, the species survived.'

Bathos (a sudden change in mood from the serious or important to the trivial or ridiculous)
'Dame Judi Dench is a national treasure, like a cup of tea.'

Turning something on its head
'Celebrities are pointless, that is the point of them.'

> **Word play**
> 'Everybody who's nobody wants to be somebody.'

• Choose something from the text that amused you and explain what technique is being used (either from the list above or another technique).

6. Your own writing: How to be a ...

• Write the introduction to a new *How to be a ...* book. Here are some ideas for topics, but you could use your own: *How to be a Skateboarder*; *How to be a Teacher*; *How to be a Son/Daughter*; *How to be a Friend*; *How to be a Sibling*.

• Before you start, think about your tone, content, purpose and audience. Go round the class or your friends and family collecting some quotations on your topic.

• Use as many of the features of 'What is a Celebrity?' as you can. Use quotations, different types of humour, bullet points and headings. You could make up your own headings or use the ones below.

 – What is a ...?
 – ... food chain
 – The life cycle of a ...
 – What do you actually do?
 – What are ... for?
 – The future of ...

On a Train

Large ochre squashes sat plumply in fields of withering vines; people priming pumps and swinging buckets out of wells on long poles; tall narrow haystacks, and pepper fields in so many stages of ripeness I first took them for flower gardens. It is a feeling of utter quietness, deep rural isolation the train briefly penetrates. It goes on without a change for hours, this afternoon in Yugoslavia, and then all people disappear and the effect is eerie: roads without cars or bicycles, cottages with empty windows at the fringes of empty fields, trees heavy with apples and no one picking them. Perhaps it's the wrong time – 3.30; perhaps it's too hot. But where are the people who stacked that hay and set those peppers so carefully to dry? The train passes on – that's the beauty of a train, this heedless movement – but it passes on to more of the same. Six neat beehives, a derelict steam engine with wild flowers garlanding its smokestack, a stalled ox at a level crossing. In the heat haze of the afternoon my compartment grows dusty, and down at the front of the train Turks lie all over their seats, sleeping with their mouths open and children wakeful on their stomachs. At each river and bridge there were square brick emplacements, like Croatian copies of Martello towers, pocked by bombs. Then I saw a man, headless, bent over in a field, camouflaged by cornstalks that were taller than he; I wondered if I had missed all the others because they were made so tiny by their crops.

There was a drama outside Niš. At a road near the track a crowd of people fought to look at a horse, still in its traces and hitched to an overloaded wagon, lying dead on its side in a mud puddle in which the wagon was obviously stuck. I imagined its heart had burst when it tried to free the wagon. And it had just happened: children were calling to their friends, a man was dropping his bike and running back for a look, and farther along a man pissing against a fence was straining to see the horse. The scene was composed like a Flemish painting in which the pissing man was a vivid detail. The train, the window frame holding the scene for moments, made it a picture. The man at the fence flicks the last droplets from his penis and, tucking it in his baggy pants, begins to sprint; the picture is complete.

* * * * *

'I hate sightseeing,' said Molesworth. We were at the corridor window and I had just been reprimanded by a Yugoslav policeman for snapping a picture of a steam locomotive that, in the late afternoon sun, and the whirling dust the thousands of homeward-bound commuters had raised crossing the railway lines, stood amidst a magnificent exhalation of blue vapours mingling with clouds of gold gnats. Now we were in a rocky gorge outside Niš, on the way to Dimitrovgrad, the cliffs rising as we moved and holding occasional symmetries, like remainders of intelligent brickwork in the battlements of a ruined castle. The sight of this seemed to tire Molesworth, and I think he felt called upon to explain his fatigue. 'All that tramping around with guidebooks,' he said after a moment. 'In those horrible crocodiles of tourists, in and out of churches, museums, and mosques. No, no, no. I just like to be still, find a comfortable chair. Do you see what I mean? I like to *absorb* a country.'

He was drinking. We were both drinking, but drink made him reflective and it made me hungry. All I had had to eat during the day was a cheese bun in Belgrade, an envelope of pretzels, and a sour apple. The sight of Bulgaria, with its decrepit houses and skinny goats, did not make me hopeful of a good meal at Sofia Station, and at the fearfully named town of Dragoman a number of people, including several from Car 99, were taken off the train because they hadn't had cholera shots. Italy, the Bulgarians said, was stricken.

I found the Bulgarian conductor and asked him to describe for me a typical Bulgarian meal. Then I wrote down the Bulgarian words for the delicacies he had mentioned: cheese, potatoes, bread, sausages, salad with beans, and so forth. He assured me that there would be food in Sofia.

'This is an awfully slow train,' said Molesworth as the Direct-Orient creaked through the darkness. Here and there was a yellow lantern, a fire far off, a light in a hut at a remote halt where, barely visible, the stationmaster could be seen five paces from his hut, presenting his flag to the dawdling express.

I showed Molesworth my list of Bulgarian foods, and said I planned to buy what was obtainable at Sofia; it would be our last night on the Direct-Orient – we deserved a good meal.

'That should be very useful,' said Molesworth. 'Now, what are you going to use for money?'

'I haven't the slightest idea,' I said.

'They use the lev here, you know. But the snag is, I couldn't find a quotation for it. My bank manager said it was one of those hopeless currencies – I suppose it's not really money at all, just pieces of paper.' From the way he talked I could tell he wasn't hungry. He went on, 'I always use plastic. Plastic's incredibly useful.'

'Plastic?'

'Well, these things.' He set his drink down and took out a wad of credit cards, shuffled them, and read their names.

'Do you think the Barclaycard has hit Bulgaria yet?'

'Let's hope so,' he said. 'But if not, I still have some lire left.'

It was after eleven at night when we pulled into Sofia, and, as Molesworth and I leaped off the train, the conductor told us to hurry: 'Fifteen minutes, maybe ten.'

'You said we'd have a half-hour!'

'But we are running late now. Don't talk – hurry!'

We quick-marched down the platform, searching for food.

There was a cafeteria with a mob at the counter and then nothing more except, at the far end of the platform, a man with a steaming metal pushcart. He was bald. He held a small paper bag in one hand and with the other he flipped open the several tabernacles of his pushcart and stabbed at white buns and red, dripping sausages, the size of bananas, with pink meat showing in slightly burst seams. There were three customers ahead of us. He served them, taking his time, urging buns and sausages into the bags with his busy fork. When my turn came I showed him two fingers, changed my mind, three fingers. He bagged three of each.

'The same again,' said Molesworth and handed him a 1000-lire note.

'No, no,' said the man; he pushed my dollar away and at the same time took my bag from me and put it on the pushcart.

'He won't take our money,' said Molesworth.

'*Banka, banka,*' said the man.

He wants us to get change.'

'This is a dollar,' I said. 'Take the whole thing.'

'He won't wear it,' said Molesworth. 'Where's your *banka*, eh?'

The bald man pointed to the station. We ran in the direction his finger was pointing and found a teller's cage where a long line of disconsolate people stood clutching pieces of paper and kicking their luggage as the line inched forward.

'I think we'll have to give this up as a bad job,' said Molesworth.

'I'm dying for one of those sausages.'

'Unless you want to get duffilled*,' said Molesworth, 'you should get back on the train. I think I shall.'

We did and minutes later the whistle blew and the Bulgarian darkness swallowed Sofia. Enrico, seeing us empty-handed, got Italian crackers from his sister, the nun, and gave them to us; the Armenian lady presented a slab of cheese and even sat with us and had a drink, until her son wandered in wearing a pair of pyjamas. He saw his mother laughing; he burst into tears. 'Now I go,' she said, and went. Monique had gone to bed; so had Enrico. Car 99 was asleep, but we were picking up speed. 'And we're not badly off,' said Molesworth, slicing the cheese. 'Two more bottles of wine – that's one apiece and still some Orvieto to finish. Cheese and biscuits. We can call it a late supper.' We went on drinking, and Molesworth talked of India, how he had gone out for the first time on a P & O liner with thousands of enlisted men, tough mineworkers from the Durham coal fields. Molesworth and his fellow officers had plenty to drink, but the lower ranks were battened down. After a month they ran out of beer. There were fights, the men were mutinous, 'and by the time we reached

* Duffil is the name of another passenger they have met on the train.

Bombay most of them were in chains. But I got an extra pip on my shoulder for behaving myself.'

'This is the idea,' said Molesworth. The train was racing, and he was uncorking the last bottle. 'It's usually a good rule to drink the wine of the country you're passing through.' He glanced out the window into the blackness. 'I suppose that's still Bulgaria. What a great pity.'

Paul Theroux
The Great Railway Bazaar, 1975

Des Moines

I come from Des Moines. Somebody had to.

When you come from Des Moines you either accept the fact without question and settle down with a local girl named Bobbi and get a job at the Firestone factory and live there for ever and ever, or you spend your adolescence moaning at length about what a dump it is and how you can't wait to get out, and then you settle down with a local girl named Bobbi and get a job at the Firestone factory and live there for ever and ever.

Hardly anyone ever leaves. This is because Des Moines is the most powerful hypnotic known to man. Outside town there is a big sign that says WELCOME TO DES MOINES. THIS IS WHAT DEATH IS LIKE. There isn't really. I just made that up. But the place does get a grip on you. People who have nothing to do with Des Moines drive in off the interstate, looking for gas or hamburgers, and stay for ever. There's a New Jersey couple up the street from my parents' house whom you see wandering around from time to time looking faintly puzzled but strangely serene. Everybody in Des Moines is strangely serene.

The only person I ever knew in Des Moines who wasn't serene was Mr Piper. Mr Piper was my parents' neighbour, a leering cherry-faced idiot who was forever getting drunk and crashing his car into telephone poles. Everywhere you went you encountered telephone poles and road signs leaning dangerously in testimony to Mr Piper's driving habits. He distributed them all over the west side of town, rather in the way dogs mark trees. Mr Piper was the nearest possible human equivalent to Fred Flintstone, but less charming. He was a Shriner and a Republican – a Nixon Republican – and he appeared to feel he had a mission in life to spread offence. His favourite pastime, apart from getting drunk and crashing his car, was to get drunk and insult the neighbours, particularly us because we were Democrats, though he was prepared to insult Republicans when we weren't available.

Eventually, I grew up and moved to England. This irritated Mr Piper almost beyond measure. It was worse than being a Democrat. Whenever I was in town, Mr Piper would come over and chide me. 'I don't know what you're doing over there with all those Limeys,' he would say provocatively. 'They're not clean people.'

'Mr Piper, you don't know what you're talking about,' I would reply in my affected English accent. 'You are a cretin,' You could talk like that to Mr Piper because (1) he was a cretin and (2) he never listened to anything that was said to him.

'Bobbi and I went over to London two years ago and our hotel room didn't even have a *bathroom* in it,' Mr Piper would go on. 'If you wanted to take a leak in the middle of the night you had to walk about a mile down the hallway. That isn't a clean way to live.'

'Mr Piper, the English are paragons of cleanliness. It is a well-known fact that they use more soap per capita than anyone else in Europe.'

Mr Piper would snort derisively at this. 'That doesn't mean diddly-squat, boy, just because they're cleaner than a bunch of Krauts and Eyeties. My God, a *dog's* cleaner than a bunch of Krauts and Eyeties. And I'll tell you something else: if his Daddy hadn't bought Illinois for him, John F. Kennedy would never have been elected President.'

I had lived around Mr Piper long enough not to be thrown by this abrupt change of tack. The theft of the 1960 presidential election was a long-standing plaint of his, one that he brought into the conversation every ten or twelve minutes regardless of the prevailing drift of the discussion. In 1963, during Kennedy's funeral, someone in the Waveland Tap punched Mr Piper in the nose for making that remark. Mr Piper was so furious that he went straight out and crashed his car into a telephone pole. Mr Piper is dead now, which is of course one thing that Des Moines prepares you for.

When I was growing up I used to think that the best thing about coming from Des Moines was that it meant you didn't come from anywhere else in Iowa. By Iowa standards, Des Moines is a Mecca of cosmopolitanism, a dynamic hub of wealth and education, where people wear three-piece suits and dark socks, often simultaneously. During the annual state high school basketball tournament, when the hayseeds from out in the state would flood into the city for a week, we used to accost them downtown and snidely offer to show them how to ride an escalator or negotiate a revolving door. This wasn't always so far from reality. My friend Stan, when he was about sixteen, had to go and stay with his cousin in some remote, dusty hamlet called Dog Water or Dunceville or some such improbable spot – the kind of place where if a dog gets run over by a truck everybody goes out to have a look at it. By the second week, delirious with boredom, Stan insisted that he and his cousin drive the fifty miles into the county town, Hooterville, and find something to do. They went bowling at an alley with warped lanes and chipped balls and afterwards had a chocolate soda and looked at a *Playboy* in a drugstore, and on the way home the cousin sighed with immense satisfaction and said, 'Gee thanks, Stan. That was the best time I ever had in my whole life!' It's true.

I had to drive to Minneapolis once, and I went on a back road just to see the country. But there was nothing to see. It's just flat and hot, and full of corn and soya beans and hogs. Every once in a while you come across a farm or some dead little town where the liveliest thing is the flies. I remember one long, shimmering stretch where I could see a couple of miles down the highway and there was a brown dot beside the road. As I got closer I saw it was a man sitting on a box by his front yard, in some six-house town with a name like Spigot or Urinal, watching my approach with inordinate interest. He watched me zip past and in the rear-view mirror I could see him still watching me going on down the road until at last I disappeared into a heat haze. The whole thing must have taken about five minutes. I wouldn't be surprised if even now he thinks of me from time to time.

He was wearing a baseball cap. You can always spot an Iowa man because he is wearing a baseball cap advertising John Deere or a feed company, and because the back of his neck has been lasered into deep crevasses by years of driving a John Deere tractor back and forth in a blazing sun. (This does not do his mind a whole lot of good either.) His other distinguishing feature is that he looks ridiculous when he takes off his shirt because his neck and arms are chocolate brown and his torso is as white as a sow's belly. In Iowa it is called a farmer's tan and it is, I believe, a badge of distinction.

Iowa women are almost always sensationally overweight – you see them at Merle Hay Mall in Des Moines on Saturdays, clammy and meaty in their shorts and halter tops, looking a little like elephants dressed in children's clothes, yelling at their kids, calling out names like Dwayne and Shauna. Jack Kerouac, of all people, thought that Iowa women were the prettiest in the country, but I don't think he ever went to Merle Hay Mall on a Saturday. I will say this, however – and it's a strange, strange thing – the teenaged daughters of these fat women are always utterly delectable, as soft and gloriously rounded and naturally fresh-smelling as a basket of fruit. I don't know what it is that happens to them, but it must be awful to marry one of those nubile cuties knowing that there is a time bomb ticking away in her that will at some unknown date make her bloat out into something huge and grotesque, presumably all of a sudden and without much notice, like a self-inflating raft from which the stopper has been yanked.

Even without this inducement, I don't think I would have stayed in Iowa. I never felt altogether at home there, even when I was small. In about 1957, my grandparents gave me a Viewmaster for my birthday and a packet of discs with the title 'Iowa – Our Glorious State'. I can remember thinking even then that the selection of glories was a trifle on the thin side. With no natural features of note, no national parks, no battlefields or famous birthplaces, the Viewmaster people had to stretch their creative 3-D talents to the full. Putting the Viewmaster to your eyes and clicking the white handle gave you, as I recall, a shot of Herbert Hoover's birthplace, impressively three-dimensional, followed by Iowa's other great treasure, the Little Brown Church in the Vale (which inspired the song whose tune nobody ever quite knows), the highway bridge over the Mississippi River at Davenport (all the cars seemed to be hurrying towards Illinois), a field of waving corn, the bridge over the Missouri River at Council Bluffs and the Little Brown Church in the Vale again, taken from another angle. I can remember thinking even then that there must be more to life than that.

Then one grey Sunday afternoon when I was about ten I was watching TV and there was a documentary on about movie-making in Europe. One clip showed Anthony Perkins walking along some sloping city street at dusk. I don't remember now if it was Rome or Paris, but the street was cobbled and shiny with rain and Perkins was hunched deep in a trench coat and I thought, 'Hey, *c'est moi!*' I began to read – no, I began to *consume* – *National Geographics,* with their pictures of glowing Lapps and mist-shrouded castles and ancient cities of infinite charm. From that moment, I wanted to be a European boy. I wanted to live in an apartment across from a park in the heart of a city, and from my bedroom window look out on a crowded vista of hills and roof-tops. I wanted to ride trams and understand strange languages. I wanted friends named Werner and Marco who wore short pants and played soccer in the street and owned toys made of wood. I cannot for the life of me think why. I wanted my mother to send me out to buy long loaves of bread from a shop with a wooden pretzel hanging above the entrance, I wanted to step outside my front door and *be* somewhere.

As soon as I was old enough I left. I left Des Moines and Iowa and the United States and the war in Vietnam and Watergate, and settled across the world. And now when I came home it was to a foreign country, full of serial murderers and sports teams in the wrong towns (the Indianapolis Colts? the Toronto Blue Jays?) and a personable old fart who was President. My mother knew that personable old fart when he was a sportscaster called Dutch Reagan at WHO Radio in Des Moines. 'He was just a nice, friendly, kind of dopey guy,' my mother says.

Which, come to that, is a pretty fair description of most Iowans. Don't get me wrong. I am not for a moment suggesting that Iowans are mentally deficient. They are a decidedly intelligent and sensible people who, despite their natural conservatism, have always been prepared to elect a conscientious, clear-thinking liberal in preference to some cretinous conservative. (This used to drive Mr Piper practically insane.) And Iowans, I am proud to tell you, have the highest literacy rate in the nation: 99.5 per cent of grown-ups there can read. When I say they are kind of dopey I mean they are trusting and amiable and open. They are a tad slow, certainly – when you tell an Iowan a joke, you can see a kind of race going on between his brain and his expression – but it's not because they're incapable of high-speed mental activity, it's only that there's not much call for it. Their wits are dulled by simple, wholesome faith in God and the soil and their fellow man.

Above all, Iowans are friendly. You go into a strange diner in the South and everything goes quiet, and you realise all the other customers are looking at you as if they are sizing up the risk involved in murdering you for your wallet and leaving your body in a shallow grave somewhere out in the swamps. In Iowa you are the centre of attention, the most interesting thing to hit town since a tornado carried off old Frank Sprinkel and his tractor last May. Everybody you meet acts like he would gladly give you his last beer and let you sleep with his sister. Everyone is happy and friendly and strangely serene.

The last time I was home, I went to Kresge's downtown and bought a bunch of postcards to send back to England. I bought the most ridiculous ones I could find – a sunset over a feed lot, a picture of farmers bravely grasping a moving staircase beside the caption 'We rode the escalator at Merle Hay Mall!', that sort of thing. They were so uniformly absurd that when I took them up to the check-out, I felt embarrassed by them, as if I were buying dirty magazines, and hoped somehow to convey the impression that they weren't really for me. But the check-out lady regarded each of them with interest and deliberation – just as they always do with dirty magazines, come to that.

When she looked up at me she was almost misty-eyed. She wore butterfly glasses and a beehive hairdo. 'Those are real nice,' she said. 'You know, honey, I've bin in a lot of states and seen a lot of places, but I can tell you that this is just about the purtiest one I ever saw.' She really said purtiest. She really meant it. The poor woman was in a state of terminal hypnosis. I glanced at the cards and to my surprise I suddenly saw what she meant. I couldn't help but agree with her. They *were* purty. Together, we made a little pool of silent admiration. For one giddy, careless moment, I was almost serene myself. It was a strange sensation, and it soon passed.

My father liked Iowa. He lived his whole life in the state, and is even now working his way through eternity there, in Glendale Cemetery in Des Moines. But every year he became seized with a quietly maniacal urge to get out of the state and go on vacation. Every summer, without a whole lot of notice, he would load the car to groaning, hurry us into it, take off for some distant point, return to get his wallet after having driven almost to the next state, and take off again for some distant point. Every year it was the same. Every year it was awful.

The big killer was the tedium. Iowa is in the middle of the biggest plain this side of Jupiter. Climb onto a roof-top almost anywhere in the state and you are confronted with a featureless sweep of corn for as far as the eye can see. It is 1,000 miles from the sea in any direction, 400 miles from the nearest mountain, 300 miles from skyscrapers and muggers and things of interest, 200 miles from people who do not habitually stick a finger in their ear and swivel it around as a preliminary to answering any question addressed to them by a stranger. To reach anywhere of even passing interest from Des Moines by car requires a journey that in other countries would be considered epic. It means days and days of unrelenting tedium, in a baking steel capsule on a ribbon of highway.

In my memory, our vacations were always taken in a big blue Rambler station-wagon. It was a cruddy car – my dad always bought cruddy cars, until he got to the male menopause and started buying zippy red convertibles – but it had the great virtue of space. My brother, sister and I in the back were miles away from my parents up front, in effect in another room. We quickly discovered during illicit forays into the picnic hamper that if you stuck a bunch of Ohio Blue Tip matches into an apple or hard-boiled egg, so that it resembled a porcupine, and casually dropped it out the tailgate window, it was like a bomb. It would explode with a small bang and a surprisingly big flash of blue flame, causing cars following behind to veer in an amusing fashion.

My dad, miles away up front, never knew what was going on and could not understand why all day long cars would zoom up alongside him with the driver gesticulating furiously, before tearing off into the distance. 'What was that all about?' he would say to my mother in a wounded tone.

'I don't know, dear,' my mother would answer mildly. My mother only ever said two things. She said, 'I don't know, dear.' And she said, 'Can I get you a sandwich, honey?' Occasionally on our trips she would volunteer other pieces of intelligence like, 'Should that dashboard light be glowing like that, dear?' or, 'I think you hit that dog/man/blind person back there, honey,' but mostly she wisely kept quiet. This was because on vacations my father was a man obsessed. His principal obsession was with trying to economise. He always took us to the crummiest hotels and motor lodges, and to the kind of roadside eating-houses where they only washed the dishes weekly. You always knew, with a sense of doom, that at some point before finishing you were going to discover someone else's congealed egg-yolk lurking somewhere on your plate or plugged between the tines of your fork. This, of course, meant cooties and a long, painful death.

But even that was a relative treat. Usually we were forced to picnic by the side of the road. My father had an instinct for picking bad picnic sites – on the apron of a busy truck stop or in a little park that turned out to be in the heart of some seriously deprived ghetto, so that groups of children would come and stand silently by our table and watch us eating Hostess Cupcakes and crinkle-cut potato chips – and it always became incredibly windy the moment we stopped, so that my mother spent the whole of lunch-time chasing paper plates over an area of about an acre.

In 1957 my father invested $19.98 in a portable gas stove that took an hour to assemble before each use and was so wildly temperamental that we children were always ordered to stand well back when it was being lit. This always proved unnecessary, however, because the stove would flicker to life only for a few seconds before puttering out, and my father would spend many hours turning it this way and that to keep it out of the wind, simultaneously addressing it in a low, agitated tone normally associated with the chronically insane. All the while my brother, sister and I would implore him to take us some place with air-conditioning, linen table-cloths and ice-cubes clinking in glasses of clear water. 'Dad,' we would beg, 'you're a successful man. You make a good living. Take us to a Howard Johnson's.' But he wouldn't have it. He was a child of the Depression and where capital outlays were involved he always wore the haunted look of a fugitive who had just heard bloodhounds in the distance.

Eventually, with the sun low in the sky, he would hand us hamburgers that were cold and raw and smelled of butane. We would take one bite and refuse to eat any more. So my father would lose his temper and throw everything into the car and drive us at high speed to some roadside diner where a sweaty man with a floppy hat would sling hash while greasefires danced on his grill. And afterwards, in a silent car filled with bitterness and unquenched basic needs, we would mistakenly turn off the main highway and get lost and end up in some no-hope hamlet with a name like Draino, Indiana, or Tapwater, Missouri, and get a room in the only hotel in town, the sort of rundown place where if you wanted to watch TV it meant you had to sit in the lobby and share a cracked leatherette sofa with an old man with big sweat circles under his arms. The old man would almost certainly have only one leg and probably one other truly arresting deficiency, like no nose or a caved-in forehead, which meant that although you were sincerely intent on watching *Laramie* or *Our Miss Brooks,* you found your gaze being drawn, ineluctably and sneakily, to the amazing eaten-away body sitting beside you. You couldn't help yourself. Occasionally the man would turn out to have no tongue, in which case he would try to engage you in lively conversation. It was all most unsatisfying.

After a week or so of this kind of searing torment, we would fetch up at some blue and glinting sweep of lake or sea in a bowl of pine-clad mountains, a place full of swings and amusements and the gay shrieks of children splashing in water, and it would all almost be worth it. Dad would become funny and warm and even once or twice might take us out to the sort of restaurant where you didn't have to watch your food being cooked and where the glass of water they served you wasn't autographed with lipstick. This was living. This was heady opulence.

It was against this disturbed and erratic background that I became gripped with a curious urge to go back to the land of my youth and make what the blurb writers like to call a journey of discovery. On another continent, 4,000 miles away, I became quietly seized with that nostalgia that overcomes you when you have reached the middle of your life and your father has recently died and it dawns on you that when he went he took some of you with him. I wanted to go back to the magic places of my youth – to Mackinac Island, the Rocky Mountains, Gettysburg – and see if they were as good as I remembered them. I wanted to hear the long, low sound of a Rock Island locomotive calling across a still night and the clack of it receding into the distance. I wanted to see lightning bugs, and hear cicadas shrill, and be inescapably immersed in that hot, crazy-making August weather that makes your underwear scoot up every crack and fissure and cling to you like latex, and drives mild-mannered men to pull out handguns in bars and light up the night with gunfire. I wanted to look for Ne-Hi Pop and Burma Shave signs and go to a ball game and sit at a marble-topped soda-fountain and drive through the kind of small towns that Deanna Durbin and Mickey Rooney used to inhabit in the movies. I wanted to travel around. I wanted to see America. I wanted to come home.

So I flew to Des Moines and acquired a sheaf of roadmaps, which I studied and puzzled over on the living-room floor, drawing an immense circular itinerary that would take me all over this strange and giant semi-foreign land. My mother, meantime, made me sandwiches and said, 'Oh, I don't know, dear,' when I asked her questions about the vacations of my childhood. And one September dawn in my thirty-sixth year I crept out of my childhood home, slid behind the wheel of an ageing Chevrolet Chevette lent by my sainted and trusting mother and guided it out through the flat, sleeping streets of the city. I cruised down an empty freeway, the only person with a mission in a city of 250,000 sleeping souls. The sun was already high in the sky and promised a blisteringly hot day. Ahead of me lay about a million square miles of quietly rustling corn. At the edge of town I joined Iowa Highway 163 and with a light heart headed towards Missouri. And it isn't often you hear anyone say that.

Bill Bryson
The Lost Continent, 1989

Travelling in Ireland

Now, if you're going to go travelling in Ireland, it's important you know the correct way to ask somebody for directions. 'What you *don't* do is abruptly say, 'Excuse me! Could you tell me the way to ...?' This is an English technique, the subtext of which is: 'I'm interrupting you here in a fairly clumsy way in order to elicit a necessary fact, but otherwise this transaction is of no value and will give no pleasure. Go on, tell me then.'

The preferred approach in Ireland is to turn the encounter into a social occasion, on a par with what goes on when two strangers meet and get chatting at a party or wedding reception. A tangential preamble is essential; something along the lines of, 'Ah, that's a great hedge you're trimming', or 'Sure, it's a glorious day', especially if it isn't. Large quantities of personal information will then be exchanged, in the course of which the directions you are seeking may or may not emerge. Some of the best conversations you will have in Ireland may happen in this way.

I was once travelling in County Clare with a wonderful man called John Moriarty, a Christian mystic who is, by the way, convinced that I do carry the genetic memories of my Irish ancestors, and am therefore genuinely at home here. We were on the edge of the wilderness known as the Burren, looking for one of the ancient holy wells of Ireland, St Colman's Well. We had found nothing, and had been lost several times already in one morning, so this was shaping up to be a top travel experience.

On the road ahead of us, a man was walking. No buildings were visible for miles in any direction, so it was difficult to understand where he might be walking from or to. He must have been seventy, and was dressed in a farm labourer's tweed jacket, shiny with ordure and held around his waist with a length of string. He wore an old flat cap that may once have been shot at by Captain A. E. Percival, and the look of a man who had never been pampered. 'Ah, look,' said John. 'A bachelor.'

We pulled over and John walked across to him – none of this wind-your-window-down-and-bark-an-enquiry nonsense. They then embarked on a wide-ranging discussion that took in meteorology, natural history, anatomy, theology and chiropody, before John deftly slipped in the crucial question, for all the world as if it were an afterthought.

'We're looking for St Colman's Well.'

'Ah, yes. Ah, yes.'

'Do you know it then?'

'Sure, I do. I do.'

'Could you tell us how to find it so?'

Pause. 'What country's it in?'

So as the woman approaches the repmobile, I'm aware of the social etiquette. But will I be able to pull it off? She opens brilliantly.

'I'm just waiting for my daughter.'

Of course. So that's why she's parked in the middle of a crossroads. She has a look that is at once both blank and intense, as if perhaps she's spent too many years as a priest's housekeeper. But I don't let it get to me, and come back with details of my own family. We then banter about crops and such like for a while, until I sense that the moment is right. And then – ping! I'm in.

'I was wondering if you might be able to give me some directions.'

'Ah. Well, I'm afraid, you see, that I don't live around here.'

'Oh, I see. Where do you live, then?'

'Over there.'

She points to a white farmhouse across some fields, on a hillside about a mile away.

'Oh. Right. Well, anyway ...'

I produce the scholarly tome and show her a sketch of the Bohonagh circle, but it's clear she doesn't recognise it, even though she must have lived her whole life within eight or ten miles of it, according to the complex family history she eagerly provides. But the name itself rings a bell, though she says there's also another place that sounds similar, and it might be that. Or not. Eventually she suggests a route.

'Go back a way below there, now. Go right, and right, and I think left. Do you know the Dunmanway road?'

I nod, and smile, and only I know that I mean 'No'.

'Well, you take that. And there's an old tumbledown wreck of a pub there, and you turn away up the hill. It's painted yellow. Or at least it was twenty years ago.'

Clueless, I head off politely, happy simply to put a few country miles between me and the Michael Collins birthplace. After driving for ten minutes, I round a bend, and suddenly find myself at the Michael Collins birthplace. The Geordie waves and smiles.

I immediately implement Plan B, which in this instance is to drive at random until something happens. It's important to have a Plan B, especially when there's no Plan A. After a few minutes, I find myself at a T-junction I don't think I've passed before, though of course I can't be certain. And there's a pub – no name displayed, but almost certainly called McCarthy's. Unfortunately, it's shut. This is a difficult concept to grasp. I've never found a pub closed in Ireland before, and I'm not sure how to cope. Intellectually, I realise that the whole point of travel is to introduce you to the unknown, but emotionally I'm finding it difficult to deal with. I take a swig from my bottle of Virgin Mary mineral water, and consider my situation.

I'm lost, and the pub's shut. It's hard to see how things could get much worse. But I'm determined not to be thwarted by these elusive stones. They have come to represent the moral high ground, and I am determined to attain it. I drive a few more miles round winding lanes, until I find a sign to Rosscarbery ('Michael Collins birthplace – 1 mile'). Then, within sight of the main road I'd left earlier in the day, my eye is caught by a bright yellow sign on a noticeboard at the entrance to a field.

NOTICE IS HEREBY GIVEN THAT THE OCCUPIER OF THIS PROPERTY EXCLUDES THE DUTY OF CARE TO ALL VISITORS. NO AUTHORISED ENTRY IS ALLOWED

Inside the field, only about fifty yards away, but protected from me by a gate, barbed-wire and an electric fence, sits a huge cromlech – a boulder marking an ancient burial site. Above it, on the west of a hill, is the outline of an old ring fort. If I've got my bearings right, the place is called Templefaughnan, and Bohonagh can't be far away. The tome tells me that St Fachtna, who is credited with bringing Christianity to this area in the sixth century, is reputed to have preached the gospel in this very field.

He wouldn't have much joy if he came back today, mind you. Five modern bungalows guard the field in a protective semicircle, in case the barbed-wire and the electricity aren't enough to put you off. I think of scaling the gate for a closer look, but the thought of some beefy farmer lurking behind the net curtains, with ginger hair growing out of his ears and nostrils, just itching to exclude the duty of care to some trespassing English bastard, persuades me to drive on.

Round the first bend in the lane, opposite a bungalow with crazy-paved gateposts, is a roadside holy grotto. In marked contrast to the rugged, ancient boulder in the field, it looks as pristine as a gilt-framed picture of Daniel O'Donnell on a suburban convent mantelpiece. Either side of an altar-shaped slab stand the Virgin Mary and a chap I take to be St Fachtna himself, but who is a dead ringer for Willie Nelson. Country and western is popular out here, though, so you never know.

Searching for pagan stones in the midst of this Catholic iconography is making me feel like a devil worshipper who's sneaked into St Peter's and can't find his way out. Suddenly, the lane sweeps sharply downhill towards a junction a couple of hundred yards away. As I change down and negotiate the slope, I look up, and there ahead of me, silhouetted against the horizon on the crest of the next hill, dominating the surrounding landscape, is Bohonagh.

But by the time I've descended to the junction, it's gone. I drive along the road in both directions, but the stones can't be seen from anywhere. To find them, you've got to know they're up there, and know where to go. There's no sign or marker, so people must drive within a hundred yards of them all the time and not have a clue that they're there.

But now I know they're uphill, and just two fields away.

My way is barred by a wide ditch full of blackthorn, which is of course a sacred bush, though that isn't much consolation just now. But thirty yards away is a barred gate, and not a yellow placard in sight, so I stride up to it with a spring in my step. Then, more threatening than any official sign, I spot the fragment of ragged brown cardboard tied to the gate with baling twine. A message is printed on it in Biro, in a crabby hand that lacks generosity of spirit:

DANGER!
BULLS!!
DO NOT ENTER

Hmm.

I've never been one to mess with bulls, particularly in a Catholic country. Spain, for example, is a delightful place, but I've always been mystified by the nationwide passion for taking the piss out of bulls. Sometimes it's a prelude to killing them, of course, but often it's just for the crack.

I have a much-prized piece of home video shot a few years ago at the fiesta in Jávea, on the Costa Blanca, where they let the bulls run through the narrow back streets of the town before emerging into the main square. As the first bulls enter the square, a local sex god in tight black trousers and a puffy-sleeved white shirt unbuttoned to the scrotum leaps out in front of the lead bull, grimacing and pouting, waggling his arse, and making what I take to be the Spanish equivalent of the wanker sign.

'Wanker, eh?' enquires the bull, lunging at him and penetrating his ribs with its horns in a fairly matter-of-fact manner. Sexgod is thrown abruptly to the ground as various spectators rush to his aid and shoo the baffled bull away. Two stewards run in. One picks him up, dusts him down, staunches the wound, and asks if he's all right. He nods; at which point the other steward punches him in the face, presumably for taking the piss out of a bull in an unacceptably flamboyant manner. After all, without rules, society will collapse. As, indeed, does Sexgod, before being carried unconscious from the arena.

Now, if I'm gored by a bull here, within horn-tossing distance of the spectacular, but at this moment invisible, stones, no one's going to leap in and punch me; but no one's going to save me either. There isn't a soul to be seen in any direction. So I try to convince myself to be law-abiding, that I did my best, got as close as I could, so I can give up with honour; but I just feel pathetic. I'm scared of dogs, too. And geese.

I walk back up the steep lane I've just driven down until I can once more see the stones on the horizon, calling me to them. I'm now in a position to survey the land all around, and there isn't a bull to be seen.

It's clear that the DANGER! BULLS!! sign is just a ruse, a scam to keep New Agers, Pagans, Crusties and Whiffies from tramping all over the fields to paint each other's faces and drink Scrumpy Jack in a ritualistic manner in the centre of the stones. There isn't a problem here for me. It's just over the gate, up the hill, check out the stones, no bulls, back in the car and find a nice spot to eat my sandwich.

The first thing to catch my eye once I'm over the gate is a freshly spent shotgun cartridge, presumably fired from the gate at the back of the last person who trespassed.

Bullshit.

Not my thought, but the stuff I'm standing in. Masses of the stuff. And in the soft ground all around me, footprints I can only describe as bull-shaped. Nauseous but undeterred, I press on up the field, then surprise myself by going commando-style under an electric fence – a bit panicky, this bit, so I'm left with extensive grass stains, and a minor pulled muscle in the small of my back.

I'm now on a half-obscured path between two fields. Humming to myself in order to ward off total mental collapse, I follow it up the hill at a brisk stride, adding a little semi-cantered hitch-kick every few steps, presumably in the hope that this will render me impossibly elusive to shotguns and bulls. At the top of the hill there's a wall to the right, and beyond it, perfectly positioned to survey the countryside billowing away at 360° below it, the Bohonagh Stone Circle: thirteen slabs of granite, some of them taller than me, standing where they've been for 4,000 years.

But the dry-stone wall is lined with a single-strand electric fence, with a second wire encircling the stones themselves. Bastard farmers. What a vindictive way to treat people who only want to experience the stones at first hand. But then the thought occurs: what if the motivation was something quite different? What if it's just an attempt by a small farmer, earning an honest punt – plus massive EC subsidies, obviously – to protect the country's ancient heritage from animals?

But what animals?

The bellow comes from over my right shoulder. The beast is black and white, barrel-chested, eighty yards or so away, diagonally down the field. The gate, the repmobile, and the rest of my life are somewhere in the middle distance beyond. As is the electric fence, which I'll have to get under to give myself a chance. Anyway, can't bulls jump them? Or if not, surely they're so bloody hard that they can just crash through the flimsy tape as they thunder down on you in the mistaken belief that you're some kind of Spanish exhibitionist.

Heart pounding, back twingeing, bowels suddenly keen to get involved, I turn my back on the stupid bloody stones that have got me into this mess, and begin to edge down the hill, to my left. The bull backs off, head down, in that way that suggests backing off is just a momentum-gathering preliminary to charging forward. I speed up and head for the nearest point of the electric fence, all the while making a pitiful squeaking sound as I run, mentally reliving childhood promises never to do anything wrong ever again if only God will let me off this time.

As I go to throw myself under the electrically charged cable, I stumble in a rutted hoofprint, and catch the wire with my forehead. Nothing. Except relief. The fence is just for show. The current isn't even turned on. All over Europe, animals are being conned by farmers anxious to keep their electricity bills down, though I'll bet they're claiming the full whack from Brussels.

But what if the bull knows that?

The tape is between us, but the brute has now started to execute a distinctly threatening amble in my direction. Sprawled on my back, legs akimbo, I must make an inviting target. I couldn't feel more vulnerable if I were wearing skintight Spanish jeans with red arrows pointing to the crotch, marked 'Insert Horns Here'.

But surely the gate to the lane, and safety, must only be yards away. Keeping my body perfectly still, I begin – slowly, ever so slowly, so as not to alarm the bull – to turn my head.

There's a man at the gate, watching me.

'Have ya fallen and hurt yourself, or are ye just afraid of the cow?'

Pete McCarthy
McCarthy's Bar, 2000

Tokyo Pastoral

This is clearly one of those districts where it always seems to be Sunday afternoon. Somebody in a house by the corner shop is effortlessly practising Chopin on the piano. A dusty cat rolls in the ruts of the unpaved streetlet, yawning in the sunshine. Somebody's aged granny trots off to the supermarket for a litre or two of honourable saki. Her iron-grey hair is scraped into so tight a knot in the nape no single hair could ever stray untidily out, and her decent, drab kimono is enveloped in the whitest of enormous aprons, trimmed with a sober frill of cotton lace, the kind of apron one associates with Victorian nursemaids.

She is bent to a full hoop because of all the babies she has carried on her back and she bows formally before she shows a socially acceptable quantity of her gold-rimmed teeth in a dignified smile. Frail, omnipotent granny who wields a rod of iron behind the paper walls.

This is a district peculiarly rich in grannies, cats and small children. We are a 60 yen train ride from the Marunouchi district, the great business section; and a 60 yen train ride in the other direction from Shinjuku, where there is the world's largest congregation of strip-shows, clipjoints and Turkish baths. We are a pretty bourgeois enclave of perpetual Sunday wedged between two mega-highways.

The sounds are: the brisk swish of broom on tatami matting, the raucous cawing of hooded crows in a nearby willow grove; clickety-clackety rattle of chattering housewives, a sound like briskly plied knitting needles, for Japanese is a language full of Ts and Ks; and, in the mornings, the crowing of a cock. The nights have a rustic tranquility. We owe our tranquility entirely to faulty town planning; these streets are far too narrow to admit cars. The smells are: cooking; sewage; fresh washing.

It is difficult to find a boring part of Tokyo but, by God, I have done it. It is a very respectable neighbourhood and has the prim charm and the inescapable accompanying ennui of respectability.

I can touch the walls of the houses on either side by reaching out my arms and the wall of the house at the back by stretching out my hand, but the fragile structures somehow contrive to be detached, even if there is only a clearance of inches between them, as though they were stating emphatically that privacy, even if it does not actually exist, is, at least, a potential. Most homes draw drab, grey skirts of breeze-block walls around themselves with the touch-me-not decorum of old maids, but even the tiniest of gardens boasts an exceedingly green tree or two and the windowsills bristle with potted plants.

Our neighbourhood is too respectable to be picturesque but, nevertheless, has considerable cosy charm, a higgledy-piggledy huddle of brown-grey shingled roofs and shining spring foliage. In the mornings, gaudy quilts, brilliantly patterned mattresses and cages of singing birds are hung out to air on the balconies. If the Japanese aesthetic ideal is a subfusc, harmonious austerity, the cultural norm is a homey, cheerful clutter. One must cultivate cosiness; cosiness makes overcrowding tolerable. Symmetrical lines of very clean washing blow in the wind. You could eat your dinner off the children. It is an area of white-collar workers; it is a good area.

The absolute domestic calm is disturbed by little more than the occasional bicycle or a boy on a motorbike delivering a trayful of lacquer noodle bowls from the cafe on the corner for somebody's lunch or supper. In the morning, the men go off to work in business uniform (dark suits, white nylon shirts); in the afternoon, schoolchildren loll about eating ice-cream. High school girls wear navy-blue pleated skirts and sailor tops, very Edith Nesbitt, and high school boys wear high-collared black jackets and peaked caps, inexpressibly Maxim Gorki.

At night, a very respectable drunk or two staggers, giggling, down the hill. A pragmatic race, the Japanese appear to have decided long ago that the only reason for drinking alcohol is to become intoxicated and therefore drink only when they wish to be drunk. They all are completely unabashed about it.

Although this is such a quiet district, the streets around the station contain everything a reasonable man might require. There is a blue movie theatre; a cinema that specialises in Italian and Japanese Westerns of hideous violence; a cinema that specialises in domestic consumption Japanese weepies; and yet another one currently showing *My Fair Lady*. There is a tintinabulation of chinking *pachinko* (pinball) parlours, several bakeries which sell improbably luxurious European patisserie, a gymnasium and an aphrodisiac shop or two.

If it lacks the excitement of most of the towns that, added up, amount to a massive and ill-plumbed concept called Greater Tokyo, that is because it is primarily a residential area, although one may easily find the cluster of hotels which offer hospitality by the hour. They are sited sedately up a side street by the station, off a turning by a festering rubbish tip outside a Chinese restaurant, and no neighbourhood, however respectable, is complete without them – for, in Japan, even the brothels are altogether respectable.

They are always scrupulously clean and cosy and the more expensive ones are very beautiful, with their windbells, stone lanterns and little rock gardens with streams, pools and water lilies. So elegantly homelike are they indeed, that the occasional erotic accessory – a red light bulb in the bedside light, a machine that emits five minutes of enthusiastic moans, grunts and pants at the insertion of a 100 yen coin – seems like a bad joke in a foreign language.

Repression operates in every sphere but the sexual, even if privacy may only be purchased at extortionate rates.

There are few pleasant walks around here; the tree-shaded avenue beside the river offers delight only to coprophiles. But it is a joy to go out shopping. Since this is Japan, warped tomatoes and knobbly apples cost half the price of perfect fruit. It is the strawberry season; the man in the open fruit shop packs martial rows of berries the size of thumbs, each berry red as a guardsman, into a polythene box and wraps each box before he sells it in paper printed with the legend, 'Strawberry for health and beauty.'

Non-indigenous foods often taste as if they had been assembled from a blueprint by a man who had never seen the real thing. For example, cheese, butter and milk have such a degree of hygienic lack of tang they are wholly alienated from the natural cow. They taste absolutely, though not unpleasantly, synthetic and somehow indefinably obscene. Powdered cream (trade-named 'Creap') is less obtrusive in one's coffee. Most people, in fact, tend to use evaporated milk.

Tokyo ought not be a happy city – no pavements; noise; few public places to sit down; occasional malodorous belches from sewage vents even in the best areas; and yesterday I saw a rat in the supermarket. It dashed out from under the seaweed counter and went to earth in the butchery. 'Asoka,' said the assistant, which means, 'Well, well, I never did,' in so far as the phrase could be said to mean anything. But, final triumph of ingenuity, Megapolis One somehow contrives to be an exceedingly pleasant place in which to live. It is as though Fellini had decided to remake *Aphaville*.

Up the road, there is a poodle-clipping parlour; a Pepsi-Cola bottling plant heavily patrolled by the fuzz; a noodle shop which boasts a colour TV; a mattress shop which also sells wicker neckpillows of antique design; innumerable bookshops, each with a shelf or two of European books, souvenirs of those who have passed this way before – a tattered paperback of *The Rosy Crucifixion*, a treatise on budgerigar keeping, Marx and Engels on England; a dispenser from which one may purchase condoms attractively packed in purple and gold paper, trademarked 'Young Jelly'; and a swimming pool.

I am the first coloured family in this street. I moved in on the Emperor's birthday, so the children were all home from school. They were playing 'catch' around the back of the house and a little boy came to hide in the embrasure of the window. He glanced round and caught sight of me. He did not register shock but he vanished immediately. Then there was a silence and, shortly afterwards, a soft thunder of tiny footsteps. They groped round the windows, invisible, peering, and a rustle rose up, like the dry murmur of dead leaves in the wind, the rustle of innumerable small voices murmuring the word: '*Gaijin, gaijin, gaijin*' (foreigner), in pure, repressed surprise. We spy strangers. *Asoka*.

Angela Carter
New Society, 1970

The Toughest Trip

A couple of months ago I endured a hellish family vacation in Colorado. We had gone to the Rockies to ski for a week. As it turned out, the weather was perfect and the skiing was sublime, the food was ample and good, the beds were comfortable, the people were polite and good-natured. As I say, it was hell.

I know what you're thinking: Are you out of your mind, man? It sounds like paradise!

Paradise for you, maybe. But when you're a travel writer, there's nothing worse than a perfectly pleasant vacation. We are at our best when our trips are at their worst.

My bus blows a tire on an isolated mountain pass and I rub my hands in glee. Here's good material for a story! I mill around with all the other passengers, noting the snow-swept peaks and the growing chill in the air, the dry rocky landscape and the absolute absence of houses.

A yell comes from behind the bus, 'The spare tire's flat! We'll have to wait until the next bus comes along.'

'When's that?' someone yells back.

'About this time tomorrow!'

I can barely suppress my joy.

Think about it. What can you write about on a trip where nothing goes wrong?

'I recently spent a week skiing in Colorado. Every morning we awoke to pristine, powdery slopes. After a full day of skiing – with no waits at the lifts – we came back to our hotel for a hearty buffet dinner. Then we went to bed.'

Riveting stuff, eh?

Now consider this:

'Everything was schussing splendidly along on our week-long Colorado ski trip until day five. That morning we had taken the longest lift to the top of the range, where we intended to try some backside slopes we had never run before. Suddenly a blizzard moved in, so quickly that we barely had time to construct an igloo before 100-mph winds brought blinding snows.

'As we shivered in that igloo for the next 12 hours, doling out precious bites of the two Power bars we had stuffed into our parkas, we reflected on the comforts of the days before: the hot buffet of roast beef, salmon and turkey with corn on the cob and mashed potatoes, the unlimited wine and beer and the tables overflowing with cream puffs and cheesecake and glistening slices of chocolate decadence. We recalled the warm rooms at the inn, with its fluffy pillows and soft beds ...'

See? Without the blizzard and the igloo, there's just no story there.

That's the problem with being a travel writer. And this problem is compounded by the fact that everyone thinks it's such a glamorous job. I can't even count how many times I've been exchanging convivial cocktail banter when someone has asked what I do for a living.

'I'm a travel writer.'

Instantly the conversation stops and klieg lights beam from their eyes.

'You mean you get paid to travel around the world?'

'No, that would be a flight attendant. Travel wri –'

'You mean, you just go somewhere and write about it and you get paid to do that?'

'Well, it's really not quite that –'

'God, what a great job! You just say 'I want to go to Paris' and someone pays for you to fly there and stay there and eat out at all these great restaurants, and all you have to do is visit a few museums and then sit in some café and write about it?'

No one wants to hear about the long sleepless nights toiling over a constipated keyboard. No one wants to hear about the endless hours schlepping from Important Historic Site to Quaint Guest House to Notable Cultural Attraction. No one wants to hear about the grueling 12-hour flights in coach class, or how like a peripatetic J. Alfred Prufrock, I have measured out my life in airport waiting rooms.

And certainly no one wants to hear about the week-long ski trip in Colorado where nothing goes wrong, and how I beat my head against the columnar wall until finally I decided that the only thing I could write about would be how hard it is to write about a trip where nothing goes wrong.

I could try to explain that, but my cocktail questioners would already be in some palmy Panavision scene, the trade winds rustling the fronds, the warm waves swashing onto the sand, lush green peaks towering to their right and a coral-colored sunset splashing across the sky. Even as I sputtered, purple-prosed postcards would be blossoming in their heads.

So, let's start all over again: Have I told you about the blizzard that almost buried me alive on a recent ski trip in the Rockies?

Don George
The Lonely Planet website (www.lonelyplanet.com), 8 May 2002

Travel Activities

Before Reading

Reading extracts

The following extracts are taken from the different examples of travel writing included in this anthology.
- Read each extract and talk about the points listed here:
- what it is mainly about (for example, the place, the people, the writer)
- the purpose
- the style and tone of the writing (for example, is it descriptive or funny or poetic or factual?)
- anything which strikes you as particularly interesting about the subject or the way it is written (for example, what you can tell about the place or the impression you get of the writer).

---

1. I come from Des Moines. Somebody had to.
When you come from Des Moines you either accept the fact without question and settle down with a local girl named Bobbi and get a job at the Firestone factory and live there for ever and ever, or you spend your adolescence moaning at length about what a dump it is and how you can't wait to get out, and then you settle down with a local girl named Bobbi and get a job at the Firestone factory and live there for ever and ever.

---

2. The sounds are: the brisk swish of broom on tatami matting, the raucous cawing of hooded crows in a nearby willow grove; clickety-clackety rattle of chattering housewives, a sound like briskly plied knitting needles, for Japanese is a language full of Ts and Ks; and in the mornings, the crowing of a cock. The nights have a rustic tranquillity. We owe our tranquillity to faulty town planning; these streets are far too narrow to admit cars. The smells are cooking, sewage; fresh washing.
It is difficult to find a boring bit of Tokyo but, by God, I have done it.

3. Large ochre squashes sat plumply in fields of withering vines; people priming pumps and swinging buckets out of wells on long poles; tall narrow haystacks, and pepper fields in so many stages of ripeness I first took them for flower gardens. It is a feeling of utter quietness, deep rural isolation the train briefly penetrates. It goes on without a change for hours, this afternoon in Yugoslavia, and then all people disappear and the effect is eerie: roads without cars or bicycles, cottages with empty windows at the fringes of empty fields, trees heavy with apples and no one picking them. Perhaps it's the wrong time – 3.30. Perhaps it's too hot. But where are the people who stacked that hay and set those peppers so carefully to dry? The train passes on – that's the beauty of a train, this heedless movement – but it passes on all the same.

4. A couple of months ago I endured a hellish family vacation in Colorado. We had gone to the Rockies to ski for a week. As it turned out, the weather was perfect and the skiing was sublime, the food was ample and good, the beds were comfortable, the people were polite and good-natured. As I say, it was hell.

5. Now, if you're going to go travelling in Ireland, it's important you know the correct way to ask somebody for directions. What you don't do is abruptly say, 'Excuse me! Could you tell me the way to ...?' This is an English technique, the subtext of which is: 'I'm interrupting you here in a fairly clumsy way in order to elicit a necessary fact, but otherwise this transaction is of no value and will give no pleasure. Go on, tell me then.'
The preferred approach in Ireland is to turn the encounter into a social occasion.

• Sum up what you have learned about different styles of travel writing.

On a Train

1. Talking about the text
• Having heard the text being read aloud, work in pairs or small groups. Talk about your first responses. These might include:
- whether you enjoyed it
- what it made you feel about foreign travel
- what it made you feel about trains and train journeys.

• The text could be said to divide into two parts. Decide where you think the divide is and give a sub-heading to each part. Look at the first and second parts in turn. Decide which of these words and phrases apply, to each part.

Humorous
Dramatic
Exciting
Detailed
Poetic
Conversational
Reflective
Telling a story
Describing people
Describing places
Making you think
Creating a visual picture

• Which bit of the account did you enjoy most? Pick a short section (5-10 lines) to look at closely. Talk about what you enjoyed about it. Practise reading it aloud.

• Share the bits of the text you have chosen as a whole class. Each group should read their section aloud and explain what they liked about it.

2. Observing the events

Paul Theroux writes about his own experiences. He writes in the first person, as 'I'. How would the piece be different if it were being observed by a more distanced commentator, who narrated the events without having participated in them?

• Experiment with re-writing a small section of the text using third person narration. You could choose any bit from "'I hate sight-seeing," said Molesworth' to the end of the text. For example:

Molesworth and Theroux stood at the corridor window, Molesworth chattering away about his dislike of sightseeing whilst Theroux remained silent. He was still feeling rather irritated by the incident with the Yugoslav policeman.

• Talk about what difference it made to change the style of narration.

3. Writing a travel book

Fifteen years after writing his first travel book *The Great Railway Bazaar* Paul Theroux published an article about travel writing. In it he highlights some of the things he disliked about the travel books being published at the time and what he was trying to do in *The Great Railway Bazaar* which was rather different. Some key extracts from this article are included on page 50.

I had always somewhat disliked travel books: they seemed self-indulgent, unfunny and rather selective.

The travel writer left a great deal out of his books and put the wrong things in.

The travel book was a bore. A bore wrote it and bores read it.

It annoyed me that a traveller would suppress the moments of desperation or fear or lust, the details of meals, the names of books read to kill time, the condition of the toilets.

The truth of travel was interesting and off-key, and few people ever wrote about it.

Travel had to do with movement and truth: with trying everything, offering yourself to experience and then reporting it.

I wrote everything down – conversations, descriptions of people and places, details of trains, trivia, even criticism of the novels I happened to be reading.

• Re-read the extract from Theroux's *The Great Railway Bazaar* and talk about the extent to which you think Theroux is achieving what he sets out as his aims as a travel writer. For example, is there lots of trivia? Is it off-key? Does it avoid the trap of being boring?

• In role as Paul Theroux write a short paragraph explaining the ways in which you think the extract from *The Great Railway Bazaar* manages to avoid the failings of many travel books.

Des Moines

1. Group work on the text

• Having heard the text being read aloud to you, work in small groups, with each group exploring a different aspect. Take notes on your discussion to help you plan a presentation. Use the ideas below and on the next page to help you, then when you are ready, present your aspect of the text to the rest of the class.

Group 1: People
• Go through the text, listing all the people who are described. For each one:
– talk about what they are like.
– consider how they are presented by Bryson.
– consider why Bryson has put them into the piece about Des Moines. Pick one or two short quotes that are particularly strong expressions of what they are like.
You should also discuss what you have learned about Bryson himself.

• Plan a short presentation on the people in the text, what they have in common, why they are there and your reactions to Bryson's presentation of them.

Group 2: Purposes
• Write out these headings as a chart, with space to record quotations and your comments.

1. Describe
2. Inform
3. Entertain/amuse
4. Tell a story
5. Make you think

• For each heading, find two or three examples from the text where the writer seems to have this purpose in mind. Pick out short quotes. Talk about which of these purposes seem to you most strongly at work in this text.

• Plan a short presentation on the different purposes of the text and which you felt to be the most important and interesting.

Group 3: Stories and anecdotes

Bryson uses several little stories, or anecdotes, to tell us about Des Moines.

• Go through the text, listing each of the stories.

– What do you think he achieves by telling each of the stories?
– How does he introduce each anecdote?
– How does he use description, dialogue and commentary to tell the anecdote?
– What do they have in common, if anything?
– How effective are they?
– Which one(s) did you enjoy most and why?

• Plan a short presentation on the stories told, your reactions to them and the role they play in the text.

Group 4: Tone

This opening chapter has a range of different tones at different times.

• Go through the text finding two or three examples of each of the tones suggested below and write them on a chart, with page numbers. Discuss what makes you aware of the tone in each case. What do you think is the main tone of the piece?

– Funny/Ironic
– Serious
– Reflective
– Chatty
– Poetic
– Nostalgic

You should also think about the writer's relationship with the reader.

• Plan a short presentation on the different tones you found in the piece and which you felt to be strongest.

Group 5: Humour

Find as many examples as you can of Bryson trying to be funny in this piece. In each case, try to say what it is that makes it funny. These are some of the ways in which it might be humorous:

– the names used
– exaggeration
– funny situations
– funny characters
– teasing the reader
– humorous comparisons
– irony.

• Plan a presentation on the humour in the piece, in which you pick out some short quotations and sections and explain why you find them funny.

2. Writing about 'Des Moines'

• Write about your responses to 'Des Moines' using your discussion and notes to help you explore what the writer is trying to do and how he achieves his purposes.

3. Writing about your area

• Write an account of life in your area, using one of the angles listed below:

1. A personal account, in the style of Bryson, which sets out to present a humorous view of the place and supplies all kinds of examples and anecdotes to support that view.

2. Two different versions of your area, for example an advert to go into a Tourist Information Centre, trying to attract visitors and a letter to the local newspaper setting out the problems in the area and suggesting improvements and solutions.

Travelling in Ireland

1. Where does it belong?

Like much recent non-fiction, it is quite difficult to decide exactly what sort of book *McCarthy's Bar* is. In this anthology, it is categorised as 'travel'. However, you could argue that it should have been included as humour or autobiography or ... what else?

• In small groups talk about how you would categorise it and why. It might help to think about which section of a bookshop you would expect to find it in.

2. Group work on the text

• Use the categories for analysing Bill Bryson's piece 'Des Moines' (pages 51-52) to explore the extract from *McCarthy's Bar*. The categories are listed below.

– People
– Purposes
– Stories and anecdotes
– Tone
– Humour

• You could go on to write a detailed analysis of this passage.

3. A radio programme

A striking feature of Pete McCarthy's travel book is the tone of voice he uses to establish a relationship with the reader. Some of the ways you might describe the way it is written are suggested here:

– intimate
– rambling
– informal
– confiding
– friendly.

This sort of writing often makes very good radio – *McCarthy's Bar* and its sequel *The Road to McCarthy* have both been serialised on Radio 4.

• In small groups, prepare a dramatised reading for radio of a short section from this extract, for example from 'Now if you're going to go travelling in Ireland ...' to '... Michael Collins birthplace.'

4. Your own writing

• Imagine Pete McCarthy visited your home, the place where you live or, if you prefer, your school. What do you think he would say about it and the people who live in it? Do people behave in a way that might seem strange to an outsider? What stories or anecdotes would he find to tell about his experiences and the people he meets?

• Write a first draft, drawing on all the techniques you identified in Pete McCarthy's piece. You could go on to write this up as a piece of original writing or prepare it as an individual Speaking and Listening assignment.

Tokyo Pastoral

1. Picture postcards

• Read the text out loud or listen to it being read to you.

• Working in small groups, skim through it looking for five images of Tokyo that might make good picture postcards.

• Skim through the text looking for five images of Tokyo that might be used in a campaign leaflet to clean up the area, showing the deterioration of the community.

2. Exploring the text

• Each group will be given one area of the text to talk about, take notes on and present to the rest of the class. Pick out three or four key quotes, just short phrases, to help you explain to the class what Angela Carter is describing and how she creates a view of Tokyo and its inhabitants.

- Sounds and smells
- Japanese family life
- The physical environment
- Houses and homes
- Shops and what they reveal about life in Tokyo
- Angela Carter, the outsider
- Japanese Attitudes to sex and sexuality
- Tokyo women
- Tokyo men

3. Exploring the title
• Now you have read the article, talk about the title and what it adds to your understanding of the piece. Use the definitions included here as a starting point for your discussion.

Tokyo – the capital city of Japan
Pastoral – a description of an idealised country life.

The Toughest Trip

1. Holiday nightmares – 'I nearly ...'
For Don George, a holiday in which everything is perfect is no fun at all. He wants plenty of dramatic things to happen so that he has a good story to tell.
• Think of a holiday or school trip in which not everything went to plan. Write down in note form the bare bones of what happened. Use different coloured pens to annotate your ideas with suggestions for how you could turn this into a funny or dramatic or shocking or revolting story.

In his article Don George shows how a travel writer can turn a holiday nightmare into a good story. A short extract from this section is included here:

> As we shivered in that igloo for the next 12 hours, doling out precious bites of the two Power bars we had stuffed into our parkas, we reflected on the comforts of the days before: the hot buffet of roast beef, salmon and turkey with corn on the cob and mashed potatoes, the unlimited wine and beer and the tables overflowing with cream puffs and cheesecake and glistening slices of chocolate decadence. We recalled the warm rooms at the inn, with its fluffy pillows and soft beds ...

• Turn your holiday nightmare (or nightmare school trip) into an entertaining anecdote to tell the rest of the class. You could use the techniques suggested here to help:
– exaggeration
– challenging people's expectations
– short sentences to increase suspense
– humour.

• Tell your anecdote to the class.

Comparing Travel Texts

1. Travel truths or travel bores?

• In groups take responsibility for reading one of the following passages:

Des Moines (from *The Lost Continent*)

Tokyo Pastoral

Travelling in Ireland (from *McCarthy's Bar*)

• Talk about the passage in relation to Paul Theroux's opinions about travel books (included on page 50).

• In role as the writer, prepare a brief presentation on your piece, focusing on the points listed here:

– what you were trying to do

– how you think you achieved this

– how it meets Paul Theroux's criteria for a good travel book

– anything else which you think is important about it.

• Re-group so that there is at least one person who has worked on each piece. Take it in turns to make your presentation. The other writers should have chance to make comments and ask questions.

2. Your own writing

• Use the work you have done on travel writing to write about your own environment or a place you have travelled to. You could do it in the style of one of the writers you have read, take elements from different writers, or try to speak with a voice that is distinctively your own. These are the first two sentences from two of the texts, that could be adapted as a starting point.

I come from ... ... Somebody had to ... ...

This is clearly one of those districts where it always seems to be ... ...

Legalising Drugs

It was not the drug, but the criminalisation of it that killed my son.

I had been expecting Scott's death for some time. But when it came, just a month from his 34th birthday, it was none the less devastating. The blow was felt more keenly by his four siblings, especially his elder sister, Fiona, who was closest to him and who had tried so hard for so long to help him. But none of them, all drug-free, had suspected that he was so far down the road. The last time I saw him, just four days before he died, I knew he would not see 40 and said so. No one wanted to believe me.

Up to his early teens, his school reports would have won him a place in heaven. He was everything any parent would have wished for – sensitive, conscientious, well fitted into school life and so on. Then a fellow pupil, a doctor's son, took some Valium tablets from his father's surgery and gave some to Scott. There was the wholly-to-be-expected flurry of panic-stricken letters between headmaster and parents, and the guilty boys were separated.

But Scott had tasted the forbidden fruit and, for reasons he could never explain then or later, the taste and the danger appealed. None of the other lads involved ended up on drugs, only Scott. After another episode with pills when he was about 15, I sought advice from friends, doctors and psychiatrists. There was much hand-wringing but nothing else.

Taking a stronger tack, I marched him off to Cambridge police station, where I had arranged for a chief inspector to receive us in full uniform. A stern lecture concluded with Scott being banged up in a cell for five minutes to give him a taste of what the future might hold. He was singularly unimpressed. It began to dawn on me that the son I once had, anxious to please, keen to play by the rules, was now rapidly slipping away. Why? What had we done? What made him different from the rest of the family? We didn't know then and we don't know now.

At age 17 came his first arrest for possession of amphetamine sulphate. Stories in the local papers, family tears, public disgrace, embarrassment, humiliation for him, and more hunting around to find someone, some place, some service to help him. Nothing. A year later he was in court again on a similar charge, and this time he was found a place in a probation hostel. For a time, it looked as though he might find a new direction, but on his release he headed for London and we lost him for good.

In the years up to his death, he kept in touch by letter and telephone, particularly with Fiona, and occasionally he would visit, or he and I would meet in a pub somewhere. His conversation was always about the pain of existence in a world where two-thirds starved so one-third could live well. He hated war, poverty and injustice, and felt powerless to alter things. But he would always try to get back home for the family Christmas, and we took heart from that, happy that he hadn't rejected us completely.

On his last but one visit, I found him trying to steal from a handbag in the kitchen. I said nothing because his confusion and embarrassment said enough for both of us. I knew then, with total heartsink, that he was on heroin, because that's what heroin addicts have to do – steal from anyone or anywhere for cash to buy their stuff. This constant scraping around and the toxicity and the malnutrition is what eventually kills the addict. At his death, this tall, handsome, unaggressive misfit, who found the world so difficult to live in, had 29 convictions for theft, all to buy adulterated drugs.

He spent the last five weeks before his death on remand for theft. He turned out to be innocent and was released. I picked him up and drove him to his flat. He was drawn and tired. He didn't want to come for a meal, he said, he just wanted to get his head down. My last words to him were: 'Well, make sure you keep your head down.' His parting words were: 'Don't worry, dad. I'll be all right.' Four days later he died, asleep in the arms of the old harlot, heroin.

On the wall of his flat we found this hand-written valediction to the drug:

The hot chills and cold sweats, the withdrawal pains,
Can only be stopped by my little white grains.
There's no other way and no need to look,
For deep down inside you know you are hooked.
You'll give up your morals, your conscience, your heart,
And you will be mine until death us do part.

So why, in the wake of so much pain, do I want to see drugs legalised? Because I believe it was not the drug itself – unlike alcohol and tobacco, heroin has no known long-term side effects – but the criminalisation of it that killed my son. In fact, a number of things contributed to his death: he was stupid enough to use heroin in the first place; he had spent five weeks in prison without drugs; on release his body could not take his normal dose (the coroner's view); and the heroin was toxic (revealed by the inquest pathology report).

I am convinced that he would be alive today if all drugs had been legalised and controlled, because he would have had no need to steal and would not have been in prison, the heroin would have been controlled and therefore not toxic, and proper treatment would have been available under such a regulated system.

Drugs, for me, should be a public-health rather than a criminal matter. First, they should be removed from the monopoly clutches of crime. Second, the billions saved in the costs of law enforcement, street crime and property theft should be redirected towards regulation, licensing, education, prevention, treatment and rehabilitation. The present uncontrolled drugs free-for-all will mean that thousands more will follow my son to the grave, victims of criminally supplied impure drugs, unless western governments recognise that the so-called 'war against drugs' is unwinnable and wholly counterproductive.

Many will ask how this can be morally justified. My view is that there is more moral justification in trying to cut crime and save lives than in leaving things as they are – under the control of criminals. Those who believe legalisation will make more hard drugs available to more young people overlook the fact that drugs of all kinds are more available to more young people now than ever, even with prohibition in force. There is not a whit of evidence to support the idea that there is some massive reservoir of disaffected youth about to rush out and die. There are more pushers out there than chemists' shops, so those who want to use hard drugs are using them now and will continue to use them come what may. Therefore we should make sure the drugs they use are safe. This can only be done under legalised regulation.

Just like alcohol prohibition in America, attempts at enforcement have served largely to demonstrate the lethal impotence of the law. We are beginning to see US-style gang warfare in our towns and cities. Apart from the health costs, multibillion-pound drug cartels, by bribery and terror, are undermining and corrupting law-enforcement and political systems across the world. Prohibition is simply fuelling this fire. We are spending billions dribbling water in at one end while criminals are making billions pouring their toxic fuel in at the other.

Prohibition did not work in the past and it will not work in the future, simply because – now as in 1920s America – crime is controlling the supply. Therefore the link with crime must be broken. This would be a first step to removing the drugs issue from the monopoly control of crime and putting it where it belongs – in the area of public health, where it can be most effectively dealt with. Drug abusers, like alcoholics, should be treated as patients needing help rather than criminals to be punished. At present, we cannot control the drugs supply, either in quantity or quality, because we are not in charge of it. The Al Capones are.

So we must dump prohibition and go for control by legalisation. Setting up a royal commission would be a good start. Decriminalisation will not provide a long-term answer because it leaves the offence on the statute book and leaves supply in the hands of crime. It will mean repealing or amending a number of United Nations treaties, including the 1961 UN Single Convention on Narcotic Drugs, which prevents the unilateral legalisation of hard drugs by individual governments. But the drugs laws provide governments with powerful enforcement tools which are often used for non-drug purposes – like Nixon and Watergate – so these are tools that will not be surrendered easily. Further, there are lots of people who live off drug prohibition who will not want to give up their seats at a number of influential tables.

I am no advocate of drugs – I wish to God people wouldn't use them – because for my son the drugs road led to a very dead end. But that need not be so for thousands like him if we take control of the supply. At least we will be sure that they will get treatment and the chance of rehabilitation. And for those foolish enough to keep using, we will be sure that what they take will not kill them.

Fulton Gillespie
The Guardian, 28 March 2002

Legalising Drugs – Letters to the Paper

These letters appeared in response to a Leading Article, Comment piece and letters in *The Daily Telegraph* arguing against legalising drugs.

Re: Say no to the Inquisition

Sir – Both drug laws and drug education must be reality-based (Leading Article, May 22). Children who realise they've been lied to about cannabis often assume that harder drugs such as heroin are relatively harmless, too: a recipe for disaster.

The Commons Home Affairs committee recently concluded that 'the harm caused by illegal drugs varies immensely from one drug to another. Since most users and potential users know this, there is no point in pretending otherwise.' While Britain increasingly favours commonsense approaches to drugs, the culture wars are heating up in America. President Bush is now pushing 'compassionate coercion' for users of non-traditional drugs, with America's millions of cannabis smokers the likely target.

Like any drug, cannabis can be harmful if abused, but arrests and criminal records are hardly appropriate health interventions. Unlike alcohol, cannabis has never been shown to cause an overdose death, nor does it share the addictive properties of tobacco. Unfortunately, cannabis represents the counterculture to misguided reactionaries intent on forcibly imposing their version of morality. Britain should just say no to the American Inquisition.

Robert Sharpe, Drug Policy Alliance, Washington DC
24 May 2002

Re: Legalisation – our best hope

Sir – I would like to send my support to David Cameron for his article on 'the drugs war' (Comment, May 23). It was refreshing to see an honest perspective that did not pander to a middle-aged electorate that has no knowledge of the drugs scene.

I am 25 and have experimented with practically all the drugs currently available in Britain. I can understand why there is such a heroin problem. A fact ignored by most people is that it is very, very nice. Too nice. I made a promise to myself never to touch it again after my first try.

Even Mr Cameron dismissed the possibility of legalisation. This is a shame as it is surely our best hope. We pour millions into fighting the drug war, a war that cannot be won. We fill the pockets of smugglers, killers, slave labourers and despots.

Alternatively, we could construct drug centres, employ people currently out of work, and make huge profits for state coffers. Cocaine currently retails at £50 a gram.

The state could sell a better product at £35-£40 a gram and use the profits to invigorate the inner cities, help rural areas, strengthen the police and the NHS.

Yes, frequency of first-time users would surely increase but with a drug user database we could actually control the volume of use per individual. An over-18s policy would also exclude those whom society is most keen to protect.

To me, legalisation would mean an end to the regimes in Afghanistan and Colombia and an end to the forced labour that goes on to fulfil our hedonistic needs.

Rupert Turner, Bridgnorth, Shropshire
25 May 2002

Re: Keep your promise

Sir – Not many people write to say they have experimented with most drugs and that 'heroin is very, very nice'. Rupert Turner's letter is very frank (May 25). I hope he keeps his promise to himself not to try it again.

Only half way through his letter does the weakness of his proposal appear. First, he states that the drug war cannot be won. No attempt has been made to fight it yet in this country.

Second, when the 'drug centres' are functioning, undercutting current drug prices, selling presently illegal drugs to anyone over 18 who can pay for them, as Mr Turner writes, the number of first-time users will surely increase.

But he thinks this disadvantage can be overcome by the compilation of a drug user database that will 'actually control the volume of use per individual'.

This is absurd. The user will top up his controlled supply with illegally bought supplies. He will probably buy them from the unemployed whom Mr Turner is going to use to staff his centres.

Unless under-18s are also supplied through the drug centres, the illegal supply chain will not disappear. And why will the legalisation of supply in Britain and the increased demand mean 'an end to the regimes in Afghanistan and Colombia'? They should gain from the increase in demand.

Philip Davies, National Drug Prevention Alliance, Hatch End, Middx
29 May 2002

Re: Evidence shows the current system doesn't work

Sir – Recent letters illustrate the paucity of the arguments of those who think the current 'war on drugs' can be won if fought with increased ferocity. They trot out the same tired mantra in the face of overwhelming evidence that current policies are failing badly. Our prisons are now at the bursting point of 71,000 because 61 per cent of the inmates have committed prohibition-related or drug offences.

Two million ecstasy tablets are now consumed each week, as opposed to one million in 1995 when the Leah Betts campaign began. Our children are consuming them. Do these people really want the police to arrest all those who take them, so that half the country's children are imprisoned for up to 14 years each?

Mr Mahoney thinks we should apply the strict regime of Singapore. History shows that it is possible to regulate the populations of tiny city states such as Singapore or ancient Athens, but only for a while. You cannot oppress large and diverse populations. He might as well argue that the way to stop football hooliganism is to ban football.

I challenge the drug war proponents to come up with just one constructive argument. Maybe then we can raise the level of this debate.

Mick Humphreys, Taunton, Devon
31 May 2002

The Daily Telegraph, 24th-31st May 2002

Big Brother – a Boring Showcase for Exhibitionists

'There is nothing that Channel 4 can do to obviate the fact that all the Brotherites are skull-crushingly dumb.'

And so we arrive at chapter 102 in my massive, magisterial but pessimistic master-work, provisionally entitled *New Lows in Western Culture*. And, coming directly after my thoughts on 'Jerry Springer and the High Tide of Voyeurism', chapter 102 deals with that remarkable new nadir in popular programming, Channel 4's *Big Brother*. I will attempt to show that *Big Brother* – the show in which 10 young people are locked up together and filmed – is a uniquely damaging and vicious piece of television, pandering to the worst instincts of viewer, broadcaster and participant, degrading all three in the process.

Or maybe I won't. Because it isn't true. As a piece of television, as a cultural artefact, *Big Brother* is singularly unimportant. Not only is it not a new low, it isn't really a low at all, merely a logical extension of the docu-soap genre, in which 'ordinary people' live their lives while being constantly filmed. It isn't *The Truman Show*, because Truman didn't know that the cameras were there (the key thrill for the fictional audience). For that reason, as others have pointed out, it isn't genuinely voyeuristic.

It is, of course, the opposite: a showcase for exhibitionists. But even here it fails to go much beyond karaoke night at the Dog and Duck. True, there was a scene early on in which the bald girl persuaded several of her fellow inmates to press their naked bodies on to the wall of the living-room while covered in a brown paint (thus creating a mural worryingly reminiscent of the 'dirty protest' in the Maze). Even so, this came nowhere close to the gut-churning self-flaunting to be found in Denise Van Outen's vehicle, *Something for the Weekend*. The experience of watching an unclothed middle-aged couple telling their daughter – in front of an adrenalised studio audience – that they most liked to be kissed on their 'private parts' (what 'private' parts?) is something that only global war will efface from my memory. Thank God Channel 4 also gives us *The Sopranos*.

Nor do I think *Big Brother* represents a technological breakthrough. And I don't say this just because I spent a fruitless morning trying to catch the nubile Melanie in the shower on the Web – and signally failing to catch anyone anywhere. Webcams have been around for half a decade, allowing the terminally boring to entertain the fatally bored. So it ain't new.

Of course, there has been significant media interest (of which – I am perfectly well aware, thank you – this article is an example), and once one hound barks, the rest tend to follow. This has created one of those strange loops in which the media's interest in the story gradually becomes part of the story. Yesterday *The Sun* – which had flown a model helicopter over Stalag Luft 14 and dropped leaflets calling for one particular participant to be voted out – boasted about their own appearance on *Big Brother* and quoted *The Guardian*, which had complimented them on doing it. Yet such media circularity is hardly a new story either.

The broadcasters, I suppose, might be accused of a degree of cynicism in the way in which *Big Brother* has been structured and presented. In the first instance it is odd, and slightly reprehensible, that – just as the nation worries about the alcohol intake of the young – *Big Brother* should be sponsored by Southern Comfort. I think Waterstone's or the Co-op should have been invited instead.

Far worse, though, is the punctuation of *Big Brother* by the 'expert' vapourings of academics who ought to know better. My favourite cod-phrase this week was from the clinical psychologist at Manchester University. 'The real turning point of the relationship is by the chicken coop,' he said of Melanie and (the now-departed) Andrew. Apparently, she scratched her nose just after he'd scratched his, and we all know what that means, don't we? This was followed by the observation (when one of the men suggested that the washing-up ought to be done), that 'what Darren is doing is adopting the role of the parent'.

Yes, it really is that interesting.

The best-selling computer game for PC machines at the moment is something called *The Sims*. In *The Sims* you take charge of an individual or family, house them, choose their furniture, give them hobbies, move them around the neighbourhood and introduce them to other folks. They shower and urinate (covered by a localised pixellation), throw their rubbish on the floor and – if denied company, activity or sleep – go bonkers. And Channel 4's producers have learnt from *The Sims*. So their real Sims are given displacement tasks (this week it was learning semaphore, next week it's gutting wildebeest), told to perform certain chores, and forbidden from campaigning against other Sims.

Even so, many believe (and I'm one of them) that Channel 4 has introduced an agent provocateur into the house to stir things up when they go flat, or introduce topics of conversation that might lead to interesting encounters. On Monday night Nicholas (whom I am sure I've met somewhere) was to be found engaging three fellow Sims in a discussion about condom etiquette. This is almost exactly the kind of thing producers traditionally want mixed households of young people to discuss on camera.

And it's here that we at long last arrive at what is genuinely significant about *Big Brother*. Not its contribution to cultural decline, not its role within the media village, not what it says about broadcaster or audience. What is really interesting about *Big Brother* is what it tells us about young people in Britain, what it tells us about the Sim generation itself. Because poor old Nicholas (a tad older than most of them) wound up talking to himself about condoms. There is nothing that he, Channel 4 or the psychologists can do to obviate the fact that all the Brotherites are staggeringly, skull-crushingly, die-on-a-sofa dumb. You might as well talk to trilobites.

For a kick-off, they're all the same. Every one of them looks and sounds and dresses like an aerobics instructor at a third-rate health centre. In three weeks I have yet to hear any of them venture anything so radical as an opinion on something outside themselves, or anything so entertaining as a genuine insight or a flash of wit. The only art they're interested in is their own, the only time is now, and the only place is here.

Three of the men and one of the women are actually functionally incoherent. When Darren soliloquises, the words die on his lips and drop, cold, on the floor in front of him. On Monday, the lesbian ex-nun Anna, tempted to leave the house (or at least, tempted to tell everyone she was tempted to leave the house) said: 'I'm not that interesting and I don't think I will be missed when I go.'

Any one of them could have expressed that opinion with complete truth. You would have thought that it was statistically impossible to find such uniform bores, such conformists. The one 'character' or rebel – 35-year-old Caroline – is only different in that she is noisily self-obsessed. Nevertheless, she, too, represents a generation in which adolescence seems to drag on into early middle age.

There is, however, an upside to all this. What the Channel 4 kids also demonstrate is far less inhibition than earlier generations (I might have liked to do that body-art stuff, but I'd never have dared), much greater openness and – yes – more tolerance. And perhaps blandness is a price worth paying for that. Just.

David Aaronovitch
The Independent, 9 August 2000

The Man With No Name

When it was raining hard the other day, a familiar silhouette appeared at my front door. I knew it was him, because, having rung the bell, he retreated to the gate: a defensive habit gained on the streets. 'It's the man', said my young daughter, 'with no name.'

He had on his usual tie and tweed jacket and was leaning against the hedge, though he said he hadn't had a drink. 'Just passing through,' he said as usual, and money passed between us with the customary clumsy handshake. 'I'd better give that a trim,' he said, as he always did, pointing at the hedge, and again I thanked him and said no; he was too unsteady for that. Collar up, he turned back into the rain.

I have known him for about three years. He comes to my door at least every week, and I see him out on the common in all weathers, asleep or reading or looking at the traffic. I see him nodding as if in silent discussion with himself on a weighty matter; or waving and smiling at a procession of women with small children in buggies. Understandably, women hurry away from him; others look through him.

He has no home, though he once told me he lived 'just around the corner'. That turned out to be a hostel. From what I can gather, he sleeps rough most of the time, often on a bench in front of a small powerboats clubhouse, or in a clump of large trees where sick and alcoholic men go and where there was a murder some years back. In winter, he has newspapers tucked inside his jacket. Perhaps he is fifty, or more; it's difficult to tell.

He vanishes from time to time, as the homeless tend to do; and when I last asked him about this, he said he went to 'visit my sister'. I very much doubted this; I know he goes to one of several seaside towns for a few weeks at a time. There he scans the local newspaper small ads for 'unemployed guests wanted'. These are inserted by the owners of bed-and-breakfast hotels and hostels, where homeless people are sent by local authorities and by the Department of Health and Social Security.

I can imagine a little of what it must be like for him. As a reporter I once ended up in one of these 'hotels'. When I couldn't produce the Social Security form that would allow the owner to collect every penny of his 'guest's' state benefit, I was thrown out. This wholesale diversion of public money is acknowledged as one of the fastest ways of getting rich in Britain since the Thatcher Government stopped councils spending on housing more than ten years ago. Hotel owners are said to make about £120 million a year. In the Enterprise Society, homelessness, like drinking water, has been 'privatised'; or is it 'restructured'?

My friend is one of 80,000 people who are officially homeless in London. This is the equivalent of the population of Stevenage, in Hertfordshire; the true figure is greater, of course. The national figure for homeless households is 169,000, ten times higher than a decade ago. The homeless are now a nation within a nation, whose suffering makes a good television story at Christmas or when there is snow and ice.

I have never been made homeless. To have nowhere to go, perhaps for the rest of my life, to face every day the uncertainty of the night and fear of the elements, is almost unimaginable. I say 'almost', because in writing about the homeless I have gleaned something of their powerlessness once they are snared in what used to be known as the 'welfare state'. This was true before Thatcher.

The difference these days is that there are no 'typical' homeless any more. They are also from the middle classes and the new software classes. They are both old and young – an estimated 35,000 children are homeless in London alone. My friend is typical in that he bears the familiar scars of homelessness: such as a furtiveness that gives the impression of a person being followed; a sporadic, shallow joviality that fails to mask his anxiety; and a deferential way that does not necessarily reflect his true self. The latter, because it is out of character, is occasionally overtaken by melodramatic declarations of independence. When he told me he had to go to hospital one day for a stomach operation and I offered to take him, he said, 'No! I can walk! Of course I can!' And he did.

I didn't know who or what he was until recently. It seemed an intrusion to ask. My place in his life was simply as a source of a few quid from time to time. Then one day he was telling me about a television programme about Asia he had seen, and it was clear he had been there in the Army. And that led to a statement of pride about what he had done with his life on leaving the Army. He had worked in a garage, training apprentice mechanics, until this was thwarted by a string of personal tragedies: a divorce and finally his 'redundancy': that wonderful expression of the Enterprise Society. He was then too old to start again; and he was taking to drink.

He has turned up with cuts and bruises, and blood caked on his cheek. Once, when I said I would go and call a doctor, I returned to the door to find him gone. On the common and in the streets, he is prey to thugs and to the police. He has little of the protection the rest of us assume as a right, provided by a civilised society. The defences that have been built up for the likes of him since the great Depression of sixty years ago continue to be dismantled with platitudes that are spoken, unchallenged, on the news almost every night.

Recently it was National Housing Week. The junior housing minister, Tim Yeo, said the government's 'rough sleepers initiative', which was launched during the freezing conditions of last winter, had halved the numbers of homeless sleeping out in London.

Anyone driving through London's West End knows this to be untrue. The homeless in the capital have become a tourist curiosity. Europeans are incredulous at having to step over so many human bundles on the pavement, in the Underground, on the steps of galleries and museums. Eavesdrop on a French tour guide describing the sights in the shopfronts of the Strand. 'They were hosed away,' she says, 'but they have come back.'

With the maximum publicity, the government allocated £300 million for 'rough sleepers'. As the London Housing Unit has pointed out, this has been wiped out by the £138 million in cuts in long-term housing investment by councils and by the abolition of £100 million-worth of special allowances for London boroughs. The minister, Tim Yeo, said: 'You will see a similar priority given to housing as to education and health between now and the general election.' In the circumstances this had to be irony; but it was not.

John Pilger
New Statesman, 14 June 1991

Beggars of Britain

Punk Beggars, drunk beggars, beggars with babies. Beggars in shell suits and beggars in rags. Beggars stinking of cheap lager with snot on their chin and a mangy mutt on the end of a piece of string. Lots of them.

And gypsy beggars who try to stuff a ratty flower into your button hole with some sentimental line – 'For the children,' coos some obese hag. Old beggars too shagged out to beg, young beggars who look like they could run a four-minute mile if they ever made it up off their fannies. Beggars in King's Cross, beggars in Covent Garden, beggars on the street where you live. All kinds of beggars everywhere in this city, and they will be with us forever now. They have no shame. Because begging is no longer taboo.

I think that my father would rather have seen us go hungry than have to go out there and ponce for our supper. I think that the old man, may he rest peacefully, would have preferred to rob, cheat or watch us wither with malnutrition before standing on a street corner with a Uriah Heep look in his eye asking for a hand-out. He would have been happier seeing us sleeping in a shoebox full of shit than he would have been *begging*.

The fact is that my father's generation was incapable of begging. The children they raised were also incapable of begging. There were standards that were not negotiable. There were certain lines you never crossed; there were taboos. Respect the elderly. Don't rat on your friends. Never hit a woman. Never stand on a street corner with snot on your chin and a dog on the end of a piece of string asking passers-by if they have any change. Of all the taboos, *don't beg* was the greatest of all. You could sleep with your sister before you went begging.

Somewhere between then and now, between our childhood and our thirties, all the old taboos disappeared. But taboos are good, taboos are the no-go areas that mark the parameters of society's moral code. When taboos fall, civilisation is built on dangerously shifting sands.

Liberals would blame the fall of the begging taboo on the let-the-bloody-orphans-take-care-of-themselves ethics of Thatcherism. Conservatives would blame the hey-you-guys-let's-catch-crabs permissiveness of the '60s. What is certain is that violence against women, children and the wrinklies is at an all-time high; and that begging is suddenly shame-free, an acceptable way to make a living. It is now quite all right to earn a crust with the crumbs you can ponce from strangers. Begging is a vocation. Soon beggars will have agents and accountants who will write off the food for their dogs-on-a-rope against tax. How low can you go? The British have become a nation of nappy-wearers.

In that underrated comedy classic *American Psycho,* Patrick Bateman is plagued by beggars at every turn. In the exchanges between Bateman and the beggars, Bret Easton Ellis reveals that he is really an old softie at heart. The beggars are invariably homeless and hungry and deserving of sympathy, easily reduced to tears of shame and regret. Meanwhile, the American Psycho himself is an archetype of right-wing heartlessness, saying things to the cry-baby beggars like, 'Listen – do you think it's fair to take money from people who do have jobs? Who do work?' just before he slices out their eyeballs with a platinum Am Ex card.

The most unrealistic thing about the beggars in *American Psycho* is their shame. It is quite believable that they are outside every restaurant. It is perfectly credible that they inspire nausea and disgust in Bateman. What smacks of pure invention, however, are the tears of self-loathing that course down their cheeks whenever Bateman gives them a stern look. I never saw a beggar yet who would recognise guilt if it bit him on his unwashed ass. In real life – over here and over there – beggars have no shame. Their whole schtick is a transference of guilt. Shame is meant to be in the eye of the beholder. Twenty years ago – *five years ago!* – the beggar might have felt guilty. Now it's the *beggee* who's meant to feel bad. Well, I'm sorry, but any liberal guilt I might feel about brushing past yet another beggar – and there are so many of the bastards – has long been overwhelmed by compassion fatigue.

Now that begging is an acceptable career option it is worth considering a few tips from poncing masterclass. Place yourself somewhere the public can't miss you, say outside a West End theatre or at the foot of some tube station steps. Consider the use of props – a child is good, a baby even better, though you would be surprised at the well of compassion you plumb when you have some flea-bitten mongrel at your side. Signs are fine. Knock out ones that say, 'Please give generously – No home, no job, no shame' or 'Take pity – Mohawk with run in tights' or 'Dog on a rope to support'. Make eye contact and be persistent, friendly – don't be too specific. Ask the beggees for 'loose change', rather than money for a cup of coffee or money to catch the bus to the Job Centre. Everybody knows you are going to piss it away.

You can always sing a little song or do a little dance, but a true beggar frowns on these gimmicks. Busking is begging with music (give me money because I am entertaining you) just as mugging is begging with menace (give me money or I will fill your face in). But begging purists want you to give them money because – what? Because you are better off than they are? Because life has dealt them a bad hand?

Well, I don't buy it. I don't believe that the people begging are the unluckiest people in town. They are merely the people with the least pride, dignity, self-respect – all the intangibles that hold the human spirit together.

It's strange, but I don't recall ever seeing a black beggar in London, or a Hong Kong Chinese beggar or an Indian beggar. I must have seen hundreds, thousands of beggars in this town, and they have all been white trash. But when you look at the sick-making state of the white working class – all the men turning into fat farts at 20, all the girls turning into their mothers a year later – what possible hope could there be for the next rung down on the caste system? If the people with jobs have the aesthetic beauty and intellectual ability of a cow pat, what chance is there for the people without a job? Though of course by now begging *is* a job – the newest profession.

I used to give, I used to give generously. These people disgusted me, but still I gave. I was appalled, but I felt sorry for them – and they knew it! Oh, they could spot old muggins a mile off! It was feeding frenzy time at the zoo when I came down the road! I was a soft touch – I thought it was the correct emotional response. In a way, my concern has simply been exhausted. So sorry, *no change!* Ponce your next bruise-blue can of Vomit Brew from some other sucker. There's just *too many* of them. But it goes beyond mere compassion fatigue. I think I have grown to truly hate them.

I hate the way they make a beautiful city ugly, the way they shuffle about in a lager haze first thing in the morning – booze is a bigger factor than bad luck in the begging world – and I hate it that my son came home one day saying he had given his tube fare to a man who really really needed it. I wish he could grow up thinking all men are brothers. But it is hard to think of a man as your brother when he has a brain addled by alcohol, snot on his chin and a dog on a rope. Then every man feels like an only child.

Begging defaces the city, degrades the spirit. It dehumanises you as well as them; it brutalises us all. You learn to walk past these people, you have to, and it makes it easier to turn away from the truly needy. These professional leeches, big strapping lads some of them, harden your heart, put callouses on your soul. They make every cry for help seem like junk mail.

In Africa you see beggars with deformed legs crawling, literally crawling, by the side of the road. In Africa you see old men with their eyes turned a horrible milky blue by river blindness being led around by their grandchildren. You see sights that make you feel like weeping – you see beggars with every excuse for begging. But London isn't the Third World. It just smells that way.

In America they have beggars who are suffering from AIDS – that's probably a couple of years away for us – which begs the question, what's so special about AIDS? Of course it's terrible, all terminal, all tragic. Because there is no social network to take care of these people, you say. Because the medical services can't cope. Well, you can believe that if you want. Or you can believe that begging is like eating human flesh, being cruel to animals or pushing your granny while she's shaving – something that no-one in the developed world should ever do, under any circumstances. The virus that we are truly blighted by is the one that attacks the human spirit. It is reflected in the general degeneracy of life in our capital, in the pathetically unctuous faces of all these healthy grown men whose best friend is a dog on a piece of string.

But it may not be very long before we look back on the good old days when the only beggars we had to contend with were gypsies, punks and drunks. The new hard times are not a northern, working-class, trouble-at-mill thing this time around. This time the recession has hit the middle class – it's wonderful, it's never been so easy to hail a black cab – and now that the last taboo is gone, how long before you are asked for loose change by a Channel 4 commissioning editor or a *South Bank Show* researcher, or an editor at Random House? How long before you look into the face of a beggar on Old Compton Street and realise – the horror, the horror – that you have had *lunch* with this person?

The taboos are coming down, and so are all the borders. The other day I saw a family of East Europeans jabbering away in some Slavic dialect. You wouldn't believe these people. The woman was wearing a little Porsche badge on clothes so synthetic they were a fire hazard. If you think that Thatcher has made us a nation of nappy wearers, then wait till you get a load of the paragons of dependency that Marx and Lenin have produced. The opening up of Europe creates all sorts of possibilities for the begging industry.

We owe it to ourselves to walk past them, metaphorically gobbing in the grubby palms of their outstretched hands, chanting our protest against a world that is forever changing for the worst. No change, we say, no change. Just say no change.

Tony Parsons
Arena, September/October 1991

Argument Activities

An Introduction to Argument

1. Arguing in talk and writing

• In pairs or small groups, talk about what you understand by the word 'argument'. Come up with a list of the types of situation in which you listen to, read, or take part in 'argument' in your daily life:

– at home
– at school
– in the street, or other public places
– in things that you read in comics, magazines and newspapers
– in what you watch on television.

• What strategies do you use when you're arguing? For instance, do you use sarcasm, do you yell, do you exaggerate or do you make your views known by piling up lots of reasons? Make a list of your strategies.

• Now read this dictionary definition of argument and decide which meaning most closely matches the kinds of argument you've been talking about in the previous activities.

1. A quarrel, altercation.
2. A discussion in which reasons are put forward in support of and against a proposition, proposal, or case; debate.
3. A point or series of propositions presented to support or oppose a proposition.
4. A process of reasoning in which the conclusion can be shown to be true or false.

Argument in the sense of definitions 2, 3 and 4 happens both in speech and writing.
• List a few examples of each, for example:

Speech	Writing
A public enquiry on the building of a road	A newspaper editorial
A judge's summing up of a trial	

Both personal arguments and argument in the sense of 'debate', use a range of strategies.
• Look at the list below. How many match the list you came up with for your own arguments?

– Logic
– Emotion
– Humour
– Irony/sarcasm
– Exaggeration
– Rhetorical devices (such as repeating words or phrases, or asking questions you don't really want answered)
– Appealing to the audience
– Facts and figures
– Personal experience
– Expert witnesses
– Examples of similar things which have happened in the past or in different places

• When you read the pieces of argument in this section of the book, keep in mind what you've discovered about:
– what argument is
– the strategies people use when they argue.

Legalising Drugs

1. Before reading
You are going to read an article from a national newspaper about a man whose son died of drug abuse.
• Brainstorm what you think he might want to argue as a result of his and his son's experiences.

2. Reading the article
• Listen to the article being read aloud.

• When you have finished listening, talk about your first responses to the writer's experiences and the argument he is making.

3. Yes but ...
• In pairs or small groups read the second half of the article aloud. While one person reads a paragraph in turn, the others should interrupt with possible alternative arguments. For instance, when he says, 'I am convinced that he would be alive today if all drugs had been legalised and controlled because he would have had no need to steal ...', one of you might interrupt with 'Yes but ...'

4. Personal experience, fact and opinion
• Look through a photocopy of the article. Put an E beside each paragraph which is mainly about personal experience. Put an F beside each paragraph which mainly

states objective facts. Put an O beside the paragraphs which seem to you to express the writer's opinions.

• What conclusions can you draw about:
– how much of the article is based on experience, fact or opinion – you could estimate proportions, e.g. is it 50% -25%?
– where in the article there is most experience, fact and opinion
– what effect this has on the reader.

• Do you feel that the personal experience strengthens or weakens the argument? Would you have liked more or less information about Scott Gillespie and way that he died?

5. Signposting where the argument is going
• On your photocopy of the article underline all the words and phrases that help move his argument on and show how it is developing logically. For instance, 'So ...'

• Where in the article do these words appear? Do you think the writer signals the direction of his argument early enough? Why do you think he doesn't do so at the beginning?

6. Taking a different view
• Brainstorm all the arguments against Fulton Gillespie's viewpoint on legalising drugs.

• Write a letter to Fulton Gillespie, responding to his story and his views about drugs in which you disagree with his conclusions. Try to find an appropriate tone of voice, to match the personal nature of his argument.

7. Arguing from experience
• Think of something that you've experienced that has shaped your views and led you to feel strongly about an issue. Here are some examples to start you thinking.

– A difficult encounter with someone important to you, that has shaped your views on relationships or friendships.
– A serious accident, or incident that happened to you or a friend.
– A book or a film that has shaped the way you see the world.
– Your experience of facilities for young people in your locality and what it has led you to feel about what needs changing.

• Describe the experience and its impact on your life and opinions. Think about how to select and order the detail of your narrative so that it has maximum impact on the argument you are presenting. For instance, will you follow Fulton Gillespie's example and have the whole narrative at the beginning, followed by the argument?

Legalising Drugs – Letters to the Paper

'Legalising Drugs' ('It was not the drug') is a newspaper article; it makes its case using personal experience. Another quite different form of argument is letters to a newspaper. They are usually:

– short
– to the point
– clearly focused on replying to points made either in an article or in other letters to the newspaper.

1. Reading letters on the issue of legalising drugs

The letters on pages 61-63 are all replies to a series of articles and letters on the issue of legalising drugs, in *The Daily Telegraph* (24th-31st May, 2002). In the letters, the articles are referrred to as 'the Leading Article' and 'Comment'.

• Some of the letters are written in quite complex language. Read each letter, without worrying too much about whether you understand every single word. See if you can decide whether each letter is for legalisation of drugs, against it, or undecided.

• For each letter, decide which of these statements you think are most relevant. Choose up to three statements for each letter.

---

1. It mainly argues using personal experience.
2. It mainly uses facts, statistics and other 'objective' evidence.
3. It makes fresh arguments of its own.
4. It knocks down the arguments raised by other letter writers or the writer of the leading article.
5. It uses language powerfully to argue its case.
6. It is too emotional and nasty in its attacks on other writers.
7. It is nice and simple and clear in its argument.
8. It makes too many points – it's easy to lose the thread of the argument.
9. The language is unnecessarily complicated.
10. It is punchily written and makes a strong impact.

---

2. Writing a letter of your own

• Write a short, punchy letter of your own, on the subject of the legalisation of drugs. You could reply to one of the ones you've read.

3. Argument consequences

The people who write letters to a newspaper are responding either to articles or letters published in the paper. Newspapers like *The Guardian* and *The Independent* also have special 'Debate' sections of their websites where readers can 'post' their opinions and reply to those expressed by other people. These debate 'threads' often form arguments.

• Write a statement expressing an opinion on a subject about which you feel strongly. You should also explain why this is your opinion. Some possible topics are suggested here.

- Education should be compulsory until 18 years.
- Pupils learn better in single sex schools.
- Sex education is best left to parents.

• Now pass your piece of paper on to the person sitting next to you. Read the statement you have been given and add one of your own on the same topic. It doesn't matter whether you agree or disagree but you should make sure that the two statements are linked together so that they make sense, for example, I agree/disagree with xx because xx ...

• Carry on for as long as possible, then listen to the arguments being read out loud.

Big Brother – a Boring Showcase for Exhibitionists

1. Before reading
• David Aaronovitch tackles the subject of *Big Brother* and reality TV. Before reading the article consider the following statements in pairs and rank them in order of importance. Then share your top four with another pair and see if you can come up with a final list of the three most important statements for you on reality TV.

1. It brings the country together with a running topic of conversation.
2. It creates real situations for the viewer to observe and learn from.
3. It deepens our understanding of human nature.
4. It reduces the dignity of the viewers by turning them into voyeurs, spying on other people and the way they behave.
5. It is humiliating for the participants because it exposes them to public hostility and judgement.
6. Reality TV depends on recruiting show-offs rather than ordinary people.
7. The participants are usually very boring which makes their conversation uninteresting.
8. *Big Brother* has successfully created a new form of television which has made TV, as a whole, much worse.
9. *Big Brother* gives real interactive power to the viewer who can play a part in shaping the plot.
10. Reality TV gives ordinary people opportunities to show what they can do.
11. Reality TV is a sad reflection on British society because more people voted in the *Big Brother* show than voted in the General Election of 2001.
12. It calls itself 'reality TV' but in fact it's highly edited – the directors select from the 26 cameras and also edit the footage – so how real is it?

2. Understanding the argument

• Write out the first sentence of each paragraph on alternate lines to leave space for you to jot down a few ideas. Analyse how each of these first sentences works:
– to intrigue the reader and rouse their curiosity?
– to be challenging?
– to signpost the argument?
For each sentence, jot down what argument is being raised and what the sentence seems to be doing for the reader. The first sentence has been done for you as an example.

'And so we arrive at chapter 102 in my massive, magisterial but pessimistic master-work, provisionally entitled *New Lows in Western Culture*.'

It seems to be arguing that *Big Brother* is one of the worst things we've seen yet in western culture. It's unusually written and is designed to be amusing and capture the reader's interest.

3. Arguing for fun

Aaronovitch uses a very direct form of address to the audience. His argument is only partly serious – he's also arguing to entertain.
• On a photocopy of the text, underline the phrases which mark this as a particularly informal piece of argument.

• Underline any phrases that show Aaronovitch entertaining the reader. For each phrase, try to explain how it works (for instance, by using sarcasm, irony, exaggeration, absurdity and so on).

4. Argument as a play

Aaronovitch writes as though he were having a conversation with the reader. Sometimes, catching the flavour of a speaking voice can give colour and life to writing.
• Try working out how you would argue with Aaronovitch by composing your arguments as a scripted duologue. For instance:

ME: How can you say it's a showcase for exhibitionists at the same time as saying all the contestants are completely and utterly dull? If they were so dull, people wouldn't bother watching.

AARONOVITCH: Ah, but there are lots of boring exhibitionists. Take Chris Evans, for instance …

5. Arguing against Aaronovitch

• Apart from the last paragraph you get the impression that Aaronovitch really dislikes *Big Brother*. Put the case for the defence of *Big Brother* and programmes like it. First brainstorm all your ideas, then work out how you can make your case in a really lively, persuasive way.

• Present your case, either as an article in the newspaper, or as an oral argument in front of your class.

6. Making a case for a new reality TV show
• In pairs think up some reality television ideas that you might try and persuade a TV company to adopt. Anticipate objections and build answers into a proposal for a two minute presentation. If you can't think of any ideas try the following as starters.

– A murderer is released from prison and is hunted by professional criminals who have auditioned for the part.
– School students are selected to live alone on a desert island. How will they manage without adults? (*Lord of the Flies* rides again!)
– So you think you can teach! Volunteers enlist to run a school.

The Man With No Name

Magazines and newspapers try to attract readers by asking well known journalists to write articles giving their opinions and views about a variety of social issues. Journalists who write this kind of column become well known to the reader, who looks forward to reading what they have to say about topical issues and events. The final two articles in this section are by two such writers, John Pilger and Tony Parsons, both writing on the subject of begging. Both pieces were written and first published in 1991, under a Conservative government. Pilger's piece, which is included in his book *Distant Voices*, was first published in the *New Statesman*, a left of centre weekly magazine. Tony Parson's article was written in the same period and comes from *Arena*, a fortnightly style magazine aimed at men.

1. Homelessness today
• In groups of three exchange any personal experiences you may have had of seeing or talking to beggars or the homeless.

2. What the Bible says
In the New Testament, the treatment of the poor is seen as being a very important test of Christian faith.
• Look at these quotes from the bible, in which Jesus preaches to his followers. Talk about what the quotes tell us about Christian beliefs about the poor and about charity.

> '‌Blessed are the meek: for they shall inherit the earth.'
> *St. Matthew 5:3*

> 'It is easier for a camel to go through the eye of a needle, than for a rich man to enter into the kingdom of God.'
> *St. Matthew 19:24*

> 'For I was an hungred, and ye gave me meat:
> I was thirsty and ye gave me drink:
> I was a stranger, and ye took me in:
> Naked, and ye clothed me: I was sick and ye visited me:
> I was in prison, and ye came to me.'
> *St Matthew 25:35*

> 'Inasmuch as ye have done it unto one of the least of these my brethren, ye have done it unto me.'
> *St Matthew 25:40*

3. What is the argument?

• Having read the article, or heard it read aloud, work in small groups and see if you can decide what points John Pilger is trying to make. For each of the statements below, decide whether you agree or disagree and why.

Pilger is arguing that:

... the homeless are to blame for their plight and shouldn't be given money when they beg.

... the Department of Health and Social Security's rules help to make people homeless.

... it's a disgrace that public money from the Department of Health and Social Security is going into the pockets of hotel owners, rather than being spent on homes for the homeless.

... it's really only a very small part of the population that is homeless.

... homelessness and begging will decrease if the Government makes tougher laws to stop people from loitering on the streets and begging.

... the 'welfare state', which was supposed to help people has trapped the homeless in their situation.

... homeless people can't be identified as a typical group. Anyone can become homeless, from any class or age group.

... homeless people are people who are especially inadequate and that's why they have become homeless.

... the homeless are not given the same rights as the rest of society.

... homeless people shouldn't have the same rights as everyone else.

4. Making a point with a story

John Pilger uses a particular incident to make a general point about society, in this case the plight of the homeless and the government's response to the problem. By telling a story Pilger intends to get the sympathy of the reader which in turn enables him to make his point.
• Find two examples of Pilger telling the story of the man and two examples of Pilger giving his broader viewpoint on homelessness and government policy.

• List the ways that Pilger tries to create the sense of a real human being in his description of the homeless man.

• Where do the comment and story appear in the article? For example, is it all story at the beginning and comment at the end? Talk about why you think Pilger has structured the article in this way.

5. No name's story

When a writer uses a slice of someone's life to make a point it is possible that the people being written about might have another point of view.
• Re-read 'The Man with No Name' and write a piece of your own, as if written by the homeless man. How might he see 'The Middle-Class Journalist with No Name'? It might help to imagine it as a dialogue with another homeless person in a hostel.

6. Writing about homelessness

Included below is some more recent information on homelessness and street homelessness from Shelter, the national homelessness charity. It is taken from *Housing and Homelessness in England: the facts* and *Street Homelessness* (2002).
• Read the information and talk about the main issues it raises.

• Use the information from Shelter and your own experiences of seeing people on the streets to do one of the tasks suggested here:
– talk about how much has changed since Pilger wrote his piece
– write a short article on the continuing problem of homelessness.

Housing and Homelessness in England: the Facts
Homelessness affects families and single people alike, and is the most acute indicator of a shortage of affordable housing.

Broadly, the homelessness legislation defines a person as homeless if 'there is nowhere where they (and anyone who is normally with them) can reasonably be expected to live'. We do not know the total number of people who are homeless according to this definition. Many people do not approach local authorities for help, because they do not know about their rights or because they think they won't get any help.

Of those who approach local authorities, 184,290 households were found to be homeless by local authorities in England in 2001. Shelter estimates that this represents over 440,000 people.

Street Homelessness
All initiatives to tackle street homelessness have been bedevilled by problems of how to accurately measure the numbers of people sleeping on the streets. How do you find people who are scattered over wide areas, often hidden for privacy and protection? How do you measure the numbers on any given night? How many people are sleeping out over longer periods? [...]
• In 1966, the National Assistance Board counted 300 people sleeping on the streets in Inner London and six outer boroughs, and 965 people throughout the rest of Britain.
• The 1991 census which counted the number of people sleeping on the streets for the first time, found 2,674 people in this situation in England.
• In June 1998, the Department of Environment, Transport and the Regions (DETR) estimated there were 1,850 street homeless people in England, of whom 621 were in Greater London.
• In March 2001 government figures estimated that there were 380 people sleeping on the streets in London.
• In 1999/2000 Shelter England worked with 19,725 individuals or households who said they had nowhere to go that night when they got in touch.
• In the first four months of 2001 Shelter's services were contacted by 1,320 people in London who had experienced street homelessness. Of these 337 had been street homeless for between a week and three months, and 174 had been street homeless for six months or more.

Beggars of Britain

1. The title
When this article first appeared, it was called 'Street Trash', with the words 'Beggars of Britain' as a smaller title.
• Talk about your response to the full title. What expectations does it raise for you?

2. The tone of voice
• In threes read the first two paragraphs aloud. Each person should try reading it with a different tone of voice. Which one seems most appropriate to the way the author uses words?

Angry
Sneering and full of contempt
Patronising
Cruel
Sympathetic and concerned
Depressed

3. Who is he talking to?
• *Arena* is a magazine aimed at men. Can you learn anything about the readership of the article from Parson's:
– use of language
– use of vocabulary
– level of formality
– emotional appeal.

• What does his language tell you about the way he sees the reader?

4. How strong is his case?
• Make a list of the reasons why Tony Parsons dislikes begging. Do they add up to a reasonable case against begging?

• Do you feel that the author is breaking any taboos in this article, saying things that most people would feel shouldn't be said?

5. Shock tactics
Tony Parsons is determined to make the reader sit up and take notice. He uses shock tactics to do this.
• Find some examples of this and talk about how they work.

6. The weapon of sarcasm
At one point Parsons seems to be writing a guide on how to beg. Clearly, given his point of view, these instructions are not meant to be taken seriously. He is pretending to give advice but is in fact only using this as a device to reinforce his argument. This technique is called sarcasm or irony.
• Write 'A Beginner's Guide to Being ...'. Choose from the list on page 85.

– Politicians
– Dentists
– Bullies
– DJs
– Chat show hosts.

• Use sarcasm as away of expressing your view of that group.

7. Parsons and Pilger meet
• Write an imaginary dialogue between John Pilger and Tony Parsons about the subject of begging and homelessness. Use all the work you have done on the two texts to help you identify what is different about their viewpoints and their likely styles of arguing with each other.

Gather Together in My Name

The midmorning sun was deceitfully mild and the wind had no weight on my skin. Arkansas summer mornings have a feathering effect on stone reality.

After five days in the South my quick speech had begun to drag, and the clipped California diction (clipped in comparison) had started to slur. I had to brace myself properly to 'go downtown'. In San Francisco, women dressed particularly to shop in the Geary and Market streets' big-windowed stores. Short white gloves were as essential a part of the shopping attire as girdles, which denied cleaved buttocks, and deodorant, which permitted odorless walkings up and down the steep hills.

I dressed San Francisco style for the nearly three-mile walk and proceeded through the black part of town, past the Christian Methodist Episcopal and African Methodist Episcopal churches and the proud little houses that sat above their rose bushes in grassless front yards, on toward the pond and the railroad tracks which separated white town from black town. My postwar Vinylite high heels, which were see-through plastic, crunched two inches into the resisting gravel, and I tugged my gloves all the way up to my wrist. I had won over the near-tropical inertia, and the sprightly walk, made a bit jerky by the small grabbing stones, the neat attire and the high headed position, was bound to teach the black women watching behind lace curtains how they should approach a day's downtown shopping. It would prove to the idle white women, once I reached their territory, that I knew how things should be done. And if I knew, well, didn't that mean that there were legions of Black women in other parts of the world who knew also? Up went the Black Status.

When I glided and pulled into White Town, there was a vacuum. The air had died and fallen down heavily. I looked at the white windows expecting to see curtains lose strained positions and resume their natural places. But the curtains on both sides of the street remained fixed. Then I realized that the white women were missing my halting but definitely elegant advance on their town. I then admitted my weariness, but urged my head higher and my shoulders squarer than before.

What Stamps' General Merchandise Store missed in class it made up in variety. Cheap grades of thread and chicken feed, farming implements and hair ribbons, fertilizer, shampoo, women's underwear, and B.V.D.s. Socks, face powder, school supplies and belly-wrenching laxatives were shoved on and under the shelves.

I pitied the poor storekeeper and the shop attendants. When I thought of the wide aisles of San Francisco's Emporium and the nearly heard, quiet conversations in the expensive City of Paris, I gave the store a patronizing smile.

A young, very blond woman's mournful countenance met me in the middle of a crowded aisle. I gave her, 'Good morning,' and let a benign smile lift the corners of my lips.

'What can I do for you?' The thin face nodded at me like a sharp ax descending slowly. I thought, 'The poor shabby dear!' She didn't even form her words. Her question floated out like a hillbilly song,' 'Whakin I dew fer yew?'

'I'd like a Simplicity pattern, please!' I could afford to be courteous. I was the sophisticate. When I gave her the pattern number out of my head and saw her start at my Western accent, regained for the moment, I felt a rush of kindness for the sorrowful cracker girl. I added, 'If you please.'

She walked behind a counter and riffled through a few aging sewing patterns, her shoulders rounding over the drawer as if its contents were in danger. Although she was twenty, or more likely eighteen, her stance and face spoke of an early surrender to the poverty of poor-white Southern life. There was no promise of sex in her hip span, nor flight in her thin short fingers.

'We ain't got it here. But I can put in a order to Texarkana for it for you.'

She never looked up and spoke of the meager town twenty five miles away as if she meant Istanbul.

'I would so much appreciate that!' I did feel grateful and even more magnanimous.

'It'll be back in three days. You come in on Friday.'

I wrote my name, Marguerite A. Johnson, without flourishes on the small pad she handed me, smiled encouragement to her and walked back into the now-serious noon sunshine. The heat had rendered the roads empty of pedestrians, and it assaulted my shoulders and the top of my head as if it had been lying in wait for me.

The memory of the insensate clerk prodded me into exaggerated awareness and dignity. I had to walk home at the same sprightly clip, my arms were obliged to swing in their same rhythm, and I would not under any circumstances favor the shade trees which lined the road. My head blurred with deep pains, and the rocky path swam around me, but I kept my mind keen on the propriety of my position and finally gained the Store.

Momma asked from the cool, dark kitchen, 'What'd you buy, Sister?'

I swallowed the heat-induced nausea and answered, 'Nothing, Momma.'

* * * * *

The days eased themselves around our lives like visitors in a sickroom. I hardly noticed their coming and going. Momma was as engrossed as she'd allow herself in the wonder of my son. Patting, stroking, she talked to him and never introduced in her deep voice the false humor adults tend to offer babies. He, in turn, surrendered to her. Following her from kitchen to porch to store to the backyard.

Their togetherness came to be expected. The tall and large dark-brown woman (whose movement never seemed to start or stop) was trailed one step by the pudgy little butter-yellow baby lurching, falling, now getting himself up, at moments rocking on bowed legs, then off again in the wave of Momma. I never saw her turn or stop to right him, but she would slow her march and resume when he was steady again.

* * * * *

My pattern had arrived from old exotic Texarkana. And I dressed for the trek downtown, and checked my hair, which was straightened to within an inch of its life and greased to desperation. From within the Store, I felt the threat of the sun but walked out into the road impelled by missionary zeal.

By the time I reached the pond and Mr. Willie Williams' Dew Drop In, the plastic seemed to have melted to the exact shape of my feet, and sweat had popped through the quarter inch of Arrid in my armpits.

Mr. Williams served me a cold drink. 'What you trying to do? Fry your brains?'

'I'm on my way to the General Merchandise Store. To pick up an order.'

His smile was a two-line checkerboard of white and gold. 'Be careful they don't pick you up. This sun ain't playing.'

Arrogance and stupidity nudged me out of the little café and back on the white hot clay. I drifted under the shade trees, my face a mask of indifference. The skin of my thighs scudded like wet rubber as I walked deliberately by the alien white houses and on to my destination.

In the store the air lay heavily on the blades of two sluggish overhead fans, and a sweet, thick odor enveloped me at the cosmetic counter. Still, I was prepared to wander the aisles until the sun forgave our sins and withdrew its vengeance.

A tall saleswoman wearing a clerk's smock confronted me. I tried to make room for her in the narrow corridor. I moved to my left, she moved to her right. I right, she left, we jockeyed a moment's embarrassment and I smiled. Her long face answered with a smile. 'You stand still and I'll pass you.' It was not a request for cooperation. The hard mountain voice gave me an order.

To whom did she think she was speaking? Couldn't she see from my still-white though dusty gloves, my starched clothes, that I wasn't a servant to be ordered around? I had walked nearly three miles under a sun on fire and was neither gasping nor panting, but standing with the cool decorum of a great lady in the tacky, putrid store. She should have considered that.

'No, you stand still and I'll pass around you,' I commanded.

The amazement which leaped upon her face was quickly pushed aside by anger. 'What's your name? Where you from?'

A repetition of 'You stand still and I'll pass around you' was ready on my tongue, when the pale woman who had taken my order slack-butted down the aisle toward us. The familiar face brought back the sympathy I had felt for her and I explained the tall woman into limbo with 'Excuse me, here comes my salesgirl.'

The dark-haired woman turned quickly and saw her colleague approach. She put herself between us, and her voice rasped out in the quiet store: 'Who is this?'

Her head jerked back to indicate me. 'Is this that sassy Ruby Lee you was telling me about?'

The clerk lifted her chin and glanced at me, then swirled to the older woman. 'Naw, this ain't her.' She flipped the pages of a pad in her hand and continued, 'This one's Margaret or Marjorie or something like that.'

Her head eased up again and she looked across centuries at me. 'How do you pronounce your name, gal? Speak up.'

In that moment I became rootless, nameless, pastless. The two white blurs buoyed before me.

'Speak up,' she said. 'What's your name?'

I clenched my reason and forced their faces into focus. 'My name' – here I drew myself up through the unrevenged slavery – 'is Miss Johnson. If you have occasion to use my name, which I seriously doubt, I advise you to address me as Miss Johnson. For if I need to allude to your pitiful selves, I shall call you Miss Idiot, Miss Stupid, Miss Fool or whatever name a luckless fate has dumped upon you.'

The women became remote even as I watched them. They seemed actually to float away from me down the aisle; and from watching their distant faces, I knew they were having trouble believing in the fact of me.

'And where I'm from is no concern of yours, but rather where you're going. I'll slap you into the middle of next week if you even dare to open your mouths again. Now, take that filthy pattern and stick it you-know-where.'

As I strode between the two women I was sheathed in satisfaction. There had been so few critical times when my actions met my approval that now I congratulated myself. I had got them told and told correctly. I pictured the two women's mouths still open in amazement. The road was less rocky and the sun's strength was weakened by my pleasure. Congratulations were in order.

There was no need to stop at Mr. Williams' for a refreshing drink. I was as cool as a fountain inside as I headed home.

Momma stood on the porch facing the road. Her arms hung at her sides and she made no motions with her head. Yet something was wrong. Tension had distorted the statue straightness and caused her to lean leftward. I stopped patting myself on the back and ran to the Store.

When I reached the one-step porch, I looked up in her face. 'Momma, what's the matter?'

Worry had forced a deep line down either side of her nostrils past her stiffly held lips.

'What's wrong?'

'Mr. Coleman's granddaughter, Miss June, just called from the General Merchandise Store.' Her voice quaked a little. 'She said you was downtown showing out.'

So that's how they described my triumph to her. I decided to explain and let her share in the glory. I began, 'It was the principle of the thing, Momma –'

I didn't even see the hand rising, and suddenly it had swung down hard against my cheek.

'Here's your principle, young miss.'

I felt the sting on my skin and the deep ache in my head. The greatest hurt was that she didn't ask to hear my side.

'Momma, it was a principle.' My left ear was clogged, but I heard my own voice fuzzily.

The hand didn't surprise me the second time, but the same logic which told me I was right at the white store told me I was no less right in front of Momma. I couldn't allow myself to duck the blow. The backhand swing came down on my right cheek.

'Here's your principle.' Her voice had a far-away-tunnel sound.

'It was a principle, Momma.' Tears poured down my burning face, and ache backed up in my throat.

The hand came again and again each time I mumbled 'principle', and I found myself in the soft dust in front of the porch. I didn't want to move. I never wanted to get up again.

She stepped off the porch and caught my arms. 'Get up. Stand up, I say.'

Her voice never allowed disobedience. I stood, and looked at her face. It glistened as if she had just dashed a pan of water over her head.

'You think 'cause you've been to California these crazy people won't kill you? You think them lunatic cracker boys won't try to catch you in the road and violate you? You think because of your all-fired principle some of the men won't feel like putting their white sheets on and riding over here to stir up trouble? You do, you're wrong. Ain't nothing to protect you and us except the good Lord and some miles. I packed you and the baby's things, and Brother Wilson is coming to drive you to Louisville.'

That afternoon I climbed into a horse-drawn wagon, and took my baby from Momma's arms. The baby cried as we pulled away, and Momma and Uncle Willie stood waving and crying good-bye.

Maya Angelou
Gather Together in My Name, 1974

And When Did You Last See Your Father?

A hot September Saturday in 1959, and we are stationary in Cheshire. Ahead of us, a queue of cars stretches out of sight around the corner. We haven't moved for ten minutes. Everyone has turned his engine off, and now my father does so too. In the sudden silence we can hear the distant whinge of what must be the first race of the afternoon, a ten-lap event for saloon cars. It is quarter past one. In an hour the drivers will be warming up for the main event, the Gold Cup – Graham Hill, Jack Brabham, Roy Salvadori, Stirling Moss and Joakim Bonnier. My father has always loved fast cars, and motor-racing has a strong British following just now, which is why we are stuck here in this country lane with hundreds of cars.

My father does not like waiting in queues. He is used to patients waiting in queues to see him, but he is not used to waiting in queues himself. A queue, to him, means a man being denied the right to be where he wants to be at a time of his own choosing, which is at the front, now. Ten minutes have passed. What is happening up ahead? What fathead has caused this snarl-up? Why are no cars coming the other way? Has there been an accident? Why are there no police to sort it out? Every two minutes or so my father gets out of the car, crosses to the opposite verge and tries to see if there is movement up ahead. There isn't. He gets back in and steams some more. The roof of our Alvis is down, the sun beating on to the leather upholstery, the chrome, the picnic basket. The hood is folded and pleated into the mysterious crevice between the boot and the narrow back seat where my sister and I are scrunched together as usual. The roof is nearly always down, whatever the weather: my father loves fresh air, and every car he has owned has been a convertible, so that he can have fresh air. But the air today is not fresh. There is a pall of high-rev exhaust, dust, petrol, boiling-over engines.

In the cars ahead and behind, people are laughing, eating sandwiches, drinking from beer bottles, enjoying the weather, settling into the familiar indignity of waiting-to-get-to-the-front. But my father is not like them. There are only two things on his mind: the invisible head of the queue and, not unrelated, the other half of the country lane, tantalizingly empty.

'Just relax, Arthur,' my mother says. 'You're in and out of the car like a blue-tailed fly.'

But being told to relax only incenses him. 'What can it be?' he demands. 'Maybe there's been an accident. Maybe they're waiting for an ambulance.' We all know where this last speculation is leading, even before he says it. 'Maybe they need a doctor.'

'No, Arthur,' says my mother, as he opens the door again and stands on the wheel-arch to crane ahead.

'It must be an accident,' he announces. 'I think I should drive up and see.'

'No, Arthur. It's just the numbers waiting to get in. And surely there must be doctors on the circuit.'

It is one-thirty and silent now. The saloon race has finished. It is still over an hour until the Gold Cup itself, but there's another race first, and the cars in the paddock to see, and besides ...

'Well, I'm not going to bloody well wait here any longer,' he says. 'We'll never get in. We might as well turn round and give up.' He sits there for another twenty seconds then leans forward, opens the glove compartment and pulls out a stethoscope, which he hooks over the mirror on the windscreen. It hangs there like a skeleton, the membrane at the top, the metal and rubber leads dangling bow-legged, the two ivory earpieces clopping bonily against each other. He starts the engine, releases the handbrake, reverses two feet, then pulls out into the opposite side of the road.

'No,' says my mother again, half-heartedly. It could be that he is about to do a three-point turn and go back. No it couldn't ...

My father does not drive particularly quickly past the marooned cars ahead. No more than twenty miles an hour. Even so, it *feels* fast, and arrogant, and all the occupants turn and stare as they see us coming. Some appear to be angry. Some are shouting. 'Point to the stethoscope, pet,' he tells my mother, but she has slid down sideways in her passenger seat, out of sight, her bottom resting on the floor, from where she berates him.

'God Almighty, Arthur, why do you have to do this? Why can't you wait like everyone else? What if we meet something coming the other way?' Now my sister and I do the same, hide ourselves below the seat. Our father is on his own. He is not with us, this bullying, shaming undemocratic cheat. Or rather, we are not with him.

My face pressed to the sweet-smelling upholstery, I imagine what is happening ahead. I can't tell how far we have gone, how many blind corners we have taken. If we meet something, on this narrow country lane, we will have to reverse past all the cars we have just overtaken. That's if we can stop in time. I wait for the squeal of brakes, the clash of metal.

After an eternity of – what? – two minutes, my mother sticks her head up and says, 'Now you've had it,' and my father replies, 'No, there's another gate beyond,' and my sister and I raise ourselves to look. We are up level with the cars at the head of the queue, which are waiting to turn left into the brown ticket holders' entrance, the plebs' entrance. A steward steps out of the gateway towards us, but my father, pretending not to see him, doesn't stop. He drives ahead, on to a clear piece of road where, two hundred yards away, half a dozen cars from the opposite direction are waiting to turn into another gateway. Unlike those we have left behind, these cars appear to be moving. Magnanimous, my father waits until the last of them has turned in, then drives through the stone gateposts and over the bumpy grass to where an armbanded steward in a tweed jacket is waiting by the roped entrance.

'Good afternoon, sir. Red ticket holder?' The question does not come as a shock: we have all seen the signs, numerous and clamorous, saying RED TICKET HOLDERS' ENTRANCE. But my father is undeterred.

'These, you mean,' he says, and hands over his brown tickets.

'No, sir, I'm afraid these are brown tickets.'

'But there must be some mistake. I applied for red tickets. To be honest, I didn't even look.'

'I'm sorry, sir, but these are brown tickets, and brown's the next entrance, two hundred yards along. If you just swing round here, and – .'

'I'm happy to pay the difference.'

'No, you see the rules, say ...'

'I know where the brown entrance is, I've just spent the last hour queueing for it by mistake. I drove up here because I thought I was red. I can't go back there now. The queue stretches for miles. And these children, you know, who'd been looking forward ...'

By now half a dozen cars have gathered behind us. One of them parps. The steward is wavering.

'You say you applied for red.'

'Not only applied for, paid for. I'm a doctor, you see' – he points at the stethoscope – 'and I like being near the grandstand.'

This double *non-sequitur* seems to clinch it.

'All right, sir, but next time please check the tickets. Ahead and to your right.'

*　*　*　*　*

This is the way it was with my father. Minor duplicities. Little fiddles. Money-saving, time-saving, privilege-attaining fragments of opportunism. The queue-jump, the backhander, the deal under the table. Parking where you shouldn't, after hours, accepting the poached pheasant and the goods off the back of a lorry. 'They' were killjoys, after all – 'they' meaning the establishment to which, despite being a middle professional, a GP, he didn't belong; our job, as ordinary folk trying to get the most out of life, was to outwit them. Serious lawbreaking would have scared him, though he envied and often praised to us those who had pulled off ingenious crimes, like the Great Train Robbers or, before them, the men who intercepted a lorry carrying a large number of old banknotes to the incinerator (Still in currency, you see, but not new so there was no record of the numbers and they couldn't be traced. Nobody got hurt, either. Brilliant, quite brilliant). He was not himself up to being criminal in a big way, but he was lost if he couldn't cheat in a small way: so much of his pleasure derived from it. I grew up thinking it absolutely normal, that most Englishmen were like this. I still suspect that's the case.

My childhood was a web of little scams and triumphs. The time we stayed at a hotel situated near the fifth tee of a famous golf-course – Troon, was it? – and discovered that if we started at the fifth hole and finished at the fourth we could avoid the clubhouse and green fees. The private tennis clubs and yacht clubs and drinking clubs we got into (especially on Sundays in dry counties of Wales) by giving someone else's name: by the time the man on the door had failed to find it, my father would have read the names on the list upside-down – 'There, see, Wilson – no Wilson, I said, not Watson'; if all else failed, you could try slipping the chap a one-pound note. With his innocence, confidence and hail-fellow cheeriness, my father could usually talk his way into anything, and usually, when caught, out of anything.

He failed only once. We were on holiday, skiing, in Aviemore and he treated us to a drink in one of the posher hotels. On his way back from the lavatories, he noticed a sauna room for residents near a small back entrance. For the rest of the week, we sneaked in to enjoy residents' saunas. On the last day, though, we were towelling ourselves dry when an angry manager walked in: 'You're not residents, are you?'

I waited for some artless reply – 'You mean the saunas aren't open to the public, like the bars? I thought ...' – but for once my father stammered and looked guilty. We ended up paying some exorbitant sum *and* being banned from the hotel. I was indignant. I discovered he was fallible. I felt conned.

* * * * *

Oulton Park, half an hour later. We have met up with our cousins in the brown car park – they of course got here on time – and brought them back to the entrance to the paddock. My father has assumed that, with the red tickets he's wangled, we are entitled to enter the paddock for nothing, along with our guests. He is wrong. Tickets to the paddock cost a guinea. There are ten of us. We're talking serious money.

'We'll, buy *one*, anyway,' my father is saying to the man in the ticket-booth, and he comes back with it, a small brown paper card, like a library ticket, with a piece of string attached to a hole at the top so you can thread it through your lapel. 'Let me just investigate,' he says, and disappears through the gate, the steward seeing the lapel-ticket and nodding him through: no stamp on the hand or name-check. In ten minutes or so my father is back. He whispers to my Uncle Ron, hands him the ticket and leads the rest of us to a wooden-slatted fence in a quiet corner of the car park. Soon Uncle Ron appears on the other side of the fence, in an equally quiet corner of the paddock, and passes the ticket through the slats. Cousin Richard takes the ticket this time and repeats the procedure. One by one we all troop round: Kela, Auntie Mary, Edward, Jane, Gillian, my mother, me. In five minutes, all ten of us are inside.

'Marvellous,' my father says. 'Three pounds eleven shillings and we've got four red tickets and ten of us in the paddock. That'd be costing anyone else twenty guineas. Not bad.'

We stand round Jack Brabham's Cooper, its bonnet opened like a body on an operating table, a mass of tubes and wires and gleamy bits of white and silver. I touch the metal behind the cockpit and think of my green Dinky car, no. 8, which I call Jack Brabham in the races I have on the carpet against the red Ferrari no. 1 (Fangio) and the silver Maserati no. 3 (Salvadori) and the yellow Jaguar no. 4 (Stirling Moss). I like Jack Brabham to win, and somehow he always does, though I swear I push the cars equally. It is quiet at home, pretending. Here at Oulton Park it's not quiet: there's a headachy mix of petrol and sun and engine roar.

Later, Moss overtakes Brabham on lap six, and stays there for the next sixty-nine laps. A car comes off the circuit between Lodge Corner and Deer Leap, just along from where we're standing. There is blood, splintered wood and broken glass. My father disappears – 'just to see if I can help.' He comes back strangely quiet, and whispers to my mother: 'Nothing I could do.'

Blake Morrison
And When Did You Last See Your Father?, 1993

Black Boy

One winter morning in the long-ago, four-year-old days of my life I found myself standing before a fireplace, warming my hands over a mound of glowing coals, listening to the wind whistle past the house outside. All morning my mother had been scolding me, telling me to keep still, warning me that I must make no noise. And I was angry, fretful, and impatient. In the next room Granny lay ill and under the day and night care of a doctor and I knew that I would be punished if I did not obey. I crossed restlessly to the window and pushed back the long fluffy white curtains – which I had been forbidden to touch – and looked yearningly out into the empty street. I was dreaming of running and playing and shouting, but the vivid image of Granny's old, white, wrinkled, grim face, framed by a halo of tumbling black hair, lying upon a huge feather pillow, made me afraid.

The house was quiet. Behind me my brother – a year younger than I – was playing placidly upon the floor with a toy. A bird wheeled past the window and I greeted it with a glad shout.

'You better hush,' my brother said.

'You shut up,' I said.

My mother stepped briskly into the room and closed the door behind her. She came to me and shook her finger in my face.

'You stop that yelling, you hear?' she whispered. 'You know Granny's sick and you better keep quiet!'

I hung my head and sulked. She left and I ached with boredom.

'I told you so,' my brother gloated.

'You shut up,' I told him again.

I wandered listlessly about the room, trying to think of something to do, dreading the return of my mother, resentful of being neglected. The room held nothing of interest except the fire and finally I stood before the shimmering embers, fascinated by the quivering coals. An idea of a new kind of game grew and took root in my mind. Why not throw something into the fire and watch it burn? I looked about. There was only my picture book and my mother would beat me if I burned that. Then what? I hunted around until I saw the broom leaning in a closet. That's it ... Who would bother about a few straws if I burned them? I pulled out the broom and tore out a batch of straws and tossed them into the fire and watched them smoke, turn black, blaze, and finally become white wisps of ghosts that vanished. Burning straws was a teasing kind of fun and I took more of them from the broom and cast them into the fire. My brother came to my side, his eyes drawn by the blazing straws.

'Don't do that,' he said.

'How come?' I asked.

'You'll burn the whole broom,' he said.

'You hush,' I said.

'I'll tell,' he said.

'And I'll hit you,' I said.

My idea was growing, blooming. Now I was wondering just how the long fluffy white curtains would look if I lit a bunch of straws and held it under them. Would I try it? Sure. I pulled several straws from the broom and held them to the fire until they blazed; I rushed to the window and brought the flame in touch with the hems of the curtains. My brother shook his head.

'Naw,' he said.

He spoke too late. Red circles were eating into the white cloth; then a flare of flames shot out. Startled, I backed away. The fire soared to the ceiling and I trembled with fright. Soon a sheet of yellow lit the room. I was terrified; I wanted to scream but was afraid. I looked around for my brother; he was gone. One half of the room was now ablaze. Smoke was choking me and the fire was licking at my face, making me gasp.

I made for the kitchen; smoke was surging there too. Soon my mother would smell that smoke and see the fire and come and beat me. I had done something wrong, something which I could not hide or deny. Yes, I would run away and never come back. I ran out of the kitchen and into the back yard. Where could I go? Yes, under the house! Nobody would find me there. I crawled under the house* and crept into a dark hollow of a brick chimney and balled myself into a tight knot. My mother must not find me and whip me for what I had done. Anyway, it was all an accident; I had not really intended to set the house afire. I had just wanted to see how the curtains would look when they burned. And neither did it occur to me that I was hiding under a burning house.

Presently footsteps pounded on the floor above me. Then I heard screams. Later the gongs of fire wagons and the clopping hoofs of horses came from the direction of the street. Yes, there was really a fire, a fire like the one I had seen one day burn a house down to the ground, leaving only a chimney standing black. I was stiff with terror. The thunder of sound above me shook the chimney to which I clung. The screams came louder. I saw the image of my grandmother lying helplessly upon her bed and there were yellow flames in her black hair. Was my mother afire? Would my brother burn? Perhaps everybody in the house would burn! Why had I not thought of those things before I fired the curtains? I yearned to become invisible, to stop living. The commotion above me increased and I began to cry. It seemed that I had been hiding for ages, and when the stomping and the screaming died down I felt lonely, cast forever out of life. Voices sounded near-by and I shivered.

'Richard!' my mother was calling frantically.

I saw her legs and the hem of her dress moving swiftly about the back yard. Her wails were full of an agony whose intensity told me that my punishment would be measured by its depth. Then I saw her taut face peering under the edge of the house. She had found me! I held my breath and waited to hear her command me to come to her. Her face went away; no, she had not seen me huddled in the dark nook of the chimney. I tucked my head into my arms and my teeth chattered.

'Richard!'

The distress I sensed in her voice was as sharp and painful as the lash of a whip on my flesh.

'Richard! The house is on fire. Oh, find my child!'

Yes, the house was afire, but I was determined not to leave my place of safety. Finally I saw another face peering under the edge of the house; it was my father's. His eyes must have become accustomed to the shadows, for he was now pointing at me.

'There he is!'

'Naw!' I screamed.

'Come here, boy!'

'Naw! '

'The house is on fire!'

'Leave me 'lone!'

He crawled to me and caught hold of one of my legs. I hugged the edge of the brick chimney with all of my strength. My father yanked my leg and I clawed at the chimney harder.

'Come outta there, you little fool!'

'Turn me loose!'

I could not withstand the tugging at my leg and my fingers relaxed. It was over. I would be beaten. I did not care any more. I knew what was coming. He dragged me into the back yard and the instant his hand left me I jumped to my feet and broke into a wild run, trying to elude the people who surrounded me, heading for the street. I was caught before I had gone ten paces.

From that moment on things became tangled for me. Out of the weeping and the shouting and the wild talk, I learned that no one had died in the fire. My brother, it seemed, had finally overcome enough of his panic to warn my mother, but not before more than half the house had been destroyed. Using the mattress as a stretcher, Grandpa and an uncle had lifted Granny from her bed and had rushed her to the safety of a neighbour's house. My long absence and silence had made everyone think, for a while, that I had perished in the blaze.

'You almost scared us to death,' my mother muttered as she stripped the leaves from a tree limb to prepare it for my back.

I was lashed so hard and long that I lost consciousness. I was beaten out of my senses and later I found myself in bed, screaming, determined to run away, tussling with my mother and father who were trying to keep me still. I was lost in a fog of fear. A doctor was called – I was afterwards told – and he ordered that I be kept abed, that I be kept quiet, that my life depended upon it. My body seemed on fire and I could not sleep. Packs of ice were put on my forehead to keep down the fever. Whenever I tried to sleep I would see huge wobbly white bags, like the full udders of cows, suspended from the ceiling above me. Later, as I grew worse, I could see the bags in the daytime with my eyes open and I was gripped by the fear that they were going to fall and drench me with some horrible liquid. Day and night I begged my mother and father to take the bags away, pointing to them, shaking with terror because no one saw them but me. Exhaustion would make me drift toward sleep and then I would scream until I was wide awake again; I was afraid to sleep. Time finally bore me away from the dangerous bags and I got well. But for a long time I was chastened whenever I remembered that my mother had come close to killing me.

Each event spoke with a cryptic tongue And the moments of living slowly revealed their coded meanings. There was the wonder I felt when I first saw a brace of mountainlike, spotted, black-and-white horses clopping down a dusty road through clouds of powdered clay.

There was the delight I caught in seeing long straight rows of red and green vegetables stretching away in the sun to the bright horizon.

There was the faint, cool kiss of sensuality when dew came on to my cheeks and shins as I ran down the wet green garden paths in the early morning.

There was the vague sense of the infinite as I looked down upon the yellow, dreaming waters of the Mississippi River from the verdant bluffs of Natchez.

There were the echoes of nostalgia I heard in the crying strings of wild geese winging south against a bleak, autumn sky.

There was the tantalising melancholy in the tingling scent of burning hickory wood.

There was the teasing and impossible desire to imitate the petty pride of sparrows wallowing and flouncing in the red dust of country roads.

There was the yearning for identification loosed in me by the sight of a solitary ant carrying a burden upon a mysterious journey.

There was the disdain that filled me as I tortured a delicate, blue-pink crawfish: that huddled fearfully in the mudsill of a rusty tin can.

There was the aching glory in masses of clouds burning gold and purple from an invisible sun.

There was the liquid alarm I saw in the blood-red glare of the sun's afterglow mirrored in the squared panes of whitewashed frame houses.

There was the languor I felt when I heard green leaves rustling with a rainlike sound.

There was the incomprehensible secret embodied in a whitish toadstool hiding in the dark shade of a rotting log.

There was the experience of feeling death without dying that came from watching a chicken leap about blindly after its neck had been snapped by a quick twist of my father's wrist.

There was the great joke that I felt God had played on cats and dogs by making them lap their milk and water with their tongues.

There was the thirst I had when I watched clear, sweet juice trickle from sugar cane being crushed.

There was the hot panic that welled up in my throat and swept through my blood when I first saw the lazy, limp coils of a blueskinned snake sleeping in the sun.

There was the speechless astonishment of seeing a hog stabbed through the heart, dipped into boiling water, scraped, split open, gutted, and strung up gaping and bloody.

There was the love I had for the mute regality of tall, mossclad oaks.

There was the hint of cosmic cruelty that I felt when I saw the curved timbers of a wooden shack that had been warped in the summer sun.

There was the saliva that formed in my mouth whenever I smelt clay dust pitted with fresh rain.

There was the cloudy notion of hunger when I breathed the odour of new-cut, bleeding grass.

And there was the quiet terror that suffused my senses when vast hazes of gold washed earthward from star-heavy skies on silent nights ...

Richard Wright
Black Boy, 1970

A Passage to Africa

Long, long before I came to know and love Africa as a place, I yearned for it as an idea. It was to be, for my family, a place of deliverance, a promised land. From that day in May 1961 when my father announced that we were to leave our island home, Ceylon, for the distant shores of Africa, it began to work a sort of magic on me.

In the seven months before our departure, I began to conjure up a vision of Africa and what it would mean for us. Even as a child of five I think I knew that it represented something better than the divided island we were about to leave. I was conscious that the reason we were going had something to do with us being different; that somehow we didn't fit in.

I knew this in the way a child knows these things. I learned from half-heard conversations between my parents that Ceylon was not somewhere that we Tamils would prosper. So Ceylon was bad; Africa was good. Now we were poor; in Africa we would be rich. Africa became one of my favourite things, like slurping buffalo curd with dark, sweet *kitul pani,* the nectar of the *kitul* palm tree, out of a cool, clay pot or beating my grandmother at *carom,* a tabletop game like billiards in which wooden discs are bounced into pockets with a flick of the finger. I was ready for Africa long before I knew where it was or how we would get there. I embraced it as only a child can – with the unquestioning certainly that everything will be all right in the morning.

Such optimism is shared, at varying levels of sophistication, by all those who have sought refuge in a new land. A migrant does much more than move from one place to another; his journey is a journey from despair to hope, from oppression to opportunity.

Of course, my parents never said we were leaving forever. Very few people leave the land of their birth saying that they'll never return. Most people who head for new shores believe that one day they will be able to go back 'home'. This is what my parents told our relatives in Ceylon, partly because it was a way of alleviating the pain of separation but also because that is what they thought, perhaps even hoped would happen. It was not Ceylon we had rejected, but what it had become. And that could change.

Actually, what happened was that we ourselves changed. It was true of all of us, but especially of my sisters and me. From the minute we were made aware of this place called Africa and the prospects it held in store, our young minds began to look forward, not backwards. Our mental horizons expanded as we got closer and closer to this new land of opportunity. Like Africa's vast, dawn-red sky, which we could see as our plane tilted towards Accra, our vision of what was now possible seemed limitless. Africa would be everything that Ceylon had not been: a place where we could start again. All of us, together, as a family.

* * * * *

So the thing I remember above all about the land of my birth is the fact that I left it. That is to say, my parents left it, taking with them their five children: four girls and me, the only son. Other episodes do bob up to the surface, vestigial impressions of an early childhood in Ceylon, but it's the leaving of the place that dominates my recollections. It's a bit like trying to recall a dream: wisps of unconscious thought float by but it's the image that sticks in your mind.

Yes, I can remember standing by the well at my grandfather's home in the little eastern town of Kalmunai as he poured buckets of cold water over me. From where I stood I'd look up to see this vast expanse of belly hanging over the knot of a sarong and, further up, a kindly, indulgent face smiling down at me. There was always a black cigar in his mouth, even at bathtime.

And, yes, I remember our house in Colombo, the one with the stinking gully running by its side. In the monsoon season the gully would become a torrent of water into which we would throw our paper boats. I recall how, as these fragile little constructions were swept away, I thought of my Uncle John, who was in the merchant navy. Was this what it was like for him? Please God, let him be safe.

And there was the skinny, grizzled, filthy, smelly, half-naked old man, or sometimes his wife, who would come to slop out our latrine each morning. He was just one of a succession of people who came to our home every day. I remember the sounds he made – the squeak of his metal bucket as he walked up the path to our outside loo, his footsteps on the way back and, finally, the clash of metal against metal as he threw the contents of the bucket into the two-wheeled tank. In a culture where everyone had a place in the intricate and stifling hierarchy of caste, these people were the lowest of the low. They were the Tamils from south India, the untouchables whom Mahatma Ghandi had vowed to liberate. Nobody in Ceylon, not even the low-caste local Tamils, and certainly no Sinhalese, would stoop so low as to clean out someone else's toilet.

The *dhobi* collected our clothes for washing. I even remember the mark by which our clothes were distinguished from all the others that would be thrashed and dried next to some riverbed: a cross with dots in each quarter.

Then there was the chap who came round to take the tiffin box to my father's workplace. This was the takeaway service with home cooking. My mother would prepare a meal of rice and curries which was decanted into a stack of stainless-steel tins. These were collected by tiffin-carriers who, in bicycle relays, would ensure that food was delivered, still warm, to my father's office at the other end of town. The tins were held together by a clasp and stacked next to all the other boxes destined for men who couldn't do without the fruits of their wives' culinary talents.

But, as I say, more than anything else I remember the *frisson* of departure, the combination of fear and nerves that I sensed in my parents as they prepared us for emigration to Ghana.

George Alagiah
A Passage to Africa, 2001

Saroeun's Story

I. The first move

I was born in Pnom-Penh, the capital city of Cambodia. My life has been sad, horrible and lonely. I begin my story in 1975 when I was five years old, and the Khmer-Rouge invaded Cambodia. My family were all together when the Khmer-Rouge invaded the country by force, and they told us to move to the countryside with guns pointing at our backs. When we left the city it was ruined and people were dying and dead along the road. The corpses were starting to smell. The road to the countryside was jammed with traffic, and the sun was burning hot. The journey took three days, with very little rest.

We arrived in a town named Ta-Kaiv where my grandfather lived. We were all welcome there. The house was small and not everybody got a bed or a room on their own. Every morning my parents went to work from 5am to 6pm and had two hours rest for dinner at home. Everybody had to work not for themselves, but for everybody. After we had stayed there for six months we had to move to another town named Kor.

The house we lived in was made of wood and brick. When the rain came it was leaking, because it was old. We lived in the town, where the family had to work and steal for a living. We had no free time except a break for lunch time and dinner. Even though I was only five or six years old I had to work for my lunch and dinner. I was working in the town for a few months, where I had to carry bricks and clay. Then I had to leave town and my family to work in another town away from my family.

2. Being alone

There were about twenty children the same age as me and two leaders to look after us. The first night I spent sleeping with them I was frightened, cold and lonely. At night no one came and kissed you goodnight and nobody tucked you into bed. The job we had to do was cutting grass and taking it across the irrigation ditch to the cows. Once when I crossed the irrigation ditch, I fell and nearly drowned at the bottom but I managed to kick myself up and down until I got to the other side. Even though I was out of my breath I had to carry on my work or I would get a whip on my back and no dinner or lunch for a day. This kind of thing carried on too much. My body was suffering from malnutrition and I had to go to the hospital.

When I arrived there it was hot and raining. They took me to the big room. There were six beds in a row, and people were crying with pain. Just as I arrived in the hospital one young boy died and they replaced me on his bed. It was horrible sleeping on somebody's bed who just died. At night you couldn't sleep because of the people screaming and moaning.

I stayed there for a week and no medicine could cure me because they were all old fashioned medicines instead of the new ones. I stayed there for about a month but when I got better I had to go back to the team and work. My mum had heard about this so she asked the leader to let me stay at home and work because I was not yet fit and cured enough to work hard. I stayed in town quite a long time then I had to go back to my team. Once again I was alone. When I went back life was much, much harder than before.

3. My sister

I was working in the field when I heard that my sister had died. First of all I didn't believe it, because my sister was fit and very healthy. Then one of my best friends said it was true because his mother had told him so. I asked the leader if I could see my sister before she was buried but he told me to wait until I had my dinner. So I waited with tears running down my eyes like water. When he said I could go I ran with tears, and on the way the border guard stopped me and asked for a letter but I didn't have one because I was in a hurry. They wouldn't let me go, but one of them knew me and knew my sister was dead and he let me go.

When I arrived there my father and mother were crying and weeping, but my sister was not there. Her corpse had been buried. It was so sad not to see her before she'd gone for good. It was so sad that I hadn't much time to play with her. She was only four or five and I had been so cruel to her and now she'd gone. I felt so ashamed of myself. My sister died of poison because she had eaten potato leaves, but I don't believe it now. I think she died of starvation or some disease.

4. 'Where's my father?'

It took me at least a year to forget my sister. This year I had permission to stay at home with my parents because I was ill. I could only do light work because if I did hard work I would be badly ill. Sometimes I stayed at home because I was so weak that I couldn't do light work. So when I went for my lunch and dinner they wouldn't let me have any. Then I just stayed at home.

But my mother never let me be hungry. She took me to the dinner hall and let me eat her dinner.

One day my father was sent from the village to a large farm somewhere far from us. My mother was working in the village. It was a warm night when my father went missing. On that day he had come home because he was ill. He'd been sent home from the camp. At dinner time he went to the hall and had his dinner. When he returned he told my mother that the Ankar wanted to have a meeting with those that were ill. He was meant to come home at 8pm and my mother was looking for him when it was 11pm. She asked me where my father was. I said, 'I don't know,' and was so nasty to her and unhelpful. She was looking everywhere for him but he was gone.

A few days later I saw my mother crying in her room. The sound didn't come out but the tears were dripping like water. When I saw this I couldn't stand it so I cried with her, making much sound. She told me not to cry loudly in case the Ankar heard. The Ankar, who ruled the town, had his spies everywhere. If he thought you were suspicious, he would immediately find out everything about you. He didn't trust our family because we had been well educated.

About a week later my mother told me that her friend had found out that my father was driven in a cart with the other men and some guards. He was taken away, for something he had done. Later my mother found out he had broken a pump machine paddle and he had been killed for it or maybe he'd been accused of being a soldier. My father was never seen again. With pain and tears I slept and waited and hoped he would return.

5. Close to hell

About a month after my father went missing, the Ankar sent his spies and dug up my parents' belongings. My father must have told them because they threatened his life. After they found our precious belongings, they treated us very badly and watched everything we did.

When one week had passed, they told us to move to another place, but my mother begged them not to move us because it meant we were going to die. Most people who were moved to another place were never seen in that place again. But the leader said we must move because the house was too full for three families. Then he brought our cart and the lady whose husband was missing with my father. She had a child in beside her and a baby in her arms. She was waiting for us in the ox cart, ready to go. My mum knew the time had come for us to die so she just sat down and played with the dust on the ground. The leader told her to move down quickly, but she was too weak to stand up. So they moved everything for us. Now the time had come for us to go, we sat on the ox cart and were about to go, when the Ankar riding on his bicycle told us that we could stay for a month or so. It was like we were born again. So from that day we were never moved again.

6. The escape from Cambodia

In 1979 the Vietnamese were fighting with the Khmer Rouge and we had to move along as the battles came closer and closer. So now everybody went away and there was no Ankar or Leader, because they were frightened of the Vietnamese and the people, so they ran away to some forest or mountain and hid themselves until the war was over. When we were free, we went and gathered our family and made a plan to escape from the town to the city. One by one we went to the city. When they asked each of us, 'Where are you going?' some said to visit a friend a family or to do some trading or to visit someone in the nearby city.

When we had all arrived in the city, we tried to find our relatives and asked them if we could stay there for a while. Once we had a place to rest and some money we tried to do some business and make more money for our next journey. When we got some money we decided to make another long journey to Thailand near Cambodia.

The first thing we did was to buy about five bicycles. Then, without telling anyone, we packed up and went quietly one by one. We cycled nearly twenty four hours a day and every day the Vietnamese asked us where we were going and had we got our identity cards. We told them that we wanted to visit our friends or family and if they didn't let us go we gave them some money and the problem was over. At night we slept along the road or in the field, sometimes in the market. Every day we got up early and started cycling. Each bicycle carried three people, the driver and the little one in front of the driver near the wheel and another on the back seat. We had many problems with the wheel. The tyre kept on bursting and we had to change it.

One day I was so tired when I sat on the front of the bicycle that I fell asleep and my leg went into the wheel and bent it. I thought my foot was broken, but it was not because I could move it. Everybody was at the front, but me and my mother were the last ones. My mother had no medicine for my foot but she managed to get some wine and pour it on my foot to make it stop swelling up. Then she bandaged me with some torn up shirt. She asked me if it hurt a lot. I said no because if I said yes I knew she would take me to the hospital and we would never make the journey. So with pain we carried on. Night and day we carried on riding with little rest. At last we got to the border, but we couldn't cross to Thailand because they wouldn't let us out unless we gave some money. We didn't have any money left now, so we had to run quietly. When we ran they fired guns at us but they missed.

Eventually we arrived at the house of one of our cousins – and they asked someone to take us to the camp called Nongchan. On the way we had to walk very low because the Vietnamese were waiting to shoot anyone passing the Khmer border. There was one woman with us who had her one year old baby and she cried so loud that the Vietnamese heard us and fired at us. We were running away and our guide had left us. Now we didn't know which way to go so we just carried straight on. An hour now we had been travelling. Then we saw the camp. It was lucky that we kept going straight.

7. The camp in Thailand

When we arrived there my cousin bought me things and food to eat. Everywhere we went we had to dig a ditch to hide in because you didn't know what was going to happen in that place. It was not safe at the border. We stayed there for about a week. Then my mother said she wanted to go and visit her friend and do some trading because we had run out of money. She left me and my brother and my uncle who was a doctor. We couldn't go with her because it was dangerous. My uncle was working with the French doctors when they told him that he should move to Khao-I-Dang with them and the family. But my uncle said we must wait for my mother.

So we did. But then the Thai soldiers came and talked with the Para but they didn't understand each other so they fired at each other and we were in the middle. Some of the people died but not us. I was running to one of the ditches but they kicked me out and the bullet was chasing after me but I managed to fall into my own ditch and was safe. At that time I wasn't frightened of bullets because I'd seen so many and I played with so many.

In the middle of the war we decided we'd better go because everybody had gone except my family. Then we followed the people to the camp called Khao-I-Dang. When we got there, there were no places to sleep except in the middle of the field. When we slept that night I was crying in my dream for my mother.

A few days later we managed to build a shelter and stay there. It was about two weeks later that we found my mother. She told us that she thought we were dead and she started to look around the Thai border. Then someone told her that most people had moved to Khao-I-Dang. And so she found us there. She had got a lot of money with her and she gave us each twenty pounds.

We spent the money on food which we bought from children in the road. It was the best day of my life. We ate sweet watermelons, mangoes, bananas and rambutans which are red with spikes on the outside but inside is white flesh with seeds. It is very sweet, crisp and cold. We also bought 'noah-sam' which is made of rice and pork (a bit like a sausage roll) wrapped in a banana leaf. We ate so much that we got a fever but we didn't care, and it had gone the next day.

We stayed in Khao-I-Dang for about two years. It seemed much longer. We never thought we'd see our relatives again. We knew that they were in England and France because my mum had an old letter which had my uncle's address in France. We had sent word to them, but there was no reply. Every day we waited, and every day we went to look at the Red Cross board. But every day we were disappointed.

Then one day just as we were about to give up hope, my cousin went to look at the board and instead of finding his own letter, he found ours with a picture of my uncle looking like a stranger. We felt that at last we might have another chance, so we went straight to the Red Cross and asked for more information. They told us everything they knew, and we started writing letters to him telling him who had survived and who was missing.

He sent us what we needed, lots of money and also wrote to the authorities to arrange our passage to France. At the same time my auntie in England was also writing letters. Then one day we received a letter telling us we had an appointment with the English officer in charge of refugees. One by one they asked us questions about ourselves and our relatives, testing us, because if we had given different answers we would have failed the test and lost the chance of going to England. I felt very nervous. I was praying as I never had before and to my joy the man smiled at us and told us we would have to wait for just a few months longer.

All this time I didn't know the date but I'll never forget the day we looked at the board and saw, typed very tidily and clearly, 'ING FAMILY – Flight to England'. From that time we moved into another camp near to the capital of Bangkok. I enjoyed the coach ride and the meal they gave us. For the first time in my life I tasted foreign food! It was bread, with jam in small containers and an orange. It was so sweet and I ate so much that I got a headache. Of course I got coach sick too but I didn't care. I was so excited to be on the way.

The place we stayed in was quite small. We didn't stay in the house but in an open shelter packed with refugees, from not only Cambodia but also from Laos and Vietnam. It was damp, smelly and crowded. People were lying anywhere they could, with only a little space for walking. This was not what I'd expected, after the luxury of the coach. We seemed never to be leaving. Every day people left, but we were never called.

8. Escape to England

One day, when most people had gone, the moment finally came for us. We had one hour to pack. My brother and I put on our plimsolls instead of our flip-flops, but we couldn't tie them, as we'd never worn them before – they were our 'England shoes' which the Red Cross had given us, with a woolly jumper. They were the kindest people I'd experienced in my life.

The coach was moving fast, and all of a sudden we were in Bangkok. It was so similar to Pnom Phen before it was ruined. It reminded us that our city was a lost one. Then, suddenly, we were at the airport. What a shock! If I describe it now I'd say it was like something from the space age, but then I didn't know anything of this, I didn't even know people had been to the moon. I wasn't scared, I was enjoying it, but I was a bit worried about being sent back as we heard stories about that happening. That would have been the shock of my life.

After a few hours, we finally went through immigration, onto a bus which took us to the plane, bigger than I had ever imagined. The steps up to the plane were like steps up to heaven. When we got inside there were very nice hostesses who took us to our seats at the back where the tail was. We waited for another two hours before the plane took off. I was very careful with my seat belt.

Once we were in the air I wanted to go to the toilet. I was a bit worried because I could not read the sign, and this would be the first time I would use a European toilet. I had had a lesson in the camp telling us how to use it. It seems very funny to think about it now.

Now comes my big moment! I put on my coat I brought from Thailand and my plimsolls. The first time that I felt the air of England it was cold and foggy. I was freezing but in my mind I was sure this was a country I would like. I had seen so many English films in Thailand about the way people lived and their houses and gardens seemed like Paradise. I didn't know anything about unemployment or council flats.

There was a man waiting for us at the airport. We could only say 'Yes' or 'No,' and he couldn't speak Kmer so he just took us to the Cambodian centre in Gravesend. When we arrived in the centre, my dream was coming true – the house was what I expected, the garden was large and full of snow, and the people were kind. Cambodian people made us food and showed us around but we were too tired and hungry to look much. So we had our dinner and went straight to bed. The bed was not what I expected because we were used to sleeping on the floor. I felt sick in bed because of the bouncing on the mattress but of course I got used to it.

9. London and the present

I moved from the centre to London in 1982 to the house in South Kensington where I live now. When I first saw the house it was so big and beautiful, like palaces I had seen in books but it was only a hotel. We lived on unemployment benefit while the family learnt English and other subjects.

Now I am fourteen and in the third year at school. I wrote this story because I want the world to know what people can do to each other and how cruel people can be. I wish the Khmer Rouge could read my story and stories of others who suffered like me, to see what they have done. I'm telling the truth. I know it's hard to believe, but it did happen.

Saroeun Ing, Aged 14
More Lives, 1987

Don't Let's Go to the Dogs Tonight

Mum says, 'Don't come creeping into our room at night.'
They sleep with loaded guns beside them on the bedside rugs. She
says, 'Don't startle us when we're sleeping.'

'Why not?'

'We might shoot you.'

'Oh.'

'By mistake.'

'Okay.' As it is, there seems a good enough chance of getting shot on
purpose. 'Okay, I won't.'

So if I wake in the night and need Mum and Dad I call Vanessa, because she
isn't armed. 'Van! Van, hey!' I hiss across the room until she wakes up. And
then Van has to light a candle and escort me to the loo, where I pee sleepily
into the flickering yellow light and Van keeps the candle high, looking for
snakes and scorpions and baboon spiders.

Mum won't kill snakes because she says they help to keep the rats down (but
she rescued a nest of baby mice from the barns and left them to grow in my
cupboard, where they ate holes in the family's winter jerseys). Mum won't kill
scorpions either; she catches them and lets them go free in the pool and
Vanessa and I have to rake the pool before we can swim. We fling the scorps
as far as we can across the brown and withering lawn, chase the ducks and
geese out, and then lower ourselves gingerly into the pool, whose sides wave
green and long and soft and grasping with algae. And Mum won't kill spiders
because she says it will bring bad luck.

I tell her, 'I'd say we have pretty rotten luck as it is.'

'Then think how much worse it would be if we killed spiders.'

I have my feet off the floor when I pee.

'Hurry up, man.'

'Okay, okay.'

'It's like Victoria Falls.'

'I really had to go.'

I have been holding my pee for a long, long time and staring out of the window to try and guess how close it is to morning. Maybe I could hold it until morning. But then I notice that it is the deep-black-sky quiet time of night, which is the halfway time between the sun setting and the sun rising when even the night animals are quiet – as if they, like day animals, take a break in the middle of their work to rest. I can't hear Vanessa breathing; she has gone into her deep middle-of-the-night silence. Dad is not snoring nor is he shouting in his sleep. The baby is still in her crib but the smell of her is warm and animal with wet nappy. It will be a long time until morning.

* * * * *

Then Vanessa hands me the candle – 'You keep boogies for me now' – and she pees.

'See, you had to go, too.'

'Only 'cos you had to go.'

There is a hot breeze blowing through the window, the cold sinking night air shifting the heat of the day up. The breeze has trapped midday scents; the prevalent cloying of the leach field, the green soap which has spilled out from the laundry and landed on the patted-down red earth, the wood smoke from the fires that heat our water, the boiled-meat smell of dog food.

We debate the merits of flushing the loo.

'We shouldn't waste the water.' Even when there isn't a drought we can't waste water, just in case one day there is a drought. Anyway, Dad has said, 'Steady on with the loo paper, you kids. And don't flush the bloody loo all the time. The leach field can't handle it.'

'But that's *two* pees in there.'

'So? It's only pee.'

'*Agh sis*, man, but it'll be smelly by tomorrow. And you peed as much as a horse.'

'It's not my fault.

'You can flush.'

'You're taller.'

'I'll hold the candle.'

Van holds the candle high. I lower the toilet lid, stand on it and lift up the block of hardwood that covers the cistern, and reach down for the chain. Mum has glued a girlie-magazine picture to this block of hardwood: a blond woman in few clothes, with breasts like naked cow udders, and she's all arched in a strange pouty contortion, like she's got backache. Which maybe she has, from the weight of the udders. The picture is from *Scope* magazine.

* * * * *

We aren't allowed to look at *Scope* magazine.

'Why?'

'Because we aren't those sorts of people,' says Mum.

'But we have a picture from *Scope* magazine on the loo lid.'

'That's a joke.'

'Oh.' And then, 'What sort of joke?'

'Stop twittering on.'

A pause. 'What sort of people are we, then?'

'We have breeding,' says Mum firmly.

'Oh.' Like the dairy cows and our special expensive bulls (who are named Humani, Jack, and Bulawayo).

'Which is better than having money,' she adds.

I look at her sideways, considering for a moment. 'I'd rather have money than breeding,' I say.

Mum says, '*Anyone* can have money.' As if it's something you might pick up from the public toilets in OK Bazaar Grocery store in Umtali.

'*Ja*, but we don't.'

Mum sighs. 'I'm trying to read, Bobo.'

'Can you read to me?'

Mum sighs again. 'All right,' she says, 'just one chapter.' But it is teatime before we look up from *The Prince and the Pauper*.

*   *   *   *   *

The loo gurgles and splutters, and then a torrent of water shakes down, spilling slightly over the bowl.

'*Sis* man,' says Vanessa.

You never know what you're going to get with this loo. Sometimes it refuses to flush at all and other times it's like this, water on your feet.

I follow Vanessa back to the bedroom. The way candlelight falls, we're walking into blackness, blinded by the flame of the candle, unable to see our feet. So at the same moment we get the creeps, the neck-prickling terrorist-under-the-bed creeps, and we abandon ourselves to fear. The candle blows out. We skid into our room and leap for the beds, our feet quickly tucked under us. We're both panting, feeling foolish, trying to calm our breathing as if we weren't scared at all.

Vanessa says, 'There's a terrorist under your bed, I can see him.'

'No you can't, how can you see him? The candle's out.'

'*Struze* fact.'

And I start to cry.

'*Jeez*; I'm only joking.'

I cry harder.

'Shhh, man. You'll wake up Olivia. You'll wake up Mum and Dad.'

Which is what I'm trying to do, without being shot. I want everyone awake and noisy to chase away the terrorist-under-my-bed.

'Here,' she says, 'you can sleep with Fred if you stop crying.'

So I stop crying and Vanessa pads over the bare cement floor and brings me the cat, fast asleep in a snail-circle on her arms. She puts him on the pillow and I put an arm over the vibrating, purring body. Fred finds my earlobe and starts to suck. He's always sucked our earlobes. Our hair is sucked into thin, slimy, knotted ropes near the ears.

Mum says, 'No wonder you have worms all the time.'

I lie with my arms over the cat, awake and waiting. African dawn, noisy with animals and the servants and Dad waking up and a tractor coughing into life somewhere down at the workshop, clutters into the room. The bantam hens start to crow and stretch, tumbling out of their roosts in the tree behind the bathroom to peck at the reflection of themselves in the window. Mum comes in smelling of Vicks VapoRub and tea and warm bed and scoops the sleeping baby up to her shoulder.

I can hear July setting tea on the veranda and I can smell the first, fresh singe of Dad's morning cigarette. I balance Fred on my shoulder and come out for tea: strong with no sugar, a splash of milk, the way Mum likes it. Fred has a saucer of milk.

'Morning, Chookies,' says Dad, not looking at me, smoking. He is looking far off into the hills, where the border between Rhodesia and Mozambique melts blue-gray, even in the pre-hazy clear of early morning.

'Morning, Dad.'

'Sleep all right?'

'Like a log,' I tell him. 'You?'

Dad grunts, stamps out his cigarette, drains his teacup, balances his bush hat on his head, and strides out into the yard to make the most of the little chill the night has left us with which to fight the gathering soupy heat of day.

Alexandra Fuller
Don't Let's Go to the Dogs Tonight, 2002

Bad Blood

First there was dinner money, then the register. Then Miss Myra would hang up a cracked oilcloth scroll with the Lord's Prayer printed on it in large curly letters. She prompted, we mumbled our way through, getting out of sync during the trespasses and catching up with each other to arrive in unison at 'For ever and ever. Amen.' Next we'd be set to copy it out with chalk on jagged slices of slate. If you got to the end you simply started from the beginning again and went on until it was time to stop. You spat on your slate and rubbed it with your finger when you made mistakes, so sooner or later the letters all got lost in a grey blur. Not many in the babies' class learned to read or write by this method. That didn't matter too much, though. Hanmer Church of England School was less concerned with teaching its pupils reading, writing or arithmetic than with obedience and knowing things by heart. Soon you'd be able to recite 'Our Father' and the multiplication tables with sing-song confidence, hitting the ritual emphasis right: 'And *twelve* twelves are a *hund*red and forty-*four*. Amen.'

After a couple of years in Miss Myra's room you moved to her sister Miss Daisy's, and after that to the biggest class, belonging to the headmaster, Mr Palmer. He was a figure of fear, an absentee deity. Offenders from the lower classes were sent to him for the stick and were known to wet themselves on the way. His own class, too, regarded him with dread. He liked to preside over them invisibly from his house next door, emerging when the noise reached a level deafening enough to disturb him, to hand out summary punishment.

The further up the school you went, the less you were formally taught or expected to learn. There was knitting, sewing and weaving for older girls, who would sit out winter playtimes gossiping round the stove, their legs marbled with parboiled red veins from the heat. The big boys did woodwork and were also kept busy taking out the ashes, filling coke buckets and digging the garden. None of the more substantial farmers sent their children to Hanmer school. It had been designed to produce domestic servants and farm labourers, and functional illiteracy was still part of the expectation, almost part of the curriculum.

Not long after I started there, this time-honoured parochial system was shaken up when some of the older children were removed to a secondary modern school over the nearest border, in Shropshire. This thinned out the population and damped down the racket in Mr Palmer's room, although quite a few restive overgrown kids still stayed on until they were fourteen and the law allowed them to leave. Passing the eleven-plus ('the scholarship') was unheard of; and anyway harder than it might have been, since grammar schools in neighbouring counties had quotas for children from the real sticks, i.e. the Maelor district. When my time came, Mr Palmer graciously cheated me through. Strolling past my desk on his invigilation rounds, he trailed a plump finger down my page of sums, pointed significantly at several, then crossed two fingers behind his back as he walked away. So I did those again.

Perhaps the record of failure was starting to look fishy. The world was changing, education was changing, and the notion that school should reflect your ready-made place in the scheme of things and put you firmly back where you came from was going out of fashion even in Hanmer. It was against the grain to acknowledge this, though. The cause of hierarchy and immobility was served by singling out the few children whose families didn't fit and setting them homework. Mr Palmer drew the line at marking it, however. The three of us were given sums to do, then told to compare the results in a corner next morning. If all three, or two of us, arrived at the same answer then that was the correct one. If – as often happened – all three of us produced different answers then that particular long division or fraction retreated into the realm of undecidability. Most of our answers were at best odds-on favourites. I developed a dauntingly Platonic conception of arithmetical truths. The real answer must exist, but in some far-removed misty empyrean. Praying ('... and forty-*four*. Amen') seemed often as good a route as any to getting it right.

Sums were my cross [...] with sums I struggled like the rest, since it was never part of Mr Palmer's plan (the school's plan) to reveal that the necessary skills were *learnable*. If you passed the scholarship, that was because you were somebody who should never have been at Hanmer school in the first place, was his theory.

One day he lined up his class and went down the line saying with gloomy satisfaction 'You'll be a muck-shoveller, you'll be a muck-shoveller ...' and so on and on, only missing out the homework trio. As things turned out he was mistaken – by the time my Hanmer generation grew up there were very few jobs on the land, the old mixed labour-intensive farming had finally collapsed, farmers had gone over to machinery, and the children he'd consigned to near-illiteracy and innumeracy had to re-educate themselves and move on. Which they did, despite all the school had done to inculcate ignorance. Back there and then in our childhoods, though, in the late Forties, Mr Palmer seemed omniscient. He ruled over a little world where conformity, bafflement, fear and furtive defiance were the orders of the day. Every child's ambition at Hanmer school was to avoid attracting his attention, or that of Miss Myra or Miss Daisy. We all played dumb, the one lesson everyone learned.

Lorna Sage
Bad Blood, 2000

Arithmetic Town

In September Favourite Teacher handed out workbooks, and said to us, *when you're done with these exercises you can go out on the field and have free play*. Free play is when you have fun instead of playing kickball.

This is easy is a dumb thing to say, you should always be afraid when you hear yourself saying that, it AUTOMATICALLY means that what you're doing is impossible, and you are blowing it, and people are going to ridicule you. And EVERYTHING. I was so messed up, the problems on those three pages looked short. I knew what I was doing, I whipped through them, I couldn't believe it, my heart was singing.

I put my workbook on Her desk. She really had little inkling of the boundless scope of my difficulties as yet, this was still fall. She knew I wasn't great at arithmetic but She didn't know the picture I had of it on my mind dial, the crater of a volcano, confusion, lumps of things, muffled cries from all the people who always told me how to do it. Mom, Dad, Julie, Fard, lost to me. Then sometimes it was the inky blackness of the ocean, where the wreck of my arithmetic lay, a grim reminder there was something wrong with me. But I listened to my heart SING that I could solve these problems, that *understanding had come to me in the night*. Now I was going to be like everybody else.

I went out to the field, which seemed beautiful, great, like a day from a movie. A couple of kids were swinging, and Billy Williamson was playing football with the Czechoslovak kid from the other room, the kid who called everyone FARMERS when he meant FARTERS. Or so we thought. I got on a swing. Man, I thought, all you have to do is fill in those *blanks*, with those little *answers*, now that I understood that, I'd hardly done any thinking, maybe that was the secret. Then you come out here, and things are really neat. I felt like I'd made friends with the world. After a while more people came out, and She came with them, Her hair in the breeze and the pile of workbooks in Her arms. Her eyes like the little flowers that grew next to the crabgrass on the dirt of the field. I was swinging and swinging, talking to Fard now he'd come out, no one had said anything to me, ME, about being one of the first guys out here, I was so stupid I didn't even think about that myself, the IMPOSSIBILITY. She hadn't even given me a look when I put the workbook on Her desk. She called to a couple of people, minor corrections, they stayed with Her for a minute and then went back to their free play, She must have looked at my book already. Then I heard Her sweet voice calling *Joe? Joe Lake? Come over here please,* and there was a new tone to it, PAIN is what it was. Something a little bad started to happen way at the back of my head, it wasn't exactly that arithmetic sickness, but maybe She –

Cripe, here was my workbook open in her flowered lap.

Joe, what were you thinking when you handed these in?

She didn't sound mad, She hardly ever gets mad and when She does it's kind of funny, Her forehead gets larger and it de-powders, and She gets a really weird pink colour as Fard always points out. He makes a science of Her skin. But Her voice was hurt, She couldn't believe I would turn in the wrong answers, not just wrong answers but answers *which revealed* I had not read the directions, that I have understood nothing since 1958. Answers which showed I hadn't listened to a thing She said all day, all week, all month.

All year. I couldn't believe it either, how come these small problems were so difficult, why can't you just answer them the way they look like they OUGHT to be answered, small easy ANSWERS in just a second? Now the crappy feelings started, not only was I really dumb but I'd hurt Her, betrayed Her, She would have to be RESCUED by Fard, from me. Without being mean She told me to get back to work, which I couldn't do, because the way I did the problems was the only way I could do them. And I could only do them once.

What are you supposed to say, I asked Fard on the way home. It doesn't do any good to tell them you wouldn't even be able to get THOSE answers again. How could my brain do this to me, and why?

Todd McEwen
Granta 55: Childhood, Autumn 1996

Autobiography Activities

First Sentences

1. Reading the sentences
• Read the opening sentences of these pieces of autobiographical writing, some of which are included in this anthology.

A. One winter morning in the long-ago, four-year-old days of my life I found myself standing before a fireplace, warming my hands over a mound of glowing coals, listening to the wind whistle past the house outside.

B. Long, long before I came to know and love Africa as a place, I yearned for it as an idea.

C. A hot September Saturday in 1959 and we are stationary in Cheshire.

D. Mum says, 'Don't come creeping into our room at night.'

E. I was born in Pnom-Penh, the capital city of Cambodia.

> F. Under the volcanoes, beside the snow-capped mountains, among the huge lakes, the fragrant, the silent, the tangled Chilean forest ...

> G. When my mum died an alcoholic in 1978, it annoyed and upset me that a number of journalists started sniffing into our family background, trying to find this reason or that for why she started drinking and why I drank.

• Talk about what these sentences tell you about the person writing (e.g. Male? Female? Age? Culture? Personality?)
• Write as many statements as you can about these sentences, in this form:

Sentence A is ..., whereas Sentence C is ...

For example:

Sentence E starts simply with the person's birth, whereas Sentence F is more unusual and intriguing — you want to find out more about it.

• Which of these openings makes you most interested to read on?

Openings F and G are by Pablo Neruda and George Best.

2. Writing your own first sentence
• Try some opening sentences as if you were writing your own autobiography. Experiment with four or five different versions, for instance:
– using suspense
– being descriptive
– using humour
– being surprising or a bit quirky
– being reflective.

Gather Together in My Name

I Know Why the Caged Bird Sings is one of the most well-known and best loved autobiographies of recent times. Maya Angelou's account of her early childhood, growing up as a black girl in the American South, has had a powerful impact on its readers. Less well known perhaps are the later volumes of her autobiography, in which she describes her amazingly rich and varied experiences as a cook, shopworker, dancer and, at one point, prostitute, struggling to bring up her son on her own and make her way in the world. The extract in this book is taken from the second volume, *Gather Together in My Name* and describes a short visit to her family in the Deep South, leaving her new, more liberated urban life in San Francisco and returning to the old ways of her past.

1. The opening
• Before reading the whole piece, read the opening, up to 'Up went the Black Status'.

• Look back at her preparations to go into town. Talk about:
– how she presents herself. Does she want the reader to admire her or be amused by her or question her actions in any way? How do you know?
– what you think is likely to happen in this episode.
– what issues are being raised at this stage in the piece.

2. The structure of the episode
• Look at this way of describing the structure of the story. Talk about how the events of the story might fit this description.

Pride and self importance.

↓

An event that confirms this.

↓

An event that challenges this.

↓

Seeming to overcome the challenge.

↓

A moment of self-discovery where self-importance is shattered.

3. Asking why?
Asking the question 'why?' can give you a fresh way of thinking about the choices a writer has made.
• Try answering the following 'why?' questions and see where the answers take you.

– Why include so much description of her clothes?
– Why include the dialogue between Marguerite and the store assistants?
– Why end the description of the first visit to town with Momma's question and Marguerite's answer?
– Why include the stop-off at Mr. Willie Williams' Dew Drop In?
– Why, in the second trip to the store, does Angelou say, '... here I drew myself up through the unrevenged slavery'?

– Why end the episode with a paragraph simply describing her departure rather than explaining or reflecting on what the episode had meant?

• Try writing three or four of your own 'why?' questions, then see if you can answer them.

4. What the episode is about

• What do you think Maya Angelou is trying to say, in recounting this episode? Discuss these statements and choose the three you most agree with. Find three pieces of evidence for each of the statements you choose.

1. Angelou is showing how Marguerite is naïve and irresponsible in her behaviour.
2. Angelou shows the injustice towards black people in the Deep South in the 1940s.
3. Angelou is more sympathetic to her mother and the people of Stamps than she is towards her younger self.
4. Angelou is showing how important it is to challenge racism.
5. Marguerite is presented as a strong, independent minded and admirable young woman.
6. This is a surprisingly humorous account of a serious incident.

5. A film adaptation

Maya Angelou tells the story in a way that is very visual. Her descriptions of small details create a strong mental picture.

• Make a list of the visual images she conjures up for you. In each case, try to explain what makes that image so strong. You could use a chart like the one below to set out your ideas.

Visual image	How Maya Angelou creates it
Her awkward walk along the road because her heels sink into the gravel	The detail of the 'Vynilite' see-through plastic shoes
Her description of how she 'glided and pulled into White Town'	The 2 verbs sound very different, one almost regal and elegant, the other suggesting a struggle.
The inside of Stamps General Merchandise Store	

• Choose one small part of the extract that conjures up particularly strong images in your head. Try creating a shooting script, or storyboard to show how it might be turned into a short film sequence of just a few minutes. If you do a shooting script, include: a written list of shots (with descriptions); details of camera position, shot length and transitions, and the soundtrack.

And When Did You Last See Your Father?

1. The father
• Talk about what this incident reveals about the father. Come up with a list of adjectives to describe him, for example pig-headed and irritable.

2. Getting inside people's heads
• The father is the central figure in the narrative but whose feelings do we hear most of? Give a score to each person, from one to five (five being the highest), to indicate whose feelings we find out most about. Then, for each of the characters, jot down a few words to describe what they seem to be feeling. Pull out a quotation from the text to illustrate this. You might find it helpful to record your discoveries as a chart.

The narrator
The mother
The sister
The steward
The father

• Choose one of these people, other than the narrator and try writing a paragraph in that person's voice, describing the events of the afternoon. For instance, the father might tell it from his point of view and justify his actions, the mother might show her misery and despair.

3. Making it vivid
Blake Morrison uses a variety of techniques to capture the interest of the reader. Some of them are listed below.

– Present tense
– Dialogue
– Blunt statements
– Writing as if inside the father's head
– Description of physical things – the way they look, sound, smell or feel
– The reactions of other people (e.g. the mother)
– Reflecting from an adult perspective

• Work in pairs. Share out the techniques among the pairs. Take responsibility for finding two or three quotations or examples of your technique to share with the rest of the class.

4. Your own memories
Everyone gets embarrassed by their parents, family or even their friends sometimes.
• Think of times when you've been embarrassed by something one of these people has said or done, for instance making a scene in a shop, shaming you in public or talking to you in the wrong way in front of your friends.

• Share the memory orally with one or two other people. You could go on to write it up as a piece of original writing.

Black Boy

1. Reading the extract in stages – first stage
• Read the first few paragraphs of the extract, up to the point when the boy tells his brother 'You shut up', on page 96. Predict what you think might happen next.

• Now read the next section, up to the bottom of page 97. Talk about what happened and how well it was described. Predict what you think might happen next.

• Read on to the end of this incident at the top of page 99.

• Talk about times when you did something naughty and got into serious trouble.

2. Reading the extract in stages – second stage
The second part of the extract is quite different from the beginning.
• Read it aloud, in pairs or small groups, with each person speaking one sentence in turn.

• Talk about what's special or different about the style of this section.

• Share your ideas as a whole class.

3. Ideas for writing
• Choose one of these suggestions for writing about your life.

– Try writing about one of your own experiences of doing something naughty, making it as exciting or entertaining as you can.
– Have a go at imitating Richard Wright's way of capturing what it felt like to be a small child in the second part of the extract. For instance, you could use the same sentence structure, starting, 'There was the ...'

To come up with ideas, make a list of all the things you associate with being small, then choose ones that you think you can bring to life poetically.

A Passage to Africa

George Alagiah is famous as a news broadcaster. In this extract, the opening of his autobiography, he describes how his family moved from Ceylon, (now called Sri Lanka) to Africa.

1. Ceylon v Africa

The chapter is structured around a contrast between two places – the place he left and the place he was going to – Africa and Ceylon.

• Use a chart like the one below to talk about and note down the differences in his feelings about the two places.

Africa	Ceylon
A promised land	A divided island
A magical place	A place where he didn't belong

2. Memories of Ceylon

Alagiah offers five separate memories of Ceylon:
– grandfather and his home
– the house in Colombo
– the latrine cleaner
– the washing
– the tiffin-carriers.

• In small groups, focus on one of these memories and look closely at how Alagiah creates a strongly evocative memory. (You could think about how he appeals to different senses – sight, sound, feeling, taste or smell.)

Saroeun's Story

Saroeun Ing wrote this autobiography when he was 14 years old. He entered it for the English and Media Centre's WRITE '85 competition and it was published in a book of autobiographical writing by school students called *More Lives*.

1. The context for Saroeun's story

Saroeun came to England from Cambodia. From 1969 to 1973 the country was heavily bombed by the Americans, in an effort to wipe out their Vietnamese enemies who had crossed the border into Cambodia looking for refuge. The intensive bombing increased the determination of the Khmer Rouge, the communist party, to seize power. In 1975 they overthrew the existing government. The Khmer Rouge ruled the country in a particularly cruel way, forcing thousands of people out of the city and murdering hundreds and thousands of people. They brutally suppressed any opposition. In 1979 the Vietnamese invaded Cambodia and with the help of many Cambodian people, forced the Khmer Rouge out of power.

2. Talking about Saroeun's story

• Talk about what Saroeun describes and the impact it made on you to read it.

• Talk about how well you think Saroeun conveys to the reader his experiences, his feelings and the places and people he writes about.

Saroeun divides up his narrative into nine sections, almost like chapters.
• Look at the titles and talk about what aspect of the story each one focuses on. For instance, some are about a stage in his story, whereas others focus on a person or a feeling.

3. The experience of changing places or changing schools

This activity will involve you in listening to other people's experiences, as well as sharing your own. Give each person time and space to talk. Try asking a few questions to help them share their memories. Be sensitive – some things might be quite hard to explain or even talk about. You could do this in pairs, small groups or as a whole class, depending on how comfortable you feel about sharing your memories.

• Talk about what it was like to leave one place and come to another, whether it's leaving a school, a home or a country. You might say something about:
– the place or school you left and your thoughts and feelings about it
– your reasons for leaving
– the place or school you were going to and your feelings about going there – what you had heard about it and what you expected it to be like
– what it was like when you got there
– one memorable thing that happened to you, perhaps something funny or frightening or shocking or sad
– your feelings now about the experience of changing places/schools.
You may want to go on to write about your memories, as George Alagiah and Saroeun Ing have done. Or, if you listened to a friend's story and found it particularly interesting or powerful, you could write about it as a third person account, asking them for help and support with details and ideas.

4. Writing about childhood

• Choose four tiny memories of scenes from your own early childhood. Write a short paragraph about each one, trying to evoke a strong sense of what it looked like and felt like.

Don't Let's Go to the Dogs Tonight

Alexandra Fuller's autobiography is about her life in Zimbabwe (previously called Rhodesia) during times of conflict and turmoil. As the daughter of a white farmer, she and her family were caught up in struggles over ownership of the land, when the white government was replaced in 1979. These fights to take over the land have continued, in recent years, supported by the government of Robert Mugabe.

1. Exploring the title
• Talk about the phrase, 'We're going to the dogs'. Share your ideas as a whole class.

• Now talk about the title of the book, *Don't Let's Go to the Dogs Tonight*. What expectations does it give you about the book?

2. The opening
• Read just the first nine lines of the extract.

• Talk about what effect this opening has on you as a reader. Does it make you want to read on? If so, why?

3. What view of the world?
Some of the autobiographies in this section are reflecting back on childhood. Others are written more from the point of view of a child.
• Talk about which you think this one is.

• Pick three or four short extracts as evidence for your view. For each extract, discuss exactly what the writer is doing to create this perspective.

• Present your extracts to the rest of the class. For each extract, give the class your analysis of the writer's approach and techniques.

4. Writing about painful memories
Alexandra Fuller writes about difficult experiences but instead of constantly telling the reader how difficult life was, she does the opposite. She just describes events in a simple, dead-pan, matter-of-fact sort of way.
• Find examples in the extract of one or two of these things being described in this way:
– something frightening
– something extraordinary
– something revolting.

Bad Blood and Arithmetic Town

1. Before reading – just a minute
• Before reading these two extracts from autobiographies, try talking for just a minute about your own memories of life at your junior school. Your teacher will set you off for a minute on one of these topics:
– the register
– learning your multiplication tables
– school tests
– doing sums
– the Headteacher

– the playground
– games
– sitting on the carpet.

When one person hesitates or deviates, the next person should carry on talking on the subject.

2. What kind of account of school life?

• Look at the list of statements below. For each one, decide whether it is more relevant to Lorna Sage's *Bad Blood*; more relevant to Todd McEwen's 'Arithmetic Town'; relevant to both pieces, or relevant to neither.

---

1. School is a difficult place to be.
2. It's hard to understand why things happen the way they do.
3. Teachers are nasty people.
4. Schools aren't really about teaching and learning.
5. This is about what schools were like in the past.
6. This is a comical view of school life.
7. This is a child's eye view of school life.

You could record your discoveries on a chart like the one shown here.

Statement	Relevant to Sage	Relevant to McEwen	Relevant to both	Not relevant to either

• Find evidence for your views, by looking back at each of the texts.

3. A mini-debate

• Have a five minute debate in small groups about which of the two texts you think gives the best idea of what if feels like to be at school.
(You could try nominating people to argue on each side, instead of arguing for your own viewpoint.)

4. Your own early memories of school

• Choose one school subject or one teacher or one school year to write about. Start by making a list of all the topics you might include. The example on page 129 on P.E. lessons might give you some ideas about how you might start collecting ideas for your writing.

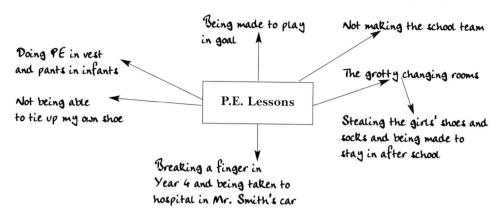

Being made to play in goal

Not making the school team

Doing PE in vest and pants in infants

The grotty changing rooms

P.E. Lessons

Not being able to tie up my own shoe

Stealing the girls' shoes and socks and being made to stay in after school

Breaking a finger in Year 4 and being taken to hospital in Mr. Smith's car

Writing Your Own Autobiography

• Use ideas from any of the extracts you have read to try writing your own autobiography. You could do it in whatever style you like. Make use of the thinking you have already done. You could follow the strategy below to help you come up with ideas and choose a style for your writing.

1. Write five or six different opening paragraphs, each taking a different angle and trying to achieve a different effect. For example, one humorous opening, one opening which begins to tell a little story from your childhood, one opening describing the physical environment, one opening which focuses on your sense of yourself (for instance your gender, your cultural identity, your feelings or beliefs). You could try writing in the style of one of the writers you have read.

2. Pick the opening that you like best and continue it, writing the whole opening section of your autobiography. When you have completed a first draft and worked on it to polish it up, write a commentary to go with it, in which you explain what you were trying to do. You should also reflect on how it compares with the openings you have read by other writers.

Reading Autobiographies

• Pick one of the extracts that you particularly enjoyed. Try reading the whole autobiography.
Alternatively, try reading one of these 'bestselling' autobiographies:
Once in a House on Fire by Andrea Ashworth
Angela's Ashes by Frank McCourt
Boy by Roald Dahl
Wild Swans by Jung Chang

You could prepare a short presentation on the book you read for the rest of your class.

The Eruption of Vesuvius

My uncle was stationed at Misenum, in active command of the fleet. On 24 August, in the early afternoon, my mother drew his attention to a cloud of unusual size and appearance. He had been out in the sun, had taken a cold bath, and lunched while lying down, and was then working at his books. He called for his shoes and climbed up to a place which would give him the best view of the phenomenon. It was not clear at that distance from which mountain the cloud was rising (it was afterwards known to be Vesuvius); its general appearance can best be expressed as being like an umbrella pine, for it rose to a great height on a sort of trunk and then split off into branches, I imagine because it was thrust upwards by the first blast and then left unsupported as the pressure subsided, or else it was borne down by its own weight so that it spread out and gradually dispersed. In places it looked white, elsewhere blotched and dirty, according to the amount of soil and ashes it carried with it. My uncle's scholarly acumen saw at once that it was important enough for a closer inspection, and he ordered a boat to be made ready, telling me I could come with him if I wished. I replied that I preferred to go on with my studies, and as it happened he had himself given me some writing to do.

As he was leaving the house he was handed a message from Rectina, wife of Tascus whose house was at the foot of the mountain, so that escape was impossible except by boat. She was terrified by the danger threatening her and implored him to rescue her from her fate. He changed his plans, and what he had begun in a spirit of inquiry he completed as a hero. He gave orders for the warships to be launched and went on board himself with the intention of bringing help to many more people besides Rectina, for this lovely stretch of coast was thickly populated. He hurried to the place which everyone else was hastily leaving, steering his course straight for the danger zone. He was entirely fearless, describing each new movement and phase of the portent to be noted down exactly as he observed them. Ashes were already falling, hotter and thicker as the ships drew near, followed by bits of pumice and blackened stones, charred and cracked by the flames: then suddenly they were in shallow water, and the shore was blocked by the debris from the mountain. For a moment my uncle wondered whether to turn back, but when the helmsman advised this he refused, telling him that Fortune stood by the courageous and they must make for Pomponianus at Stabiae. He was cut off there by the breadth of the bay (for the shore gradually curves round a basin filled by the sea) so that he was not as yet in danger, though it was clear that this would come nearer as it spread. Pomponianus had therefore already put his belongings on board ship, intending to escape if the contrary wind fell. This wind was of course full in my uncle's favour, and he was able to bring his ship in. He embraced his terrified friend, cheered and encouraged him, and thinking he could calm his fears by showing his own composure, gave orders that he was to be carried to the bathroom. After his bath he lay down and dined; he was quite cheerful, or at any rate he pretended he was, which was no less courageous.

Meanwhile on Mount Vesuvius broad sheets of fire and leaping flames blazed at several points, their bright glare emphasized by the darkness of night. My uncle tried to allay the fears of his companions by repeatedly declaring that these were nothing but bonfires left by the peasants in their terror, or else empty houses on fire in the districts they had abandoned. Then he went to rest and certainly slept, for as he was a stout man his breathing was rather loud and heavy and could be heard by people coming and going outside his door. By this time the courtyard giving access to his room was full of ashes mixed with pumice stones, so that its level had risen, and if he had stayed in the room any longer he would never have got out. He was wakened, came out and joined Pomponianus and the rest of the household who had sat up all night. They debated whether to stay indoors or take their chance in the open, for the buildings were now shaking with violent shocks, and seemed to be swaying to and fro as if they were torn from their foundations. Outside, on the other hand, there was the danger of falling pumice stones, even though these were light and porous; however, after comparing the risks they chose the latter. In my uncle's case one reason outweighed the other, but for the others it was a choice of fears. As a protection against falling objects they put pillows on their heads tied down with cloths.

Elsewhere there was daylight by this time, but they were still in darkness, blacker and denser than any ordinary night, which they relieved by lighting torches and various kinds of lamp. My uncle decided to go down to the shore and investigate on the spot the possibility of any escape by sea, but he found the waves still wild and dangerous. A sheet was spread on the ground for him to lie down, and he repeatedly asked for cold water to drink. Then the flames and smell of sulphur which gave warning of the approaching fire drove the others to take flight and roused him to stand up. He stood leaning on two slaves and then suddenly collapsed, I imagine because the dense fumes choked his breathing by blocking his windpipe which was constitutionally weak and narrow and often inflamed. When daylight returned on the 26th – two days after the last day he had seen – his body was found intact and uninjured, still fully clothed and looking more like sleep than death.

Meanwhile my mother and I were at Misenum ... After my uncle's departure I spent the rest of the day with my books, as this was my reason for staying behind. Then I took a bath, dined, and then dozed fitfully for a while. For several days past there had been earth tremors which were not particularly alarming because they are frequent in Campania: but that night the shocks were so violent that everything felt as if it were not only shaken but overturned. My mother hurried into my room and found me already getting up to wake her if she were still asleep. We sat down in the forecourt of the house, between the buildings and the sea close by. I don't know whether I should call this courage or folly on my part (I was only seventeen at the time) but I called for a volume of Livy and went on reading as if I had nothing else to do. I even went on with the extracts I had been making. Up came a friend of my uncle's who had just come from Spain to join him. When he saw us sitting there and me actually reading, he scolded us both – me for my foolhardiness and my mother for allowing it. Nevertheless, I remained absorbed in my book.

By now it was dawn, but the light was still dim and faint. The buildings round us were already tottering, and the open space we were in was too small for us not to be in real and imminent danger if the house collapsed. This finally decided us to leave the town. We were followed by a panic-striken mob of people wanting to act on someone else's decision in preference to their own (a point in which fear looks like prudence), who hurried us on our way by pressing hard behind in a dense crowd. Once beyond the buildings we stopped, and there we had some extraordinary experiences which thoroughly alarmed us. The carriages we had ordered to be brought out began to run in different directions though the ground was quite level, and would not remain stationary even when wedged with stones. We also saw the sea sucked away and apparently forced back by the earthquake: at any rate it receded from the shore so that quantities of sea creatures were left stranded on dry sand. On the landward side a fearful black cloud was rent by forked and quivering bursts of flame, and parted to reveal great tongues of fire, like flashes of lightning magnified in size.

At this point my uncle's friend from Spain spoke up still more urgently, 'If your brother, if your uncle is still alive, he will want you both to be saved; if he is dead, he would want you to survive him – why put off your escape?' We replied that we would not think of considering our own safety as long as we were uncertain of his. Without waiting any longer, our friend rushed off and hurried out of danger as fast as he could.

Soon afterwards the cloud sank down to earth and covered the sea; it had already blotted out Capri and hidden the promontory of Misenum from sight. Then my mother implored, entreated and commanded me to escape as best I could – a young man might escape, whereas she was old and slow and could die in peace as long as she had not been the cause of my death too. I refused to save myself without her, and grasping her hand forced her to quicken her pace. She gave in reluctantly, blaming herself for delaying me. Ashes were already falling, not as yet very thickly. I looked round: a dense black cloud was coming up behind us, spreading over the earth like a flood. 'Let us leave the road while we can still see,' I said, 'or we shall be knocked down and trampled underfoot in the dark by the crowd behind.' We had scarcely sat down to rest when darkness fell, not the dark of a moonless or cloudy night, but as if the lamp had been put out in a closed room. You could hear the shrieks of women, the wailing of infants, and the shouting of men; some were calling their parents, others their children or their wives, trying to recognize them by their voices. People bewailed their own fate or that of their relatives, and there were some who prayed for death in their terror of dying. Many besought the aid of the gods, but still more imagined there were no gods left, and that the universe was plunged into eternal darkness for evermore. There were people, too, who added to the real perils by inventing fictitious dangers: some reported that part of Misenum had collapsed or another part was on fire, and though their tales were false they found others to believe them. A gleam of light returned, but we took this to be a warning of the approaching flames rather than daylight. However, the flames remained some distance off; then darkness came on once more and ashes began to fall again, this time in heavy showers. We rose from time to time and shook them off, otherwise we should have been buried and crushed beneath their weight. I could boast that not a groan or cry of fear escaped me in these perils, but I admit that I derived some poor consolation in my mortal lot from the belief that the whole world was dying with me and I with it.

At last the darkness thinned and dispersed like smoke or cloud; then there was genuine daylight, and the sun actually shone out, but yellowish as it is during an eclipse. We were terrified to see everything changed, buried deep in ashes like snowdrifts. We returned to Misenum where we attended to our physical needs as best we could, and then spent an anxious night alternating between hope and fear. Fear predominated, for the earthquakes went on, and several hysterical individuals made their own and other people's calamities seem ludicrous in comparison with their frightful predictions. But even then, in spite of the dangers we had been through and were still expecting, my mother and I had still no intention of leaving until we had news of my uncle.

Of course these details are not important enough for history, and you will read them without any idea of recording them; if they seem scarcely worth putting in a letter, you have only yourself to blame for asking for them.

Pliny the Younger
Letters, 24 August, 79 AD

Beyond Belief

Yesterday's apocalyptic scenes far outstripped anything Hollywood has ever imagined. Amid the confusion, only one thing seemed certain, says Ian McEwan – the world would never be the same again.

These were the kind of events that Hollywood has been imagining these past decades in the worst of its movies. But American reality always outstrips the imagination. And even the best minds, the best or darkest dreamers of disaster on a gigantic scale, from Tolstoy and Wells to Don DeLillo, could not have delivered us into the nightmare available on television news channels yesterday afternoon. For most of us, at a certain point, the day froze, the work and all other obligations were left behind, the screen became the only reality. We entered a dreamlike state. We had seen this before, with giant budgets and special effects, but so badly rehearsed. The colossal explosions, the fierce black and red clouds, the crowds running through the streets, the contradictory, confusing information, had only the feeblest resemblance to the tinny dramas of *Skyscraper, Backdraft* or *Independence Day*. Nothing could have prepared us.

Always, it seemed, it was what we could not see that was so frightening. We saw the skyscrapers, the tilting plane, the awful impact, the cumuli of dust engulfing the streets. But we were left to imagine for ourselves the human terror inside the airliner, down the corridors and elevator lobbies of the stricken buildings, or in the streets below as the towers collapsed on to rescue workers and morning crowds. Eyewitnesses told us of office workers jumping from awesome heights, but we did not see them. The screaming, the heroism and reasonable panic, the fumbling in semi-darkness for mobile phones – it was our safe distance from it all that was so horrifying. No blood, no screams. The Greeks, in their tragedies, wisely kept these worst of moments off stage, out of the scene. Hence the word: obscene. This was an obscenity. We were watching death on an unbelievable scale, but we saw no one die. The nightmare was in this gulf of imagining. The horror was in the distance.

Only television could bring this. Our set in the corner is mostly unwatched. Now my son and I surfed – hungrily, ghoulishly – between CNN, CBC and

BBC24. As soon as an expert was called in to pronounce on the politics or the symbolism, we moved on. We only wanted to know what was happening. Numbed, and in a state of sickened wonderment, we wanted only information, new developments – not opinion, analysis, or noble sentiments; not yet. We had to know: was it two planes or three that hit the Twin Towers? Was the White House now under attack? Where was the plane the airforce was supposed to be tracking? An information junkie inside me was silently instructing the cameras: go round that tower and show me that aeroplane again; get down in the street; take me on to the roof. Never had those words, flashed by all the channels – Breaking News – meant so much. And so much, so many people, were breaking. Only briefly, in this orgy of 'fresh' developments, was there time to reflect on the misery to come for all those who would learn the news of a loved one lost, a parent or a child. There was barely time to contemplate the cruelty of the human hearts that could unleash this. Were they watching with us now, equally hungry to know the worst? The thought covered me in shame.

About that time, the news networks began to steady themselves. They had, understandably, fumbled as the wires choked with news. Anchormen, at first, had not seemed to believe the events they were presenting. The pictures obliterated the commentary. Now the operation was becoming smoother. Professionalism was surpassing sentiment. Was this a kind of acceptance? Or avoidance? Dozens of affiliated television stations began to feed in. Cameras, at last, were everywhere, just as I was sickening of this surfeit and horrified at myself for wanting it. Now it was punishment to watch, and see replayed from new angles, the imploding towers, 102 storeys enfolding into their own dust. Or see the conflagration at the 'exit hole' of the second tower. Or see two women cowering in terror behind a car.

From the vantage point of the Brooklyn Heights, we saw Lower Manhattan disappear into dust. New York, and therefore all cities, looked fragile and vulnerable. The technology that was bringing us these scenes has wired us closely together into a febrile, mutual dependency. Our way of life, centralised and machine-dependent, has made us frail. Our civilisation, it suddenly seemed, our way of life, is easy to wreck when there are sufficient resources and cruel intent. No missile defence system can protect us.

Yesterday afternoon, for a dreamlike, immeasurable period, the appearance was of total war, and of the world's mightiest empire in ruins. That sense of denial which accompanies all catastrophes kept nagging away: this surely isn't happening. I'll blink and it will be gone. Like millions, perhaps billions around the world, we knew we were living through a time that we would never be able to forget. We also knew, though it was too soon to wonder how or why, that the world would never be the same. We knew only that it would be worse.

Ian McEwan
The Guardian, 12 September 2001

My Beating by Refugees

They started by shaking hands. We said 'Salaam aleikum' – peace be upon you – then the first pebbles flew past my face. A small boy tried to grab my bag. Then another. Then someone punched me in the back. Then young men broke my glasses, began smashing stones into my face and head. I couldn't see for the blood pouring down my forehead and swamping my eyes. And even then, I understood. I couldn't blame them for what they were doing. In fact, if I were the Afghan refugees of Kila Abdullah, close to the Afghan-Pakistan border, I would have done just the same to Robert Fisk. Or any other Westerner I could find.

So why record my few minutes of terror and self-disgust under assault near the Afghan border, bleeding and crying like an animal, when hundreds – let us be frank and say thousands – of innocent civilians are dying under American air strikes in Afghanistan, when the 'War of Civilisation' is burning and maiming the Pashtuns of Kandahar and destroying their homes because 'good' must triumph over 'evil'?

Some of the Afghans in the little village had been there for years, others had arrived – desperate and angry and mourning their slaughtered loved ones – over the past two weeks. It was a bad place for a car to break down. A bad time, just before the Iftar, the end of the daily fast of Ramadan. But what happened to us was symbolic of the hatred and fury and hypocrisy of this filthy war, a growing band of destitute Afghan men, young and old, who saw foreigners – enemies – in their midst and tried to destroy at least one of them.

Many of these Afghans, so we were to learn, were outraged by what they had seen on television of the Mazar-i-Sharif massacres, of the prisoners killed with their hands tied behind their backs. A villager later told one of our drivers that they had seen the videotape of CIA officers 'Mike' and 'Dave' threatening death to a kneeling prisoner at Mazar. They were uneducated – I doubt if many could read – but you don't have to have a schooling to respond to the death of loved ones under a B-52's bombs. At one point a screaming teenager had turned to my driver and asked, in all sincerity: 'Is that Mr Bush?'

It must have been about 4.30pm that we reached Kila Abdullah, halfway between the Pakistani city of Quetta and the border town of Chaman;

Amanullah, our driver, Fayyaz Ahmed, our translator, Justin Huggler of *The Independent* – fresh from covering the Mazar massacre – and myself.

The first we knew that something was wrong was when the car stopped in the middle of the narrow, crowded street. A film of white steam was rising from the bonnet of our jeep, a constant shriek of car horns and buses and trucks and rickshaws protesting at the road-block we had created. All four of us got out of the car and pushed it to the side of the road. I muttered something to Justin about this being 'a bad place to break down'. Kila Abdulla was home to thousands of Afghan refugees, the poor and huddled masses that the war has produced in Pakistan.

Amanullah went off to find another car – there is only one thing worse than a crowd of angry men and that's a crowd of angry men after dark – and Justin and I smiled at the initially friendly crowd that had already gathered round our steaming vehicle. I shook a lot of hands – perhaps I should have thought of Mr Bush – and uttered a lot of 'Salaam aleikums'. I knew what could happen if the smiling stopped.

The crowd grew larger and I suggested to Justin that we move away from the jeep, walk into the open road. A child had flicked his finger hard against my wrist and I persuaded myself that it was an accident, a childish moment of contempt. Then a pebble whisked past my head and bounced off Justin's shoulder. Justin turned round. His eyes spoke of concern and I remember how I breathed in. Please, I thought, it was just a prank. Then another kid tried to grab my bag. It contained my passport, credit cards, money, diary, contacts book, mobile phone. I yanked it back and put the strap round my shoulder. Justin and I crossed the road and someone punched me in the back.

How do you walk out of a dream when the characters suddenly turn hostile? I saw one of the men who had been all smiles when we shook hands. He wasn't smiling now. Some of the smaller boys were still laughing but their grins were transforming into something else. The respected foreigner – the man who had been all 'salaam aleikum' a few minutes ago – was upset, frightened, on the run. The West was being brought low. Justin was being pushed around and, in the middle of the road, we noticed a bus driver waving us to his vehicle. Fayyaz, still by the car, unable to understand why we had walked away, could no longer see us. Justin reached the bus and climbed aboard. As I put my foot on the step three men grabbed the strap of my bag and wrenched me back on to the road. Justin's hand shot out. 'Hold on,' he shouted. I did.

That's when the first mighty crack descended on my head. I almost fell down under the blow, my ears singing with the impact. I had expected this, though not so painful or hard, not so immediate. Its message was awful. Someone hated me enough to hurt me. There were two more blows, one on the back of my shoulder, a powerful fist that sent me crashing against the side of the bus while still clutching Justin's hand. The passengers were looking out at me and then at Justin. But they did not move. No one wanted to help.

I cried out 'Help me Justin', and Justin – who was doing more than any human could do by clinging to my ever loosening grip asked me – over the screams of the crowd – what I wanted him to do. Then I realised. I could only just hear him. Yes, they were shouting. Did I catch the word 'kaffir' – infidel? Perhaps I was wrong. That's when I was dragged away from Justin.

There were two more cracks on my head, one on each side and for some odd reason, part of my memory – some small crack in my brain – registered a moment at school, at a primary school called the Cedars in Maidstone more than 50 years ago when a tall boy building sandcastles in the playground had hit me on the head. I had a memory of the blow *smelling*, as if it had affected my nose. The next blow came from a man I saw carrying a big stone in his right hand. He brought it down on my forehead with tremendous force and something hot and liquid splashed down my face and lips and chin. I was kicked. On the back, on the shins, on my right thigh. Another teenager grabbed my bag yet again and I was left clinging to the strap, looking up suddenly and realising there must have been 60 men in front of me, howling. Oddly, it wasn't fear I felt but a kind of wonderment. So this is how it happens. I knew that I had to respond. Or, so I reasoned in my stunned state, I had to die.

The only thing that shocked me was my own physical sense of collapse, my growing awareness of the liquid beginning to cover me. I don't think I've ever seen so much blood before. For a second, I caught a glimpse of something terrible, a nightmare face – my own – reflected in the window of the bus, streaked in blood, my hands drenched in the stuff like Lady Macbeth, slopping down my pullover and the collar of my shirt until my back was wet and my bag dripping with crimson and vague splashes suddenly appearing on my trousers.

The more I bled, the more the crowd gathered and beat me with their fists. Pebbles and small stones began to bounce off my head and shoulders. How long, I remembered thinking, could this go on? My head was suddenly struck by stones on both sides at the same time – not thrown stones but stones in the palms of men who were using them to try and crack my skull. Then a fist punched me in the face, splintering my glasses on my nose, another hand grabbed at the spare pair of spectacles round my neck and ripped the leather container from the cord.

I guess at this point I should thank Lebanon. For 25 years, I have covered Lebanon's wars and the Lebanese used to teach me, over and over again, how to stay alive: take a decision – any decision – but don't do nothing.

So I wrenched the bag back from the hands of the young man who was holding it. He stepped back. Then I turned on the man on my right, the one holding the bloody stone in his hand and I bashed my fist into his mouth. I couldn't see very much – my eyes were not only short-sighted without my glasses but were misting over with a red haze – but I saw the man sort of cough and a tooth fall from his lip and then he fell back on the road. For a second the crowd stopped. Then I went for the other man, clutching my bag under my arm and banging my fist into his nose. He roared in anger and it suddenly turned all red. I missed another man with a punch, hit one more in the face, and ran.

I was back in the middle of the road but could not see. I brought my hands to my eyes and they were full of blood and with my fingers I tried to scrape the gooey stuff out. It made a kind of sucking sound but I began to see again and realised that I was crying and weeping and that the tears were cleaning my eyes of blood. What had I done, I kept asking myself? I had been punching and attacking Afghan refugees, the very people I had been writing about for so long, the very dispossessed, mutilated people whom my own country – among others – was killing along, with the Taliban, just across the border. God spare me, I thought. I think I actually said it. The men whose families our bombers were killing were now my enemies too.

Then something quite remarkable happened. A man walked up to me, very calmly, and took me by the arm. I couldn't see him very well for all the blood that was running into my eyes but he was dressed in a kind of robe and wore a turban and had a white-grey beard. And he led me away from the crowd. I looked over my shoulder. There were now a hundred men behind me and a few stones skittered along the road, but they were not aimed at me – presumably to avoid hitting the stranger. He was like an Old Testament figure or some Bible story, the Good Samaritan, a Muslim man – perhaps a mullah in the village – who was trying to save my life.

He pushed me into the back of a police truck. But the policemen didn't move. They were terrified. 'Help me,' I kept shouting through the tiny window at the back of their cab, my hands leaving streams of blood down the glass. They drove a few metres and stopped until the tall man spoke to them again. Then they drove another 300 metres.

And there, beside the road, was a Red Cross-Red Crescent convoy. The crowd was still behind us. But two of the medical attendants pulled me behind one of their vehicles, poured water over my hands and face and began pushing bandages on to my head and face and the back of my head. 'Lie down and we'll cover you with a blanket so they can't see you,' one of them said. They were both Muslims, Bangladeshis and their names should be recorded because they were good men and true: Mohamed Abdul Halim and Sikder Mokaddes Ahmed. I lay on the floor, groaning, aware that I might live.

Within minutes, Justin arrived. He had been protected by a massive soldier from the Baluchistan Levies – true ghost of the British Empire who, with a single rifle, kept the crowds away from the car in which Justin was now sitting. I fumbled with my bag. They never got the bag, I kept saying to myself, as if my passport and my credit cards were a kind of Holy Grail. But they had seized my final pair of spare glasses – I was blind without all three – and my mobile telephone was missing and so was my contacts book, containing 25 years of telephone numbers throughout the Middle East. What was I supposed to do? Ask everyone who ever knew me to re-send their telephone numbers?

Goddamit, I said and tried to bang my fist on my side until I realised it was bleeding from a big gash on the wrist – the mark of the tooth I had just knocked out of a man's jaw, a man who was truly innocent of any crime except that of being the victim of the world.

I had spent more than two and a half decades reporting the humiliation and misery of the Muslim world and now their anger had embraced me too. Or had it? There were Mohamed and Sikder of the Red Crescent and Fayyaz who came panting back to the car incandescent at our treatment and Amanullah who invited us to his home for medical treatment. And there was the Muslim saint who had taken me by the arm.

And – I realised – there were all the Afghan men and boys who had attacked me who should never have done so but whose brutality was entirely the product of others, of us – of we who had armed their struggle against the Russians and ignored their pain and laughed at their civil war and then armed and paid them again for the 'War for Civilisation' just a few miles away and then bombed their homes and ripped up their families and called them 'collateral damage'.

So I thought I should write about what happened to us in this fearful, silly, bloody, tiny incident. I feared other versions would produce a different narrative, of how a British journalist was 'beaten up by a mob of Afghan refugees'.

And of course, that's the point. The people who were assaulted were the Afghans, the scars inflicted by us – by B-52s, not by them. And I'll say it again. If I was an Afghan refugee in Kila Abdullah, I would have done just what they did. I would have attacked Robert Fisk. Or any other Westerner I could find.

Robert Fisk in Kila Abdullah, Afghanistan
The Independent, 10 December 2001

On the Bottom

The journey did not last more than twenty minutes. Then the lorry stopped, and we saw a large door, and above it a sign, brightly illuminated (its memory still strikes me in my dreams): *Arbeit Macht Frei,* work gives freedom.

We climb down, they make us enter an enormous empty room that is poorly heated. We have a terrible thirst. The weak gurgle of the water in the radiators makes us ferocious; we have had nothing to drink for four days. But there is also a tap – and above it a card which says that it is forbidden to drink as the water is dirty. Nonsense. It seems obvious that the card is a joke, 'they' know that we are dying of thirst and they put us in a room, and there is a tap, and *Wassertrinken Verboten.* I drink and I incite my companions to do likewise, but I have to spit it out, the water is tepid and sweetish, with the smell of a swamp.

This is hell. Today, in our times, hell must be like this. A huge, empty room: we are tired, standing on our feet, with a tap which drips while we cannot drink the water, and we wait for something which will certainly be terrible, and nothing happens and nothing continues to happen. What can one think about? One cannot think any more, it is like being already dead. Someone sits down on the ground. The time passes drop by drop.

We are not dead. The door is opened and an SS man enters, smoking. He looks at us slowly and asks, *'Wer kann Deutsch?'* One of us whom I have never seen, named Flesch, moves forward; he will be our interpreter. The SS man makes a long calm speech; the interpreter translates. We have to form rows of five, with intervals of two yards between man and man; then we have to undress and make a bundle of the clothes in a special manner, the woollen garments on one side, all the rest on the other; we must take off our shoes but pay great attention that they are not stolen.

Stolen by whom? Why should our shoes be stolen? And what about our documents, the few things we have in our pockets, our watches? We all look at the interpreter, and the interpreter asks the German, and the German smokes and looks him through and through as if he were transparent, as if no one had spoken.

I had never seen old men naked. Mr Bergmann wore a truss and asked the interpreter if he should take it off, and the interpreter hesitated. But the German understood and spoke seriously to the interpreter pointing to someone. We saw the interpreter swallow and then he said: 'The officer says, take off the truss, and you will be given that of Mr Coen.' One could see the words coming bitterly out of Flesch's mouth; this was the German manner of laughing.

Now another German comes and tells us to put the shoes in a certain corner, and we put them there, because now it is all over and we feel outside this world and the only thing is to obey. Someone comes with a broom and sweeps away all the shoes, outside the door in a heap. He is crazy, he is mixing them all together, ninety-six pairs, they will be all unmatched. The outside door opens, a freezing wind enters and we are naked and cover ourselves up with our arms. The wind blows and slams the door; the German reopens it and stands watching with interest how we writhe to hide from the wind, one behind the other. Then he leaves and closes it.

Now the second act begins. Four men with razors, soapbrushes and clippers burst in; they have trousers and jackets with stripes, with a number sewn on the front; perhaps they are the same sort as those others of this evening (this evening or yesterday evening?); but these are robust and flourishing. We ask many questions but they catch hold of us and in a moment we find ourselves shaved and sheared. What comic faces we have without hair! The four speak a language which does not seem of this world. It is certainly not German, for I understand a little German.

Finally another door is opened: here we are, locked in, naked, sheared and standing, with our feet in water – it is a shower-room. We are alone. Slowly the astonishment dissolves, and we speak, and everyone asks questions and no one answers. If we are naked in a shower-room, it means that we will have a shower. If we have a shower it is because they are not going to kill us yet. But why then do they keep us standing, and give us nothing to drink, while nobody explains anything, and we have no shoes or clothes, but we are all naked with our feet in the water, and we have been travelling five days and cannot even sit down. And our women?

Mr Levi asks me if I think that our women are like us at this moment, and where they are, and if we will be able to see them again. I say yes, because he is married and has a daughter; certainly we will see them again. But by now my belief is that all this is a game to mock and sneer at us. Clearly they will kill us, whoever thinks he is going to live is mad, it means that he has swallowed the bait, but I have not; I have understood that it will soon all be over, perhaps in this same room, when they get bored of seeing us naked, dancing from foot to foot and trying every now and again to sit down on the floor. But there are two inches of cold water and we cannot sit down.

We walk up and down without sense, and we talk, everybody talks to everybody else, we make a great noise. The door opens, and a German enters; it is the officer of before. He speaks briefly, the interpreter translates. 'The officer says you must be quiet, because this is not a rabbinical school.' One sees the words which are not his, the bad words, twist his mouth as they come out, as if he was spitting out a foul taste. We beg him to ask what we are waiting for, how long we will stay here, about our women, everything; but he says no, that he does not want to ask. This Flesch, who is most unwilling to translate into Italian the hard cold German phrases and refuses to turn into German our questions because he knows that it is useless, is a German Jew of about fifty, who has a large scar on his face from a wound received fighting the Italians on the Piave. He is a closed, taciturn man, for whom I feel an instinctive respect as I feel that he has begun to suffer before us.

The German goes and we remain silent, although we are a little ashamed of our silence. It is still night and we wonder if the day will ever come. The door opens again, and someone else dressed in stripes comes in. He is different from the others, older, with glasses, a more civilized face, and much less robust. He speaks to us in Italian.

By now we are tired of being amazed. We seem to be watching some mad play, one of those plays in which the witches, the Holy Spirit and the devil appear. He speaks Italian badly, with a strong foreign accent. He makes a long speech, is very polite, and tries to reply to all our questions.

We are at Monowitz, near Auschwitz, in Upper Silesia, a region inhabited by both Poles and Germans. This camp is a work-camp, in German one says *Arbeitslager;* all the prisoners (there are about ten thousand) work in a factory which produces a type of rubber called Buna, so that the camp itself is called Buna.

We will be given shoes and clothes – no, not our own – other shoes, other clothes, like his. We are naked now because we are waiting for the shower and the disinfection, which will take place immediately after the reveille, because one cannot enter the camp without being disinfected.

Certainly there will be work to do, everyone must work here. But there is work and work: he, for example, acts as doctor. He is a Hungarian doctor who studied in Italy and he is the dentist of the Lager. He has been in the Lager for four and a half years (not in this one: Buna has only been open for a year and a half), but we can see that he is still quite well, not very thin. Why is he in the Lager? Is he Jewish like us? 'No,' he says simply, 'I am a criminal.'

We ask him many questions. He laughs, replies to some and not to others, and it is clear that he avoids certain subjects. He does not speak of the women: he says they are well, that we will see them again soon, but he does not say how or where. Instead he tells us other things, strange and crazy things, perhaps he too is playing with us. Perhaps he is mad – one goes mad in the Lager. He says that every Sunday there are concerts and football matches. He says that whoever boxes well can become cook. He says that whoever works well receives prize-coupons with which to buy tobacco and soap. He says that the water is really not drinkable, and that instead a coffee substitute is distributed every day, but generally nobody drinks it as the soup itself is sufficiently watery to quench thirst. We beg him to find us something to drink, but he says he cannot, that he has come to see us secretly, against SS orders, as we still have to be disinfected, and that he must leave at once; he has come because he has a liking for Italians, and because, he says, he 'has a little heart'. We ask him if there are other Italians in the camp and he says there are some, a few, he does not know how many; and he at once changes the subject. Meanwhile a bell rang and he immediately hurried off and left us stunned and disconcerted. Some feel refreshed but I do not. I still think that even this dentist, this incomprehensible person, wanted to amuse himself at our expense, and I do not want to believe a word of what he said.

At the sound of the bell, we can hear the still dark camp waking up. Unexpectedly the water gushes out boiling from the showers – five minutes of bliss; but immediately after, four men (perhaps they are the barbers) burst in yelling and shoving and drive us out, wet and steaming, into the adjoining room which is freezing; here other shouting people throw at us unrecognizable rags and thrust into our hands a pair of broken-down boots with wooden soles; we have no time to understand and we already find ourselves in the open, in the blue and icy snow of dawn, barefoot and naked, with all our clothing in our hands, with a hundred yards to run to the next hut. There we are finally allowed to get dressed.

When we finish, everyone remains in his own corner and we do not dare lift our eyes to look at one another. There is nowhere to look in a mirror, but our appearance stands in front of us, reflected in a hundred livid faces, in a hundred miserable and sordid puppets. We are transformed into the phantoms glimpsed yesterday evening.

Then for the first time we became aware that our language lacks words to express this offence, the demolition of a man. In a moment, with almost prophetic intuition, the reality was revealed to us: we had reached the bottom. It is not possible to sink lower than this; no human condition is more miserable than this, nor could it conceivably be so. Nothing belongs to us any more; they have taken away our clothes, our shoes, even our hair; if we speak, they will not listen to us, and if they listen, they will not understand. They will even take away our name: and if we want to keep it, we will have to find ourselves the strength to do so, to manage somehow so that behind the name something of us, of us as we were, still remains.

We know that we will have difficulty in being understood, and this is as it should be. But consider what value, what meaning is enclosed even in the smallest of our daily habits, in the hundred possessions which even the poorest beggar owns: a handkerchief, an old letter, the photo of a cherished prison. These things are part of us, almost like limbs of our body; nor is it conceivable that we can be deprived of them in our world, for we immediately find others to substitute the old ones, other objects which are ours in their personification and evocation of our memories.

Imagine now a man who is deprived of everyone he loves, and at the same time his house, his habits, his clothes, in short, of everything he possesses: he will be a hollow man, reduced to suffering and needs, forgetful of dignity and restraint, for he who loses all often easily loses himself. He will be a man whose life or death can be lightly decided with no sense of human affinity, in the most fortunate of cases, on the basis of a pure judgement of utility. It is in this way that one can understand the double sense of the term 'extermination camp', and it is now clear what we seek to express with the phrase: 'to lie on the bottom'.

Häftling: I have learnt that I am Häftling. My number is 174517; we have been baptized, we will carry the tattoo on our left arm until we die.

The operation was slightly painful and extraordinarily rapid: they placed us all in a row, and one by one, according to the alphabetical order of our names, we filed past a skilful official, armed with a sort of pointed tool with a very short needle. It seems that this is the real, true initiation: only by 'showing one's number' can one get bread and soup. Several days passed, and not a few cuffs and punches, before we became used to showing our number promptly enough not to disorder the daily operation of food-distribution; weeks and months were needed to learn its sound in the German language. And for many days, while the habits of freedom still led me to look for the time on my wristwatch, my new name ironically appeared instead, a number tattooed in bluish characters under the skin.

Only much later, and slowly, a few of us learnt something of the funereal science of the numbers of Auschwitz, which epitomize the stages of destruction of European Judaism. To the old hands of the camp, the numbers told everything: the period of entry into the camp, the convoy of which one formed a part, and consequently the nationality. Everyone will treat with respect the numbers from 30,000 to 80,000 : there are only a few hundred left and they represented the few survivals from the Polish ghettos. It is as well to watch out in commercial dealings with a 116,000 or a 117,000 : they now number only about forty, but they represent the Greeks of Salonica, so take care they do not pull the wool over your eyes. As for the high numbers they carry an essentially comic air about them, like the words 'freshman' or 'conscript' in ordinary life. The typical high number is a corpulent, docile and stupid fellow: he can be convinced that leather shoes are distributed at the infirmary to all those with delicate feet, and can be persuaded to run there and leave his bowl of soup 'in your custody'; you can sell him a spoon for three rations of bread; you can send him to the most ferocious of the Kapos to ask him (as happened to me!) if it is true that his is the *kartoffelschalenkommando,* the 'Potato Peeling Command', and if one can be enrolled in it.

In fact, the whole process of introduction to what was for us a new order took place in a grotesque and sarcastic manner. When the tattooing operation was finished, they shut us in a vacant hut. The bunks are made, but we are severely forbidden to touch or sit on them: so we wander around aimlessly for half the day in the limited space available, still tormented by the parching thirst of the journey. Then the door opens and a boy in a striped suit comes in, with a fairly civilized air, small, thin and blond. He speaks French and we throng around him with a flood of questions which till now we had asked each other in vain.

But he does not speak willingly; no one here speaks willingly. We are new, we have nothing and we know nothing; why waste time on us? He reluctantly explains to us that all the others are out at work and will come back in the evening. He has come out of the infirmary this morning and is exempt from work for today. I asked him (with an ingenuousness that only a few days later already seemed incredible to me) if at least they would give us back our toothbrushes. He did not laugh, but with his face animated by fierce contempt, he threw at me, '*Vous n'êtes pas à la maison.*' And it is this refrain that we hear repeated by everyone: you are not at home, this is not a sanatorium, the only exit is by way of the Chimney. (What did it mean? Soon we were all to learn what it meant.)

And it was in fact so. Driven by thirst, I eyed a fine icicle outside the window, within hand's reach. I opened the window and broke off the icicle but at once a large, heavy guard prowling outside brutally snatched it away from me. '*Warum?*' I asked him in my poor German. '*Hier ist kein warum*' (there is no why here), he replied, pushing me inside with a shove.

The explanation is repugnant but simple: in this place everything is forbidden, not for hidden reasons, but because the camp has been created for that purpose. If one wants to live one must learn this quickly and well:

'No Sacred Face will help thee here! it's not
A Serchio bathing-party ...'

Hour after hour, this first long day of limbo draws to its end. While the sun sets in a tumult of fierce, blood-red clouds, they finally make us come out of the hut. Will they give us something to drink? No, they place us in line again, they lead us to a huge square which takes up the centre of the camp and they arrange us meticulously in squads. Then nothing happens for another hour: it seems that we are waiting for someone.

A band begins to play, next to the entrance of the camp: it plays *Rosamunda*, the well known sentimental song, and this seems so strange to us that we look sniggering at each other; we feel a shadow of relief, perhaps all these ceremonies are nothing but a colossal farce in Teutonic taste. But the band, on finishing *Rosamunda*, continues to play other marches, one after the other, and suddenly the squads of our comrades appear, returning from work. They walk in columns of five with a strange, unnatural hard gait, like stiff puppets made of jointless bones; but they walk scrupulously in time to the band.

They also arrange themselves like us in the huge square, according to a precise order; when the last squad has returned, they count and recount us for over an hour. Long checks are made which all seem to go to a man dressed in stripes, who accounts for them to a group of SS men in full battle dress.

Finally (it is dark by now, but the camp is brightly lit by headlamps and reflectors) one hears the shout '*Absperre!*' at which all the squads break up in a confused and turbulent movement. They no longer walk stiffly and erectly as before: each one drags himself along with obvious effort. I see that all of them carry in their hand or attached to their belt a steel bowl as large as a basin.

We new arrivals also wander among the crowd, searching for a voice, a friendly face or a guide. Against the wooden wall of a hut two boys are seated on the ground: they seem very young, sixteen years old at the outside, both with their face and hands dirty with soot. One of the two, as we are passing by, calls me and asks me in German some questions which I do not understand;

then he asks where we come from. *'Italien,'* I reply; I want to ask him many things, but my German vocabulary is very limited.

'Are you a Jew?' I asked him.

'Yes, a Polish Jew.'

'How long have you been in the Lager?'

'Three years,' and he lifts up three fingers. He must have been a child when he entered, I think with horror; on the other hand this means that at least some manage to live here.

'What is your work?'

'Schlosser,' he replies. I do not understand. *'Eisen, Feuer'* (iron, fire), he insists, and makes a play with his hands of someone beating with a hammer on an anvil. So he is an ironsmith.

'Ich Chemiker,' I state; and he nods earnestly with his head, *'Chemiker gut.'* But all this has to do with the distant future: what torments me at the moment is my thirst.

'Drink, water. We no water,' I tell him.

He looks at me with a serious face, almost severe, and states clearly: 'Do not drink water, comrade,' and then other words that I do not understand.

'Warum?'

'Geschwollen,' he replies cryptically. I shake my head, I have not understood. *'Swollen,'* he makes me understand, blowing out his cheeks and sketching with his hands a monstrous tumefaction of the face and belly. *'Warten bis heute Abend.'*

'Wait until this evening,' I translate word by word.

Then he says: *'Ich Schlome. Du?'* I tell him my name, and he asks me: 'Where your mother?'

'In Italy.' Schlome is amazed: a Jew in Italy? 'Yes,' I explain as best I can, 'hidden, no one knows, run away, does not speak, no one sees her.' He has understood; he now gets up, approaches me and timidly embraces me. The adventure is over, and I feel filled with a serene sadness that is almost joy. I have never seen Schlome since, but I have not forgotten his serious and gentle face of a child, which welcomed me on the threshold of the house of the dead.

We have a great number of things to learn, but we have learnt many already. We already have a certain idea of the topography of the Lager; our Lager is a square of about six hundred yards in length, surrounded by two fences of barbed wire, the inner one carrying a high tension current. It consists of sixty wooden huts, which are called Blocks, ten of which are in construction. In addition, there is the body of the kitchens, which are in brick; an experimental farm, run by a detachment of privileged Häftlinge; the huts with the showers and the latrines, one for each group of six or eight Blocks. Besides these, certain Blocks are reserved for specific purposes. First of all, a group of eight, at the extreme eastern end of the camp, forms the infirmary and clinic; then there is Block 24 which is the *Krätzeblock,* reserved for infectious skin-diseases; Block 7, which no ordinary Häftling has ever entered, reserved for the *'Prominenz',* that is, the aristocracy, the internees holding the highest posts; Block 47, reserved for the *Reichsdeutsche* (the Aryan Germans, 'politicals' or criminals); Block 49, for the Kapos alone; Block 12, half of which, for use of the *Reichsdeutsche* and the Kapos, serves as canteen, that is, a distribution centre for tobacco, insect powder and occasionally other articles; Block 37, which formed the Quartermaster's office and the Office for Work; and finally, Block 29, which always has its windows closed as it is the *Frauenblock*, the camp brothel, served by Polish Häftling girls, and reserved for the *Reichsdeutsche*.

The ordinary living Blocks are divided into two parts. In one *Tagesraum* lives the head of the hut with his friends. There is a long table, seats, benches, and on all sides a heap of strange objects in bright colours, photographs, cuttings from magazines, sketches, imitation flowers, ornaments; on the walls, great sayings, proverbs and rhymes in praise of order, discipline and hygiene; in one corner, a shelf with the tools of the *Blockrisör* (official barber), the ladles to distribute the soup, and two rubber truncheons, one solid and one hollow, to enforce discipline should the proverbs prove insufficient. The other part is the dormitory: there are only one hundred and forty-eight bunks on three levels, fitted close to each other like the cells of a beehive, and divided by three corridors so as to utilize without wastage all the space in the room up to the roof. Here all the ordinary *Häftlinge* live, about two hundred to two hundred and fifty per hut. Consequently there are two men in most of the bunks, which are portable planks of wood, each covered by a thin straw sack and two blankets.

The corridors are so narrow that two people can barely pass together; the total area of the floor is so small that the inhabitants of the same Block cannot all stay there at the same time unless at least half are lying on their bunks. Hence the prohibition to enter a Block to which one does not belong.

In the middle of the Lager is the roll-call square, enormous, where we collect in the morning to form the work-squads and in the evening to be counted. Facing the roll call square there is a bed of grass, carefully mown, where the gallows are erected when necessary.

We had soon learnt that the guests of the Lager are divided into three categories: the criminals, the politicals and the Jews. All are clothed in stripes, all are Häftlinge, but the criminals wear a green triangle next to the number sewn on the jacket; the politicals wear a red triangle; and the Jews, who form the large majority, wear the Jewish star, red and yellow. SS men exist but are few and outside the camp, and are seen relatively infrequently. Our effective masters in practice are the green triangles, who have a free hand over us, as well as those of the other two categories who are ready to help them – and they are not few.

And we have learnt other things, more or less quickly, according to our intelligence: to reply *'Jawohl'*, never to ask questions, always to pretend to understand. We have learnt the value of food; now we also diligently scrape the bottom of the bowl after the ration and we hold it under our chins when we eat bread so as not to lose the crumbs. We, too, know that it is not the same thing to be given a ladleful of soup from the top or from the bottom of the vat, and we are already able to judge, according to the capacity of the various vats, what is the most suitable place to try and reach in the queue when we line up.

We have learnt that everything is useful: the wire to tie up our shoes, the rags to wrap around our feet, waste paper to (illegally) pad out our jacket against the cold. We have learnt, on the other hand, that everything can be stolen, in fact is automatically stolen as soon as attention is relaxed; and to avoid this, we had to learn the art of sleeping with our head on a bundle made up of our jacket and containing all our belongings, from the bowl to the shoes.

We already know in good part the rules of the camp, which are incredibly complicated. The prohibitions are innumerable: to approach nearer to the barbed wire than two yards; to sleep with one's jacket, or without one's pants, or with one's cap on one's head; to use certain washrooms or latrines which are *'nur für Kapos'* or *'nur für Reichsdeutsche';* not to go for the shower on the prescribed day, or to go there on a day not prescribed; to leave the hut with one's jacket unbuttoned, or with the collar raised; to carry paper or straw under one's clothes against the cold; to wash except stripped to the waist.

The rites to be carried out were infinite and senseless: every morning one had to make the 'bed' perfectly flat and smooth; smear one's muddy and repellent wooden shoes with the appropriate machine grease; scrape the mudstains off one's clothes (paint, grease and rust-stains were, however, permitted); in the evening one had to undergo the control for lice and the control of washing one's feet; on Saturday, have one's beard and hair shaved, mend or have mended one's rags; on Sunday, undergo the general control for skin diseases and the control of buttons on one's jacket, which had to be five.

In addition, there are innumerable circumstances, normally irrelevant, which here become problems. When one's nails grow long, they have to be shortened, which can only be done with one's teeth (for the toenails, the friction of the shoes is sufficient); if a button comes off, one has to tie it on with a piece of wire; if one goes to the latrine or the washroom, everything has to be carried along, always and everywhere, and while one washes one's face, the bundle of clothes has to be held tightly between one's knees: in any other manner it will be stolen in that second. If a shoe hurts, one has to go in the evening to the ceremony of the changing of the shoes: this tests the skill of the individual who, in the middle of the incredible crowd, has to be able to choose at an eye's glance one (not a pair, one) shoe, which fits. Because once the choice is made, there can be no second change.

And do not think that shoes form a factor of secondary importance in the life of the Lager. Death begins with the shoes; for most of us, they show themselves to be instruments of torture, which after a few hours of marching cause painful sores which become fatally infected. Whoever has them is forced to walk as if he was dragging a convict's chain (this explains the strange gait of the army which returns every evening on parade); he arrives last everywhere, and everywhere he receives blows. He cannot escape if they run after him; his feet swell and the more they swell, the more the friction with the wood and the cloth of the shoes becomes insupportable. Then only the hospital is left: but to enter the hospital with a diagnosis of *'dicke Füsse'* (swollen feet) is extremely dangerous, because it is well known to all, and especially to the SS, that here there is no cure for that complaint.

And in all this we have not yet mentioned the work, which in its turn is a Gordian knot of laws, taboos and problems.

We all work, except those who are ill (to be recognized as ill implies in itself an important equipment of knowledge and experience). Every morning we leave the camp in squads for the Buna; every evening, in squads, we return. As regards the work, we are divided into about two hundred *Kommandos,* each of which consists of between fifteen and one hundred and fifty men and is commanded by a Kapo. There are good and bad Kommandos: for the most part they are used as transport and the work is quite hard, especially in the winter, if for no other reason merely because it always takes place in the open. There are also skilled Kommandos (electricians, smiths, bricklayers, welders, mechanics, concrete-layers, etc.), each attached to a certain workshop or department of the Buna, and depending more directly on civilian foremen, mostly German and Polish. This naturally only applies to the hours of work; for the rest of the day the skilled workers (there are no more than three or four hundred in all) receive no different treatment from the ordinary workers. The detailing of individuals to the various Kommandos is organized by a special office of the Lager, the *Arbeitsdienst,* which is in continual touch with the civilian direction of the Buna. The *Arbeitsdienst* decides on the basis of unknown criteria, often openly on the basis of protection or corruption, so that if anyone manages to find enough to eat, he is practically certain to get a good post at Buna.

The hours of work vary with the season. All hours of light are working hours: so that from a minimum winter working day (8-12am and 12.30-4pm) one rises to a maximum summer one (6.30-12am and 1-6pm). Under no excuse are the Häftlinge allowed to be at work during the hours of darkness or when there is a thick fog, but they work regularly even if it rains or snows or (as occurs quite frequently) if the fierce wind of the Carpathians blows; the reason being that the darkness or fog might provide opportunities to escape.

One Sunday in every two is a regular working day; on the so-called holiday Sundays, instead of working at Buna, one works normally on the upkeep of the Lager, so that days of real rest are extremely rare.

Such will be our life. Every day, according to the established rhythm, *Ausrücken* and *Einrücken,* go out and come in; work, sleep and eat; fall ill, get better or die.

... And for how long? But the old ones laugh at this question: they recognize the new arrivals by this question. They laugh and they do not reply. For months and years, the problem of the remote future has grown pale to them and has lost all intensity in face of the far more urgent and concrete problems of the near future: how much one will eat today, if it will snow, if there will be coal to unload.

If we were logical, we would resign ourselves to the evidence that our fate is beyond knowledge, that every conjecture is arbitrary and demonstrably devoid of foundation. But men are rarely logical when their own fate is at stake; on every occasion, they prefer the extreme positions. According to our character, some of us are immediately convinced that all is lost, that one cannot live here, that the end is near and sure; others are convinced that however hard the present life may be, salvation is probable and not far off, and if we have faith and strength, we will see our houses and our dear ones again. The two classes of pessimists and optimists are not so clearly defined, however, not because there are many agnostics, but because the majority, without memory or coherence, drift between the two extremes, according to the moment and the mood of the person they happen to meet.

Here I am, then, on the bottom. One learns quickly enough to wipe out the past and the future when one is forced to. A fortnight after my arrival I already had the prescribed hunger, that chronic hunger unknown to free men, which makes one dream at night, and settles in all the limbs of one's body. I have already learnt not to let myself be robbed, and in fact if I find a spoon lying around, a piece of string, a button which I can acquire without danger of punishment, I pocket them and consider them mine by full right. On the back of my feet I already have those numb sores that will not heal. I push wagons, I work with a shovel, I turn rotten in the rain, I shiver in the wind; already my own body is no longer mine: my belly is swollen, my limbs emaciated, my face is thick in the morning, hollow in the evening; some of us have yellow skin, others grey. When we do not meet for a few days we hardly recognize each other.

We Italians had decided to meet every Sunday evening in a corner of the Lager, but we stopped it at once, because it was too sad to count our numbers and find fewer each time, and to see each other ever more deformed and more squalid. And it was so tiring to walk those few steps and then, meeting each other, to remember and to think. It was better not to think.

Primo Levi
If This Is A Man, 1958

Down and Out in Paris and London

Being poor

It is altogether curious, your first contact with poverty. You have thought so much about poverty – it is the thing you have feared all your life, the thing you knew would happen to you sooner or later; and it is all so utterly and prosaically different. You thought it would be quite simple; it is extraordinarily complicated. You thought it would be terrible; it is merely squalid and boring. It is the peculiar *lowness* of poverty that you discover first; the shifts that it puts you to, the complicated meanness, the crust-wiping.

You discover, for instance, the secrecy attaching to poverty. At a sudden stroke you have been reduced to an income of six francs a day. But of course you dare not admit it – you have got to pretend that you are living quite as usual. From the start it tangles you in a net of lies, and even with the lies you can hardly manage it. You stop sending clothes to the laundry, and the laundress catches you in the street and asks you why; you mumble something, and she, thinking you are sending the clothes elsewhere, is your enemy for life. The tobacconist keeps asking why you have cut down your smoking. There are letters you want to answer, and cannot, because stamps are too expensive. And then there are your meals – meals are the worst difficulty of all. Every day at meal-times you go out, ostensibly to a restaurant, and loaf an hour in the Luxembourg Gardens, watching the pigeons. Afterwards you smuggle your food home in your pockets. Your food is bread and margarine, or bread and wine, and even the nature of the food is governed by lies. You have to buy rye bread instead of household bread, because the rye loaves, though dearer, are round and can be smuggled in your pockets. This wastes you a franc a day. Sometimes, to keep up appearances, you have to spend sixty centimes on a drink, and go correspondingly short of food. Your linen gets filthy, and you run out of soap and razor-blades. Your hair wants cutting, and you try to cut it yourself, with such fearful results that you have to go to the barber after all, and spend the equivalent of a day's food. All day you are telling lies, and expensive lies.

You discover the extreme precariousness of your six francs a day. Mean disasters happen and rob you of food. You have spent your last eighty centimes on half a litre of milk, and are boiling it over the spirit lamp. While it boils a bug runs down your forearm; you give the bug a flick with your nail, and it falls plop! straight into the milk. There is nothing for it but to throw the milk away and go foodless.

You go to the baker's to buy a pound of bread, and you wait while the girl cuts a pound for another customer. She is clumsy, and cuts more than a pound. '*Pardon, monsieur,*' she says, 'I suppose you don't mind paying two sous extra?' Bread is a franc a pound, and you have exactly a franc. When you think that you too might be asked to pay two sous extra, and would have to confess that you could not, you bolt in panic. It is hours before you dare venture into a baker's shop again.

You go to the greengrocer's to spend a franc on a kilogram of potatoes. But one of the pieces that make up the franc is a Belgium piece, and the shopman refuses it. You slink out of the shop, and can never go there again.

You have strayed into a respectable quarter, and you see a prosperous friend coming. To avoid him you dodge into the nearest café. Once in the café you must buy something, so you spend your last fifty centimes on a glass of black coffee with a dead fly in it. One could multiply these disasters by the hundred. They are part of the process of being hard up.

You discover what it is like to be hungry. With bread and margarine in your belly, you go out and look into the shop windows. Everywhere there is food insulting you in huge, wasteful piles; whole dead pigs, baskets of hot loaves, great yellow blocks of butter, strings of sausages, mountains of potatoes, vast Gruyère cheeses like grindstones. A snivelling self-pity comes over you at the sight of so much food. You plan to grab a loaf and run, swallowing it before they catch you; and you refrain, from pure funk.

You discover the boredom which is inseparable from poverty; the times when you have nothing to do and, being underfed, can interest yourself in nothing [...] You discover that a man who has gone even a week on bread and margarine is not a man any longer, only a belly with a few accessory organs [...]

In the kitchens at the Hôtel X

THE HOTEL X was a vast grandiose place with a classical façade, and at one side a little dark doorway like a rat-hole, which was the service entrance. I arrived at a quarter to seven in the morning. A stream of men with greasy trousers were hurrying in and being checked by a doorkeeper who sat in a tiny office. I waited, and presently the *chef du personnel*, a sort of assistant manager, arrived and began to question me. He was an Italian, with a round, pale face, haggard from overwork. He asked whether I was an experienced dishwasher, and I said that I was; he glanced at my hands and saw that I was lying, but on hearing that I was an Englishman he changed his tone and engaged me.

'We have been looking for someone to practise our English on,' he said. 'Our clients are all Americans, and the only English we know is –' He repeated something that little boys write on the walls in London. 'You may be useful. Come downstairs.'

He led me down a winding staircase into a narrow passage, deep underground, and so low that I had to stoop in places. It was stiflingly hot and very dark, with only dim yellow bulbs several yards apart. There seemed to be miles of dark labyrinthine passages – actually, I suppose, a few hundred yards in all – that reminded one queerly of the lower decks of a liner; there were the same heat and cramped space and warm reek of food, and a humming, whirring noise (it came from the kitchen furnaces) just like the whir of engines. We passed doorways which let out sometimes a shouting of oaths, sometimes the red glare of a fire, once a shuddering draught from an ice chamber. As we went along, something struck me violently in the back. It was a hundred-pound block of ice, carried by a blue-aproned porter. After him came a boy with a great slab of veal on his shoulder, his cheek pressed into the damp, spongy flesh. They shoved me aside with a cry of '*Range-toi, idiot!*' and rushed on. On the wall, under one of the lights, someone had written in a very neat hand: 'Sooner will you find a cloudless sky in winter, than a woman at the Hôtel X who has her maidenhead.' [...]

One of the passages branched off into a laundry, where an old skulled-face woman gave me a blue apron and a pile of dishcloths. Then the *chef du personnel* took me to a tiny underground den – a cellar below a cellar, as it were where there were a sink and some gas-ovens. It was too low for me to stand quite upright, and the temperature was perhaps 110 degrees Fahrenheit. The *chef du personnel* explained that my job was to fetch meals for the higher hotel employees, who fed in a small dining-room above, clean their room and wash their crockery. When he had gone, a waiter, another Italian, thrust a fierce fuzzy head into the doorway and looked down at me.

'English, eh?' he said. 'Well, I'm in charge here. If you work well' – he made the motion of up-ending a bottle and sucked noisily. 'If you don't' – he gave the doorpost several vigorous kicks. 'To me, twisting your neck would be no more than spitting on the floor. And if there's any trouble, they'll believe me, not you. So be careful.'

After this I set to work rather hurriedly. Except for about an hour, I was at work from seven in the morning till a quarter-past nine at night; first at washing crockery, then at scrubbing the tables and floors of the employees' dining-room, then at polishing glasses and knives, then at fetching meals, then at washing crockery again, then at fetching more meals and washing more crockery. It was easy work, and I got on well with it except when I went to the kitchen to fetch meals. The kitchen was like nothing I had ever seen or imagined – a stifling, low-ceilinged inferno of a cellar, red-lit from the fires, and deafening with oaths and the clanging of pots and pans. It was so hot that all the metal-work except the stoves had to be covered with cloth. In the middle were furnaces, where twelve cooks skipped to and fro, their faces dripping sweat in spite of their white caps. Round that were counters where a mob of waiters and *plongeurs* [dishwashers] clamoured with trays. Scullions, naked to the waist, were stoking the fires and scouring huge copper saucepans with sand. Everyone seemed to be in a hurry and a rage. The head cook, a fine scarlet man with big moustachios, stood in the middle booming continuously, '*Ça marche, deux oeufs brouillés! Ça marche, un Chateaubriand pommes sautées!*' except when he broke off to curse at a *plongeur*. There were three counters, and the first time I went to the kitchen I took my tray unknowingly to the wrong one. The head cook walked up to me, twisted his moustaches, and looked me up and down. Then he beckoned to the breakfast cook and pointed at me.

'Do you see *that*? That is the type of *plongeur* they send us nowadays. Where do you come from, idiot? From Charenton, I suppose?' (There is a large lunatic asylum at Charenton.)

'From England,' I said.

'I might have known it. Well, *mon cher monsieur l'Anglais*, may I inform you that you are the son of a whore? And now, *fous-moi le camp* to the other counter, where you belong.'

I got this kind of reception every time I went to the kitchen, for I always made some mistake; I was expected to know the work, and was cursed accordingly. From curiosity I counted the number of times I was called *maquereau* during the day, and it was thirty-nine.

At half-past four the Italian told me that I could stop working, but that it was not worth going out, as we began again at five. I went to the lavatory for a smoke; smoking was strictly forbidden, and Boris had warned me that the lavatory was the only safe place. After that I worked again till a quarter-past nine, when the waiter put his head into the doorway and told me to leave the rest of the crockery. To my astonishment, after calling me pig, mackerel, etc., all day, he had suddenly grown quite friendly. I realized that the curses I had met with were only a kind of probation.

George Orwell
Down and Out in Paris and London, 1933

Night Cleaner at the Savoy

A single room at the Savoy costs £300 a night. A cleaner there earns £150 a week.

It seems somehow fitting that the hands on my watch are inching towards midnight as I plunge for the first time into the potent mix of light and dark, glamour and filth, opulence and poverty that is the Savoy. For I will be a shadowy figure here, emerging from the bowels of the building as the last few guests go yawning, sometimes staggering, to their crisply laundered beds.

Above stairs, the place is a fantasia of 1920s extravagance, every art-deco cliché played out in its ornate plasterwork, walnut-veneered lifts, custom-designed carpets and acres of pink marble. But enter through the underbelly of the building and you discover a sleazy world of dripping pipes; peeling and ancient paint; dirty linen.

Everything about the Savoy is on a grand scale. Here in its intestines, corridors are convoluted and endless, lined with mile upon mile of piping and electric wiring. Small foothills of soiled tablecloths spill from their plastic wrappings outside the hotel laundry; tottering precipices of crockery pile up in countless kitchens. Confused and already sweating, I am deposited outside the 'cleaning store'. In reality, this cramped understairs cupboard is actually far more than its name suggests, serving as both women's and men's changing room, meeting place and repository for all the anger and resentment that builds in the course of a night's work: 'Why must I always clean the toilets?'; 'Why does Mehmet never finish the American Bar on time?'; 'Why have I not been paid for my overtime?'

Tonight there are four other cleaners outside the store, ready with their vacuum cleaners and their buckets to ascend into the light. I'm introduced to Anna, a beautiful, slender Business Studies student from Benin who is to be my supervisor; Sergio, a cheerful beauty consultant from Venezuela who's hoping to go to college; Sara, a quiet woman from central Africa; a short Bangladeshi called Iqbal; and Amos, a Ugandan who's about to start a master's degree in particle physics.

As I take my own bucket and Hoover and turn to follow Anna to the lift, a cockroach darts out from a crack in the wall by the store. Amos lifts his foot to crush it, then stops. 'Ach, it has its own life to lead,' he says, philosophically.

So here I am. I have arrived. I am a night cleaner at the Savoy.

My journey here started several days ago at Brixton Job Centre. I'd passed by there countless times in the past decade, but I'd never entered. Why would I? I come from the other world that coexists on London's pavements: the comfortable, well-shod world of tapas bars, power showers and mortgages. The world where travel is mostly by car and tube, not bus and foot.

So why did I take a deep breath and push open the glass doors of the Job Centre one morning last August? Because I was on a mission: a journey to the heart of Minimum Wage London. I wanted to find out what sort of life was possible on around £4 an hour in Britain's most expensive city. How did the thousands of people living on the lowest legal wages get by? In central London, they would face some of the highest accommodation costs in Europe. If they moved out, they would have crippling transport bills. How did they stretch their meagre resources to cover the most basic living expenses, let alone anything that might be construed as a luxury – a pint of beer, a book, or a trip to the cinema?

There might have been easier ways, of course. Talking to some of the countless people who exist this way out of necessity, rather than choice, for one. But no matter how eloquent they might be, they could only tell me part of the story. If I really wanted to find out how it felt, I would have to do it myself.

I could do the sums without even straying from my word processor, of course: 40 hours' work a week at £4 an hour = £160. After paying tax and national insurance, around £140. (The minimum wage was £3.70 then, now it's £4.10. My job was advertised at £4.)

Outgoings: the big one would be rent. A cursory glance through Loot revealed the minimum for a bedsit to be around £60 a week. A bus pass would be £9.50. So that would leave around £70 for food and extras. And there was the possibility of claiming housing benefit. Didn't sound too bad on paper, but the minimum wage was supposed to mean more than just getting by. When the low pay commission published its first report in 1998, its chairman, George Bain, said it would allow people to live 'not in the margins, but in the mainstream of society'.

Getting a job was easier than I expected. Within half an hour of entering the Job Centre I was on my way to an interview, clutching a piece of paper. 'Casna Group Cleaning Services', it said. 'Reliable, presentable people required to clean public areas in 5-star hotels. Nights only.' But I wasn't the only one. A couple of dozen people were already waiting, crammed on to a bank of low, plastic-covered sofas: several Africans, both male and female, a South American woman, and a couple of students from Japan and Spain. It was two hours before I finally got interviewed by a cheerful Scottish woman called Eileen.

I started to reel off my previous hotel experience: genuine jobs I had had as a student; fictional dates. Eileen wrote them down then launched into a spiel. Wear your own black skirt, black tights, black shoes and white blouse. Bring your own rubber gloves. All the work is outwork. The hours are 11pm till 7am, five days a week, but in some hotels it's midnight to 7am.

'What's outwork?' I asked dumbly, not sure if I had got the job. Eileen pulled up short.

'Actually, I don't know,' she said. 'I'm just a freelance myself.'

Later, installed in a bedsit in Tooting, I reviewed the financial situation. I may only be working seven hours a night instead of eight, but it still felt manageable. £4 for 35 hours per week = £140. After tax and national insurance, maybe £127. Rent at £65, plus a bus pass at £9.50, left me with £52.50 to spend.

I splashed out £4 on two pairs of Marigolds and £13.50 on food at Sainsbury's. For that I got a couple of bottles of pasta sauce on a two-for-one offer, some dried lasagne, mushrooms, eggs, potatoes for baking, cheap cheddar, tea bags, milk, fruit and a huge bag of economy muesli. I cheated, of course, because I allowed myself to spend money I wouldn't be paid for several weeks. I would find out later that my colleagues didn't have this luxury. Most of them came from developing countries, and even if they'd saved up what seemed like a large sum in their own currency, their nest eggs disappeared virtually overnight. If they weren't lucky enough to have relatives to stay with, they had to find a room in a shared house and they had to pay a couple of months' rent up front. They struggled and starved through their first weeks in London.

Last night was my first night at work. It began with an 11pm meeting at a hotel in Bayswater. At 11.40pm the Casna managers arrived and gave the new recruits a 20-minute lecture on punctuality and reliability. Our first night would be a 'training' night so we wouldn't be paid, though we would be reimbursed if we stayed six weeks. There would also be a one-off £10 charge for 'payroll services'.

Then we were allocated our jobs, and I set off for the Savoy with one of the three managers, a Londoner called Marge with a smoker's cough. Along the way we chatted. She explained that we cleaned all public areas: reception, corridors, banqueting rooms, that kind of thing. Dusting, hoovering – it wouldn't be too bad.

Halfway to the Savoy, Marge checked her messages and said I was being taken to another hotel that was short-staffed, just for the night. There I was taken to the staff changing rooms by a portly Ghanaian called Esther. She found me a mop and bucket, bin bags and rags for cleaning, and left. That was my training. The men's toilets were filthy, bits of tissue paper, old shoes and coat hangers strewn everywhere. I had to unblock several of the toilets, turning my head sideways to avoid looking – or smelling – while I plunged my brush in.

At break we were joined by another west African man who introduced himself as Jean-Pierre. He was maybe about 45, tall, good-looking and confident. In France, where he had lived for years and raised a family, he was a politician – a socialist town councillor. But he needed to speak English to run his import-export business, and that was why he was here. He had been here six months, studying all day and working all night.

This morning I did my sums again. I'd reconciled myself to seven hours' work per night instead of eight, but now it seemed I would only get six hours' money because I wouldn't be paid for breaks. And I would lose a day's pay for training, plus £10 for payroll services.

In my first week, then, I'd be at work for 37 hours, including an hour on each of two consecutive nights at the Royal Lancaster waiting to be allocated my job. But eight of them would be unpaid because they would be 'training', and a further five would be unpaid breaks. That would leave 24 paid hours at £4 per hour, which would make £96. Minus £10 payroll charge makes £86, before tax and national insurance, for a full week of nights. Excluding breaks, for which employers aren't legally obliged to pay, that would be an average of £2.69 per hour. Even though I would not be earning enough to pay tax or national insurance, I would be taking home barely £11 more than I'd already spent on rent and bus pass, let alone food, rubber gloves or cleaning materials for my flat.

Tonight, though, there's no time to worry about it. Anna is thrusting a vacuum cleaner into my hand and steering me towards one of the service lifts that link the Savoy's sweltering basements with its opulent public parts. I spend the night cleaning function rooms, each of which has its own Gilbert and Sullivan-styled identity: Pinafore, Mikado, Gondolier. My favourite is Pinafore, which is lined with a beautiful, warm panelling – cherry, maybe – adorned with silver studding that loops and swirls across the woodwork.

In each room I must check for rubbish and then wipe or dust each surface before Hoovering the acres of carpet. One speck left behind could mean having to start all over again, Anna warns ominously. Left alone, I find the work strenuous but strangely beguiling. There's a constant, faintly romantic air of evenings recently passed by now-sleeping guests – a trail of purple feathers, discarded notes for a dull speech about cutlery, a single yellow Post-it note with 'Lord MacLaurin' written on it. I almost expect to hear echoes of jazz, or maybe a string quartet.

At 2am we take a break and leave all shreds of glamour behind. We have to splash through pools of filthy water in one of the main kitchens to line up for chicken nuggets and chips before taking a hike through the labyrinth to the staff canteen. Once there, we can reheat our food in a microwave if we don't want to eat it cold. No one bothers, though.

Before we can sit down to eat in the inappropriately-named Oasis, we must clear the day's accumulated rubbish from the tables. A mouse ambles casually along one side of the room, disappearing into the kitchen where staff meals are cooked during the day.

I also discover at this point that I am not the lowest creature in the Savoy hierarchy, for we are joined by a gang of African men with wellies and overalls whose job is to hose out the grunge and discarded food from the kitchens. They also trundle cartloads of unimaginably foul-smelling sludge, which I presume comes from waste-disposal units, through the miles of corridors to an equally nauseating skip room in the basement. They're Nigerians mostly, Anna says. She wrinkles her nose. There's a jovial atmosphere tonight and Anna is smiling at some gentle teasing from her male subordinates: 'The wonderful, warm and in-de-fa-tigable Anna,' Amos calls her.

My new companions want to know more about me.

'Where you from?'

'Manchester.'

'What, Manchester in England?'

'Yes, that's right.' Apart from Marge, I don't meet another English person in all my time working for Casna.

'So what do you do?' I'm floored by this question. I say, well, I suppose I'm a cleaner. Wrong answer. Shocked expressions.

'What, you not a student? Fran, you have to study!'

Next question: 'What church do you go to?'

'Er, I don't go to church. I'm not a Christian.'

'What? You a Muslim?'

'No, I'm not anything.'

More shocked expressions. Later, Anna adds becoming a Christian to my list of tasks for the night: 'Hoover in the corners! Dust the picture frames! Fran, you have to talk to Jesus! Tell him all your problems and he will make them go away!'

I sleep all the way home on the bus for the second morning running. Marge may think this is easy work, but I don't think most of her employees would agree. Iqbal is replaced by a Ghanaian girl who only lasts a couple of nights before going home with a bad back, never to be seen again. Anna puts her on polishing duties, but she doesn't get far. Mostly she just stands there clutching her right kidney and looking grey. I'm aching, too, by the end of my first night at the Savoy, but by the end of the week things are getting better. My knees are still sore but I'm starting to sleep in the daytime – unlike most of my colleagues, who spend their days at college. I even splash out £22.40 on a tube pass, which cuts my journey-to-work time by half. Most of my co-workers can't afford to do this. Some of them set off at nine o'clock to get to work by midnight, trailing across London on a series of buses.

On my first Friday night, I'm cleaning offices with Amos. He's impressed by how fast I work.

'I didn't think you could cope,' he says. 'But you're really trying. I like that. You're a strong woman.' Somehow, this small dollop of praise makes it all worthwhile.

Life takes on a pattern, each night a sort of symphony. There's an overture outside the cleaning store as we fix our badges on our tabards, ready to sally forth into our different domains. Then there's a steady, repeated theme as we warm to our allotted tasks: Sergio in the toilets; Amos polishing floors; Sara in the Thames Foyer. I've landed comfortably in reception, where it's light and airy, and the night is broken up by the comings and goings of the guests. We all work steadily till break, but later the pace swells as we all add brio in the hope of finishing on time.

As I clean the offices behind the reception desk, I can cast my eye over the daily incident log: a mouse is reported in the bar, then a 'whole family of mice' at play in the foyer. One night after they've been spotted in the River Restaurant and the Lincoln Room, one of the night managers suggests 'a blitz' while the hotel is quiet. Later the same evening he adds that he's seen a mouse running under the door of one of the bedrooms.

The climax of our night takes place in the American Bar, as everyone finishes their own areas and comes to help with dusting, wiping and Hoovering. Buckets and filled bin bags pile up by the door to the service lift as the activity in the bar builds. Sometimes on a busy night there are six people in there by 7.15am, three Hoovering, two dusting, while Anna conducts with terse commands, almost crazed by tiredness, mouth tight and eyes staring; occasionally erupting into a sudden, energetic spurt of furious table-wiping.

Then, as if by some invisible signal, the performance is over and we all line up to march through our wormhole into our other universe. We descend together in the lift, triumphant and bonded by exhaustion, with our bags and buckets stacked around us.

There are nights, though, when we are discordant, when the jagged edges of our double lives simply won't fit together. I think this is partly because we all know we don't belong here, that this is just a temporary situation. The thing is, almost none of my colleagues are cleaners. This is not just an affectation, an attempt to cover up a slightly shameful occupation. They really aren't. They're students, hairdressers, engineers, business people. Making ends meet in a strange country. As Amos tells me one night: 'Keeping body and soul.' And yet the only way we can gain in stature is by being better cleaners: faster, more efficient, producing ever more shiny surfaces. Angry spats break out over whether the tiled floors should be cleaned with a wet or a dry mop; it is whispered in corners that Sara doesn't clean under all her tables and that Anna is too slapdash in the offices.

There are times when one or another of us slips up, makes a mistake or talks back to Anna, and for that there is a standard punishment: The Gents' Urinals. Actually, cleaning toilets isn't as terrible as it might sound. Even scraping splatters of dried-up vomit from the tiled floors is perfectly bearable if you detach yourself from it. But the man – it had to be a man – who designed those urinals, a gleaming ultramodern confection of marble and chrome, put glass panels between each stall to catch the splashes. And the only way to make those sleek little windows shine is to kneel on the urine-damp floor with your head in the bowl and scrub each one with a green scourer, breathing in an overpowering essence of piss all the while. There are about 20 of them and the job takes nearly an hour, by the end of which your head is buzzing from the ammonia.

Sometimes Anna is charming and sweet-natured, sometimes tired and autocratic. Now and again I come across her in a stairway or corridor, berating some poor newcomer for poor work or for insubordination. 'You want to clean the toilets?' she will bark. 'You want to clean Sara's place?' (The foyer is universally known as 'Sara's place', and it fills the rest of us with dread, for it involves gargantuan feats of cushion-plumping and table-polishing.)

The recipients of these tirades usually disappear at the end of the night. One, a Malaysian hotel management student called Wai Li, lasts a week before walking out, leaving an angry note behind her: 'I wish to resign from cleaning job! Please send all my money straight away!' Others stay just a night or two, but nobody remarks much on their disappearance.

One night the pay slips arrive, but there's nothing for me yet. My colleagues gather in an angry knot, though, to compare notes – there are grumbles about unpaid overtime, promised pay rises not delivered. (Questioned about unpaid overtime, a spokesman for Casna says 'all our staff are eligible for overtime provided it has been approved by their on site manager'.) A little stack of furious letters to Casna piles up in the cleaning store. Sergio says he's resigning, but he's back the next night. He needs the money, short though it may be.

Anna is the longest-serving Casna member of staff at the hotel. She's been here a year. Few last that long. (A spokesman for Casna told *The Guardian* that the company has a 'relatively low turnover compared to our competitors', with length of service ranging 'from a few days to 10 years'.) One night I'm joined by a cheerfully padded and classily made-up woman from Zambia, who laughs at my frantic efforts to clean everything to Anna's satisfaction. She lies back on a bench in the Fitness Centre and tells me to take it 'slooow'.

'Don't rush-rush-rush like that! This I learned from my supervisor when I worked at the Café Royal,' she instructs. Over supper, she tells me how she's left her kids, aged 16 and 17, in Sweden with their dad. She's not at all sure she wants to work for Casna. How many hours a night do we get paid for? she asks. When I tell her it's only six because she won't be paid for breaks, she gets up and leaves, saying she doesn't need £24 this badly. As dawn breaks, Anna joins me in the American Bar, where I'm polishing tables. 'She your friend now, that woman?' she asks. I confide that as she's just walked out, I don't think I'll be seeing her again. 'She was a lazy woman,' Anna says angrily. 'I think she makes money by bitching.'

'You know,' she confides, 'in Africa they tell us we can make so much money in England that we will be buying our own houses in a few weeks. But there isn't an easy way. There isn't any easy money here. We have to work hard for everything we get.'

She looks sad for a minute, then she straightens her bony shoulders, resolute. 'But you know, if you really try,' she adds, 'after a while you can get a rise to £4.50 an hour.'

Fran Abrams
The Guardian, 28 January 2002

Reportage Activities

What is Reportage?

Reportage includes a wide range of kinds of writing. It can be the personal eyewitness record of an event or incident that is of interest to later generations, for instance accounts by ordinary people of the bombing of Dresden in the Second World War, or a description by an observer of the execution of Mary Queen of Scots. In this section there are three examples of such reportage:

- Pliny's eyewitness account of the eruption of Vesuvius in 79 AD is an individual's first hand experience of a major historical event.
- Ian McEwan describes how he watched on his TV screen the horrifying events unfolding in New York on 11 September 2001.
- Primo Levi writes about his experience of being a concentration camp survivor, as both a sufferer and a witness of one of history's most horrific periods.

Some people are paid to report on world events. Reportage in newspapers, for TV new or current affairs programmes takes different forms, depending on whether it is for TV, radio or print news. The piece by Robert Fisk was written for *The Independent* newspaper during the attacks on Afghanistan by American forces in December 2001.

There are two examples in this anthology of a different kind of reportage in which people write about aspects of ordinary people's lives, whether other people's or their own. They are reporting on what it is like to be that person, living that life. This kind of reportage is often used to comment on social issues, such as poverty or inequality. Fran Abrams' piece on working as a cleaner at the Savoy Hotel makes direct use of this style of reportage, made famous by George Orwell in the 1930s and 1940s.

The Eruption of Vesuvius

This eruption in AD 79 destroyed and buried the towns of Pompeii and Herculaneum.

1. Asking Pliny what happened

• Work in small groups. Imagine that Pliny is telling the story of what happened to a group of his friends. One person should be Pliny, reading his account aloud. The rest of the group are his friends, who interrupt him as he is talking, asking questions, adding comments and asking him to repeat things or re-phrase himself to make his story entirely clear.

2. Exploring the text

• Which bit of the account did you find most interesting or exciting? Choose one or two paragraphs.

• Look closely at what is going on in these paragraphs. Underline and annotate your chosen extract, looking closely at what makes the extract interesting.

Description:
– of people
– of places and geographical features
– of events
– of weather
– of sounds
– of feelings

Storytelling:
– use of suspense
– building up interest
– creating excitement

Voice:
– how the narrator is speaking to his audience
– who he is speaking to
– what kind of tone

• Read your extract aloud to the rest of the class and talk about what you found interesting about it.

3. Other voices

• Use the text to re-present the events in the voice of different people, for different purposes and audiences. Choose from the ideas below:

1. Pliny's mother dashes off a letter to Pliny's uncle, which she will leave for him at her house, just in case he returns and finds her gone.
2. A messenger is sent from Misenum to the next town, warning of the approaching danger.
3. Pomponianus survives and tells Pliny's mother what has happened to her brother.
4. An historian writes an introduction to this letter, commenting on what makes it interesting as an historical document.

Beyond Belief

1. Before reading

This article appeared in *The Guardian* on 12 September 2001, the day after the destruction of the Twin Towers in New York. It is by the British novelist, Ian McEwan.

The title of the article is 'Beyond Belief'
• Talk about the title and what it suggests about McEwan's article.

• Talk about your own memories of September 11th or pool your shared knowledge of what happened. (If you don't have clear memories of September 11th, think of another important world event that you have seen unfolding on TV.)

2. Reading the article
• Listen to the article being read aloud.

3. After reading – describing and analysing
McEwan describes things that many people felt when watching the events unfold. But he does more than describe – he tries to make sense of his reactions and analyse what happened and what it means for us and for the world.

Here are some phrases and sentences from the piece. Some are *descriptions* of feelings and actions that anyone watching might have felt. Some are *analyses* of feelings and events.
• Decide which you think are descriptions and which analyses.

> Now my son and I surfed – hungrily, ghoulishly – between CNN, CBC and BBC24.

> We had to know: was it two planes or three that hit the Twin Towers? Was the White House now under attack? Where was the plane the airforce was supposed to be tracking?

> Our way of life, centralised and machine-dependent, has made us frail. Our civilisation, it suddenly seemed, our way of life, is easy to wreck when there are sufficient resources and cruel intent. No missile defence system can protect us.

> From the vantage point of the Brooklyn Heights, we saw Lower Manhattan disappear into dust.

• Find two or three examples of description and analysis of your own.

4. What did McEwan want to say?

What did McEwan want to say about the events on September 11th, the day after they happened. Below are some of the points he seems to be making.

• Read each statement, then see if you can match it to a sentence or paragraph in his article.

---

1. What was so horrific was seeing such massive death and destruction at a distance and having to imagine the individuals' fate.
2. The world will be a different and worse place after September 11th.
3. As time went on, the massive TV coverage became almost too slick and left behind the raw emotion of the event.
4. Writers and filmmakers over the centuries have imagined nightmare scenarios but no-one has ever imagined anything as horrific as what actually happened on September 11th.
5. The extent of the television coverage allowed people to intrude on other people's misery in a way that became, in the end, quite shameful. There was just too much of it.
6. Modern technology has led us to be closely connected across the world. The destruction of the Twin Towers made the whole of our civilisation seem threatened.
7. It was such a horrific event that it was difficult to believe that it had actually happened.

---

5. Powerful writing?

McEwan's article made a strong impact when it appeared. It seemed to say things that echoed with people's experiences watching the events on screen. The power of his piece comes partly from the ideas and partly from the way he writes about it. Below are two extracts, each with a short commentary giving one person's views on what made them powerful.

'The screaming, the heroism and reasonable panic, the fumbling in semi-darkness for mobile phones – it was our safe distance from it all that was so horrifying.'

McEwan starts the sentence with all the things we didn't see but which we imagine. He ends the sentence with the point he wants to make. Starting with a list of the unseen horrors makes it very powerful.

'We had to know: was it two planes or three that hit the Twin Towers? Was the White House now under attack? Where was the plane the airforce was supposed to be tracking?'

McEwan gives us very directly the questions that were going through his and his son's mind while watching the TV. The questions take us right into their minds at the time.

• Choose two or three extracts of your own and write your own commentary on what makes them powerful for you.

My Beating by Refugees

Robert Fisk was *The Independent* newspaper's Middle East correspondent on the Afghan-Pakistan border, in December 2001, at the time of the U.S. military attacks on al-Qaida.

1. Reading the first paragraph
The first paragraph does two things:
- it gets the reader into the situation very quickly
- it makes clear the writer's attitude to the events he describes.
• Talk about *what* the writer's attitude seems to be and *how* he gets the reader straight into the situation.

2. Reading the article
• Listen to the article being read aloud. While you are listening, think about these issues:
- your immediate response to what's being described (e.g. horror, excitement, curiosity, sympathy, surprise)
- where do Fisk's sympathies lie: with himself? with his colleagues? with the people attacking him? with Westerners? with America? with the Afghan people?
- what Fisk wants the reader to think or feel as a result of reading the article.

• Share your ideas at the end of the reading.

3. The ending and the opening
• Read again the last two paragraphs of the article. What do they tell you about Robert Fisk's reasons for writing the piece and his attitude to the people who attacked him? What's your response to this?

• Look back at the opening paragraph. Why do you think Fisk chose to begin and end the piece in this way?

4. A close focus on extracts
• Look closely at the extracts from the article. For each one, decide:
- what it is trying to say
- what its purpose is (for instance: to describe, to explain, to argue, to analyse, to tell a story, to convey emotions)
- what writing techniques Robert Fisk has used to achieve that purpose.

Some of the Afghans in the little village had been there for years, others had arrived – desperate and angry and mourning their slaughtered loved ones – over the past two weeks. It was a bad place for a car to break down. A bad time, just before the Iftar, the end of the daily fast of Ramadan. But what happened to us was symbolic of the hatred and fury and hypocrisy of this filthy war, a growing band of destitute Afghan men, young and old, who saw foreigners – enemies – in their midst and tried to destroy at least one of them.

A film of white steam was rising from the bonnet of our jeep, a constant shriek of car horns and buses and trucks and rickshaws protesting at the road-block we had created.

The respected foreigner – the man who had been all 'salaam aleikum' a few minutes ago – was upset, frightened, on the run. The West was being brought low.

That's when the first mighty crack descended on my head. I almost fell down under the blow, my ears singing with the impact.

There were two more cracks on my head, one on each side and for some odd reason, part of my memory – some small crack in my brain – registered a moment at school, at a primary school called the Cedars in Maidstone more than 50 years ago when a tall boy building sandcastles in the playground had hit me on the head. I had a memory of the blow smelling, as if it had affected my nose.

I guess at this point I should thank Lebanon. For 25 years, I have covered Lebanon's wars and the Lebanese used to teach me, over and over again, how to stay alive: take a decision – any decision – but don't do nothing.

What had I done, I kept asking myself? I had been punching and attacking Afghan refugees, the very people I had been writing about for so long, the very dispossessed, mutilated people whom my own country – among others – was killing along with the Taliban, just across the border.

5. Other versions

Robert Fisk says he feared how other journalists might write about his experiences. As a result of his article, the write-up in *The Guardian* by Jessica Hodgson on the same day had the headline, 'Independent Journalist Excuses Attackers' and started:

> *The Independent's* distinguished Middle East correspondent, Robert Fisk, who was stoned by angry Afghan refugees at the weekend, has said he would have done just as they had if the boot had been on the other foot.
>
> In a moving dispatch, the injured veteran reporter said: 'What happened to us was symbolic of the hatred and fury and hypocrisy of this filthy war.'
>
> Fisk was attacked near the Pakistan border town of Quetta after his car broke down.

• Try writing a different version of Fisk's story, using the facts from his article but giving the events a different slant. Choose one of the following versions:
- how it might have been reported on the BBC news on the evening of December 10th
- how it might have been reported on the regular news slot on a radio channel like Radio One or XFM
- how it might have been reported by a newspaper like *The Sun*, who might be less sympathetic to the Afghan refugees and more sympathetic to America and the West.

6. Writing about Robert Fisk's article

• Write a piece analysing how Robert Fisk's article works as a piece of reportage. You could include paragraphs on:
- his attitude to the events and how he makes this clear
- how well he describes his experiences (through narrating the story, describing sights, sounds, feelings and so on)
- what kind of information he gives the reader and how he offers it
- what conclusions he draws from his experiences
- the beginning and the ending and how they work
- the impact of his writing on you as a reader and why.

On the Bottom

1. Before reading

• Here are some sentences and phrases taken from the text you are about to read. In pairs, talk about them and think about the following questions.

- What stories or ideas or historical events do they suggest to you?
- What kind of writing might this be from, for example a play, a press report, an autobiography, a conversation?
- What could this be about?

> Today, in our times, hell must be like this

> we wait for something which will certainly be terrible

> One cannot think any more. It is like being already dead

> We seem to be watching some mad play

> we had reached the bottom

• Look at this longer extract from the text. Talk about the additional information it gives you and what this adds to your view of what the text is about. What do you feel for the person describing this experience?

> Then for the first time we became aware that our language lacks words to express this offence, the demolition of a man. In a moment, with almost prophetic intuition, the reality was revealed to us: we had reached the bottom. It is not possible to sink lower than this; no human condition is more miserable than this, nor could it conceivably be so. Nothing belongs to us any more; they have taken away our clothes, our shoes, even our hair; if we speak, they will not listen to us, and if they listen, they will not understand. They will even take away our name: and if we want to keep it, we will have to find ourselves the strength to do so, to manage somehow so that behind the name something of us, of us as we were, still remains.

• Make a list for yourselves of any events in modern history or in today's world that this description could apply to.

2. Reading the text in stages: stage 1
• Listen to the text being read to you up to page 143, finishing with the sentence, 'He makes a long speech, is very polite, and tries to reply to all our questions.'

• In pairs or small groups talk about your feelings and reactions on listening to this and any questions about this text that you need to have answered.

• As a whole class, pool your knowledge of the period of history being described and the extermination of a whole people which has come to be known as 'the

Holocaust.' Either at this stage, or after reading the whole text, try to find out more, from books, from films (such as *Schindler's List*), from people you know whose relatives may have lived through it themselves, from adults who may have memories of their own of the war years.

3. Reading the text in stages: stage 2
• Listen to the text being read to you up to the beginning of the last paragraph on page 150.

Levi says, 'No human condition is more miserable than this'.
• Look back through the text to discuss these issues.

– What kinds of things does Levi describe that make you feel that this statement is true?
– Were you shocked by what you read?
– In saying, 'No human condition is more miserable than this', Levi uses the present tense. Where else does he use it? How does this alter the power of the text?

• Levi is writing about his own experiences. Explore how he does this by picking one small section of the text you have read so far and looking closely at it. For instance, you could look at the arrival, or the meeting with Schlome, or the description of the branding of numbers on the prisoners' arms and what the numbers revealed about life in the camp.

• Look closely at how much Levi tells us about what happened, describes his feelings, expresses outrage and anger, tries to analyse what was happening to him, urges the reader directly to feel sympathy for him.

4. Reading the text in stages: stage 3
• The last section of the text is just three paragraphs, in which Levi sums up the meaning of this experience of being in a concentration camp and what it does to a human being. Before reading it, talk about what kinds of things he *might* want to say to the reader and what kinds of feelings he *might* express.

• Read the very last section of the text, from the paragraph starting, 'If we were logical ...' on page 141 and talk about what Levi suggests about how a human being responds to such treatment and how s/he can survive it.

• Look closely at the last sentence of the text, 'It was better not to think.' Why do you think he says this?

5. The demolition of a man
• In small groups, look back at the whole text and talk about what Primo Levi is saying about the following:
– what it is to be human
– what demolishes or destroys a human being
– how human beings survive being 'on the bottom'
– what it is to be an oppressor, or destroyer of humanity.

• Find short key quotes that for you sum up what Levi's thinking is about these issues.

• The title of the book from which this text is taken is *If This Is A Man*. Talk about why you think Levi chose this title.

6. Language and viewpoint

There are some indications that it is very hard for Levi to write what he is writing, that the horror of his experiences is sometimes too great to bear and that he struggles to say what is almost unsayable.

• Look for moments where you think Levi is either trying to say something that is almost unbearable to say, or is extremely complicated to explain. Look closely at what happens to the language at these moments. Are there any disruptions to the normal flow? You might look for some of these language changes:

- a change of tense, from the past tense to the present, or vice versa
- repetition of something that is particularly painful or important, to get it across to the reader
- questions being asked rather than answered
- exclamations that suggest shock or dismay
- disruptions to the normal grammar of the sentence, that show him struggling to give voice to his feelings
- a shift between matter-of-fact description of what happened and expression of powerful feelings
- understatement, a quiet voice that is not strident.

7. A story that must be heard?

A very important text for all young people to read today.

Not really suitable for young people to read.

• In small groups, discuss the possible reasons for the opinions expressed above. What do you yourselves feel about this issue?

8. Primo Levi

Primo Levi was an Italian scientist, a chemist from Turin. As a young man he helped to form a resistance group, to try to fight against fascism. He was captured by the Italian fascist militia and sent to a detention camp in Italy. After a few weeks it was announced that all Jews in the camp would be sent to an unknown destination. It was only when they were on the train that they discovered that they were being taken to a place called Auschwitz, though they did not know at the time what that would mean. Levi was twenty five years old when he entered Auschwitz. The following year the camp was liberated and he was one of the few survivors who returned to Italy after the war. He resumed work as a chemist and went on to write many books including *If This Is A Man*, of which 'On the Bottom' is one chapter. In 1987, aged 68, Levi committed suicide.

• If you had been given the chance to talk to Primo Levi before his death, what would you have wanted to say to him and what questions would you have wanted to ask him?

• Look again at the last sentence of the text, 'It was better not to think.' Do you think that, writing this text thirteen years after being liberated, he still felt that? Why do you think he returned to his experiences and made his 'thinking' so public by publishing a book about them?

• Look at these comments written about Levi and talk about whether you agree with what they say about his writing.

> One of the few survivors of the Holocaust to speak of his experiences with a gentle voice.
> *The Guardian*

> Levi does not flinch from setting down the unbelievable details of that cruelty born of the 'mystique of barrenness', but then neither does he paint them in lurid colours to press his point home. The facts are surely enough.
> Paul Bailey, from the Introduction to *If This Is a Man* (Abacus)

Down and Out in Paris and London and Night Cleaner at the Savoy

1. Before reading
• Look closely at the extract below, taken from the article 'Night Cleaner at the Savoy'. It tells you why the writer chose to write the article.

> So why did I take a deep breath and push open the glass doors of the Job Centre one morning last August? Because I was on a mission: a journey to the heart of Minimum Wage London. I wanted to find out what sort of life was possible on around £4 an hour in Britain's most expensive city. How did the thousands of people living on the lowest legal wages get by?

What Fran Abrams is doing in this article is to make a powerful social comment by documenting ordinary people's experiences of poverty. She puts herself into their shoes and describes what their lives are like. This form of reportage was introduced, and most famously used, by the writer George Orwell, in the 1930s and 40s. In the book *Down and Out in Paris and London* he chose to put himself into a life of poverty in order to document what it was like. In London, he became a homeless person, living in hostels and sleeping rough; in Paris he worked as a dishwasher in hotel kitchens.

2 Being poor

• Read Orwell's account of what it is like to be poor, taken from *Down and Out in Paris and London*.

• Talk about how Orwell gives you a sense of what it feels like to have barely enough money to survive. As part of your discussion you might think about:
– why he uses 'you' as the form of address
– what kinds of details he gives
– what stories he tells and why.

3. In the kitchens at the Hôtel X

• Read Orwell's descriptions of working in the kitchens.

• Talk about what impact the description made on you.

• Work in pairs, with each pair taking responsibility for looking closely at one aspect of the text from the list below. Choose one good example from the text to share with the rest of the class, when you report back your findings.

– How the physical environment is described
– How the people are described
– How Orwell describes the tasks he had to do
– The use of speech and what effect it creates
– The description of feelings – whose feelings? How are they described?

• Share your findings as a whole class.

4. Reading 'Night Cleaner at the Savoy'

• Read Fran Abrams' account.

• Talk about the impact the description made on you. What does she suggest about what life is like for those on a minimum wage in Britain today? Come up with four or five or words or phrases to sum this up.

5. Similar or different?

• Make a chart to show similarities and differences in the way George Orwell and Fran Abrams have chosen to describe their experiences. Use the list in Activity 3 to give you ideas about what to compare. Use the chart on page 175 to help you get started.

Orwell	Abrams
Told in the past tense	Told in the present and past tense
Describes the detail of what he does chronologically	Also describes the detail of tasks chronologically

5. Writing your own piece of reportage

Here are two suggestions for writing reportage, drawing on the style of Orwell and Abrams.

---

1. School life

• Imagine that you have been asked to write an article about life in schools in the early twenty first century. What would you write about? How would you give a sense of what kinds of places schools are? What incidents would you describe? What places would you focus on? What visual images would you create? What view of schools would you put across – working environments buzzing with energy, relaxed, friendly communities, or depressing places where very little learning happens? Make a brainstormed list of ideas, then share them in a group or as a whole class, talking about what would give readers a real sense of what schools are like these days.

• Try writing a first paragraph, in which you imitate the style of either George Orwell's opening paragraph or Fran Abrams' opening two paragraphs. For instance:

Green Lane School was a vast, glass and metal construction, surrounded by tarmac and trees and at one side a large playing field, once grass but now just mud and lumpy turf. I arrived at ...

• Listen to other people's first paragraphs. Share ideas about what worked well, then edit and improve your own.

• Now write a first draft of the whole piece, bearing in mind that you should include some of each of the following:
– description of the physical environment
– description of smells, sounds, the feel of things or the taste of things
– description of what people look like
– description of the detail of people's actions and activity
– description of feelings, your own or other people's
– a viewpoint on what's right or wrong about what you describe
– general comments on what your account suggests about the current state of schools or education in general.

2. Young people and money – the struggle to get by

Abrams and Orwell both use their personal experiences to make important points about their society. Try doing the same.

• Write an article about your struggle as a young person to get by on your pocket money, allowance or wages from part-time work. You could do it by tracking what happens during one week, what you want and can't afford to buy, where the money goes and so on. Use the experiences you describe to make a series of points about young people and money. You could choose the points you want to make from the list below.

– Young people should be entitled to an agreed minimum amount of money.
– Young people should/shouldn't have to work for spending money.
– Parents should understand more about the pressures on teenagers to spend money.
– Pocket money should never be used as a bargaining tool – a bribe or threat – by parents.
– Being short of money causes serious problems for teenagers.
– It's important for young people to learn the value of money by not being given too much of it.

• You could consciously try to use some of the techniques used by Orwell and Abrams in your writing, for instance:
– using little anecdotes from your own experience
– quoting what other young people, (friends or members of your class) say about their experiences
– including a few facts and figures, drawn from your experience or that of your friends
– doing a bit of background research on the internet, on young people and money, to add in.

Finding the Tollund Man

An early spring day – 8 May 1950. Evening was gathering over Tollund Fen in Bjaeldskov Dal (dale or valley). Momentarily, the sun burst in, bright and yet subdued, through a gate in blue thunder-clouds in the west, bringing everything mysteriously to life. The evening stillness was only broken, now and again, by the grating love-call of the snipe. The dead man, too, deep down in the umber-brown peat, seemed to have come alive. He lay on his damp bed as though asleep, resting on his side, the head inclined a little forward, arms and legs bent. His face wore a gentle expression – the eyes lightly closed, the lips softly pursed, as if in silent prayer. It was as though the dead man's soul had for a moment returned from another world, through the gate in the western sky.

The dead man who lay there was 2,000 years old. A few hours earlier he had been brought out from the sheltering peat by two men who, their spring sowing completed, had now to think of the cold winter days to come, and were occupied in cutting peat for the tile stove and kitchen range.

As they worked, they suddenly saw in the peat-layer a face so fresh that they could only suppose they had stumbled on a recent murder. They notified the police at Silkeborg, who came at once to the site. The police, however, also invited representatives of the local museum to accompany them, for well-preserved remains of Iron-Age men were not unknown in central Jutland. At the site the true context of the discovery was soon evident. A telephone call was put through straight away to Aarhus University, where at that moment I was lecturing to a group of students on archaeological problems. Some hours later – that same evening – I stood with my students, bent over the startling discovery, face to face with an Iron-Age man who, two millennia before, had been deposited in the bog as a sacrifice to the powers that ruled men's destinies.

The man lay on his right side in a natural attitude of sleep. The head was to the west, with the face turned to the south; the legs were to the east. He lay 50 yds out from firm ground, not far above the clean sand floor of the bog, and had been covered by 8 or 9 ft of peat, now dug away.

On his head he wore a pointed skin cap fastened securely under the chin by a hide thong. Round his waist there was a smooth hide belt. Otherwise he was naked. His hair was cropped so short as to be almost entirely hidden by his cap. He was clean-shaven, but there was very short stubble on the chin and upper lip.

The air of gentle tranquillity about the man was shattered when a small lump of peat was removed from beside his head. This disclosed a rope, made of two leather thongs twisted together, which encircled the neck in a noose drawn tight into the throat and then coiled like a snake over the shoulder and down across the back. After this discovery the wrinkled forehead and set mouth seemed to take on a look of affliction.

Proper study of such an interesting find, and the need to preserve it for the future, called for its immediate removal to the National Museum in far away Copenhagen. Preparations were quickly begun. In the gathering dusk a local saw-mill was visited and asked to supply planks for a box to be built in the bog round the dead man and his bed of peat, so that everything could be despatched for investigation intact. As darkness encroached, this task had to be postponed. Next day a strong team from the Silkeborg Museum moved in under the direction of two museum curators, Peter Nielsen and H. Hansen, assisted by the police. The dead man and the surrounding peat were first tightly walled in between the sides of the box. Next, boards were pushed in underneath the whole. When the box had been filled right up to the top with peat blocks so that there was no possibility of its contents shifting during the journey, a lid was nailed on.

The heavy plank box weighed almost a ton when filled. It had to be raised nearly 10 ft vertically from the bottom of the bog and on to a horse-drawn cart which was to take it to the nearest railway station, in the village of Engesvang. The soft surface of the bog made it impossible to bring a crane up to the spot, and everything had to be done by hand. This was not accomplished without loss. One of the helpers overstrained himself and collapsed with a heart attack. The bog claimed a life for a life; or, as some may prefer to think, the old gods took a modern man in place of the man from the past [...]

[...] The journey of the Tollund man by rail through Denmark took a week. As soon as he reached the National Museum's laboratory in Copenhagen a thorough investigation was begun under Dr Knud Thorvildsen, the head of the laboratory. The long journey had gone well. When the plank box was taken apart the dead man was found lying on his peat bed exactly as when he was first uncovered. Examination of the block of peat which surrounded the body confirmed that he had been deposited in an old peat-cutting at some time in the Early Iron Age, that is, about 2,000 years ago. Underneath the whole body was a very thin layer of sphagnum moss, a reddish peat-stratum which was formed in Danish bogs precisely in the Early Iron Age. Danish peat-cutters call it 'dogs' flesh' because of its colour and its relatively poor quality as fuel.

The Iron-Age man's head and body were exceptionally well preserved, particularly the side which lay downwards and so was first subjected to the action of the bog water. Bog water, saturated with soil-acids, is an essential factor in the preservation of this type of ancient find. If the soil acid is not too strong, the bones are preserved. On the other hand, they may disappear completely in certain circumstances, dissolved in the water by the action of the acid and further decalcified by the roots of bog plants. This point is illustrated by a find made at Damendorf, in Schleswig. Here only the skin survived; but it was so well preserved that it might have been taken from a living man.

The Tollund man's head was especially well preserved, the best preserved human head, in fact, to have survived from antiquity in any part of the world. Majesty and gentleness still stamp his features as they did when he was alive. His cropped hair, up to 2 ins. long, was not dressed in any way. His eyebrows were partially preserved, and the very short stubble already mentioned covered his upper lip, chin and cheeks. It is the dead man's lightly closed eyes and half-closed lips, however, that give this unique face its distinctive expression, and call compellingly to mind the words of the world's oldest heroic epic, *Gilgamesh,* 'the dead and the sleeping, how they resemble one another'.

As to the condition of the body, Dr Thorvildsen writes that most of its upper part was still covered with skin. The left part of the chest and the left shoulder, however, were slightly decomposed, the epidermis being absent from considerable areas. A succession of sharp cuts could be seen down the back. These had been caused by peatcutting. The left hip-bone protruded from the skin and the stomach lay in folds. The sexual organs were in a good state of preservation.

The naked body was clad only in cap and girdle, with a skin rope fastened tightly around the neck. The pointed cap was made of eight pieces of leather sewn together, the hair side inwards, and was fastened to the head by two thin leather laces, fixed at the temples with knots and tied off in a bow, which was tucked in under the cap at the right temple. The belt lay low on the hips, in folds at the back but tight across the stomach. Made of thin hairless skin, it had one end drawn through a slot in the other and wider end and was secured with a slip-knot on the left side.

The plaited skin rope round the dead man's neck was knotted at one end to form an eyelet through which the other end was drawn, forming a noose which could be tightened from the back. It had left clear impressions in the skin under the chin and at the sides of the neck, but no mark at the nape of the neck, where the knot rested. The rope was skilfully plaited from two strips of hide about half an inch wide, and measured 5 ft from the curve of the eyelet to the opposite extremity. It had, however, been cut at this point and must originally have been longer.

The Tollund man most probably met his death by means of this rope. The vertebrae of the neck did not appear to be damaged, but the doctors and medico-legal experts who took part in the examination judged, nevertheless, from the way the rope was placed that the Tollund man had not been strangled, but hanged. An attempt was made to decide the point by radiography, carried out by a senior medical officer at Bispebjerg Hospital, Dr Baastrup. The result was indeterminate, because of the decalcified state of the vertebrae. A radiograph of the skull was taken at the same time. This showed clearly that the head was undamaged. The wisdom teeth had developed, indicating that the man must have been appreciably over twenty years old. The brain was intact but shrunken. An autopsy showed that the inner organs such as the heart, lungs and liver were very well preserved. So was the alimentary canal, which was removed by the palaeobotanist, Dr Hans Helbaek, with the object of determining the nature of the dead man's last meal. This was still contained in the stomach and in the larger and smaller intestines which, though somewhat flattened by the weight of the overlying peat, were otherwise intact.

These organs were carefully rinsed externally, to remove contamination from the surrounding peat. Their contents were then washed out and proved to consist of a blend of finely reduced plant remains and particles of seeds. The contents of the stomach and the smaller intestine were inconsiderable, occupying in volume barely 0.5 and 10 cubic centimetres respectively. The contents of the larger intestine, on the other hand, amounted to 260 cubic centimetres. All was of the same character. It was not possible to establish with certainty the proportions of the different ingredients because the plants had varied in their resistance to the digestive juices which had acted on them from the time the meal was eaten and for some while after death.

By the time it has been crushed in a hand-mill and between the teeth a meal of this kind, consisting largely of grains and seeds, is reduced to myriads of small particles. The basis of the investigation was a sample of 50 cubic centimetres taken from the larger intestine.

In collaboration with the anatomists, Drs Bjøvulf Vimtrop and Kay Schaurup, a point of great interest was established. Investigation showed that although the contents of the stomach consisted of vegetable remains of a gruel prepared from barley, linseed, 'gold-of-pleasure' *(camelina sativa)* and knotweed, with many different sorts of weeds that grow on ploughed land, it could not have contained any meat at the time of death, since recognizable traces of bone, sinew or muscular tissue would certainly have remained. It was further established, from the degree of digestion of the remains of the meal in the alimentary canal, that the Tollund man had lived for between 12 and 24 hours after eating his last meal.

In addition to the varieties of cultivated grain, it is worth noticing the unusual quantity of knotweed *(pale persicaria)* in the stomach. It must have been gathered deliberately and other plants represented may have been gathered along with it incidentally; for example, blue and green bristle-grass, dock, black bindweed, camomile and gold-of-pleasure. The gruel made from this mixture of cultivated and wild grains was no doubt the normal diet in the Early Iron Age, around the time of Christ, when the Tollund man was alive. Fish and meat were also eaten. Rich furnishings of bowls and dishes, with ribs of ox and sheep, and carving knives lying ready, are known in the graves of the time. But meat was certainly not the daily diet as it was in the time of the Stone-Age hunters. Milk and cheese, on the other hand, probably were, as the forms of the pottery vessels would seem to indicate.

It is not surprising that this 2,000 year-old 'recipe' for gruel from the Iron Age (consisting primarily of various cultivated grains together with the seeds of many types of weeds known at that time), should have been tried out in our own day, and in front of a big audience at that. Gruel made to this recipe was served up on an English television programme, in the summer of 1954, to two well-known archaeologists – Sir Mortimer Wheeler and Dr Glyn Daniel. Reports tell us that these gentlemen were not particularly smitten with the taste and had to wash it down with good Danish brandy, drunk from a cow-horn. Sir Mortimer finished up by saying that it would have been punishment enough for the Tollund man to have been compelled to eat this gruel for the rest of his life, however terrible his crime might have been. The Tollund man, though, would not have had brandy to help it down, as the archaeologists did. It was not until about a thousand years later that people learned to distil something stronger from fermented drinks. However, there was an alcoholic drink in the Iron Age, as has been revealed by analysis of sediments in bronze vessels of the period. It was half way between beer and a fruit wine. Barley and the wild plants cranberry and bog myrtle were used in its manufacture. The alcoholic content may have been increased by the addition of honey. This agrees with the account given in the Roman historian Tacitus' *Germania,* a work contemporary with Denmark's Early Iron Age. It says of the Germani that 'they drink a fluid made from wheat or barley, fermented so as to give it some resemblance to wine'.

When the exhaustive study of the Tollund man had been concluded, a decision was taken on preserving him for the future. Unfortunately it was only thought practicable to undertake the conservation of the splendid head. This was first of all placed for six months in a solution of water to which formalin and acetic acid had been added. The solution was then changed for one of 30 per cent alcohol, which was later replaced by one of 99 per cent alcohol to which toluol had been added. Finally, it was put into pure toluol progressively mixed with paraffin, for which wax heated to different temperatures was later substituted. After more than a year's treatment the head was sent to the Silkeborg Museum in central Jutland, a bare six miles from the spot where it had come to light in Tollund Fen. It can be seen there, alongside other discoveries of the Iron Age.

In the process of conservation the proportions of the head and the features of the face were happily completely retained, but the head as a whole had shrunk by about 12 per cent. In spite of this it has emerged as the best preserved head of an early man to have come down to us so far. The majestic head astonishes the beholder and rivets his attention. Standing in front of the glass case in which it is displayed, he finds himself face to face with an Iron-Age man. Dark in hue, the head is still full of life and more beautiful than the best portraits by the world's greatest artists, since it is the man himself we see.

P.V.Glob
The Bog People, 1965

The Tollund Man

I

Some day I will go to Aarhus
To see his peat-brown head,
The mild pods of his eye-lids,
His pointed skin cap.

In the flat country nearby
Where they dug him out,
His last gruel of winter seeds
Caked in his stomach,

Naked except for
The cap, noose and girdle,
I will stand a long time.
Bridegroom to the goddess,

She tightened her torc on him
And opened her fen,
Those dark juices working
Him to a saint's kept body,

Trove of the turfcutters'
Honeycombed workings.
Now his stained face
Reposes at Aarhus.

II

I could risk blasphemy,
Consecrate the cauldron bog
Our holy ground and pray
Him to make germinate

The scattered, ambushed
Flesh of labourers,
Stockinged corpses
Laid out in the farmyards,

Tell-tale skin and teeth
Flecking the sleepers
Of four young brothers, trailed
For miles along the lines.

III

Something of his sad freedom
As he rode the tumbril
Should come to me, driving,
Saying the names

Tollund, Grabaulle, Nebelgard,
Watching the pointing hands
Of country people,
Not knowing their tongue.

Out there in Jutland
In the old man-killing parishes
I will feel lost,
Unhappy and at home.

Seamus Heaney
Wintering Out, 1972

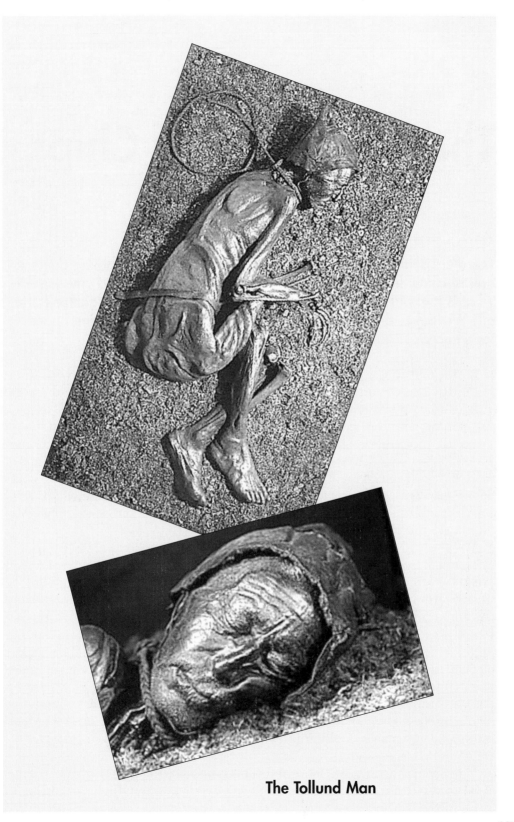

The Tollund Man

The Secret Life of Chips

There are some hungers that can only be satisfied by gobbling down a bag of chips, hot from the fryer and dredged with salt and vinegar. So what is it about fluffy starch coated in fat that makes such gluttons of us all? William Leith delves into the mystery of the most addictive finger food known to humanity.

The only time you want to eat chips is when you're really hungry. Or when you're quite hungry. Or when somebody else is eating chips in the same room. When somebody is eating chips close to you, you make a quick calculation. How well do you know that person? Will that person be offended if you ask them for a chip? Will they be offended if you ask them for another chip? Chips, being discrete units of food, rather than a single blob or lump of food, have a social element. They suggest sharing. But still, you often see chips being guarded – plates or takeaway punnets being clutched close to the chip-eater's body, out of striking range; hands being slapped across the table. You often hear the phrase, 'Get off my chips!'

We love stuffing chips into our faces. They are dry enough to pick up and soft enough to cram by the fistful into your mouth. They contain enough grease to slip down your gullet unaccompanied. Every year, as a nation, we stuff more of them into our faces than we did the year before. Chip consumption is growing in Britain by one per cent annually. This may not sound like much, but it amounts to thousands of tonnes of potatoes – preferably potatoes with a medium or high starch content, such as Maris Pipers or Pentland Dells or Idaho Russets. They are stored in vast warehouses, under strict temperature, light and humidity conditions, during which time some of the starch in the potatoes turns to sugar. This is why, when you fry them, they turn a lovely golden brown colour. And this is one of the most desirable food colours on the planet. Golden brown foods can inspire a kind of lust. Get off my chips!

When you eat chips, you feel good. This is because the carbohydrate in chips causes a rapid rise in blood glucose; chips give you a starch high. According to the nutritionist Michel Montignac, chips are a 'bad carbohydrate'. With a 'glycaemic index' of 95, almost nothing raises your blood sugar so fast. This is partly why they are so delicious. Chips are also a nutritionist's nightmare. They can be addictive. Chips are starch covered all over with fat; they are like bread which has been buttered on both sides, and around the crusts as well. Chips are starchy tubers which, typically, have been fried twice; they are potatoes from which the water has been forced out. This is why they are fluffy on the inside and crisp, or even crunchy, on the outside. They are, in a way, a culinary miracle. You just can't do this with pasta or rice.

If the West has problems with obesity and diabetes, it is because of foods like chips. This is something we've got to admit. Chips might be one of the best inventions on the planet, but they might also be killing us. When you eat chips, the graph describing the level of your blood sugar resembles a Swiss Alp; you get high, and then you crash. So you want more chips. You enter the chip cycle. Like cigarettes or cocaine, chips are delicious, not in spite of the fact that they are bad for you, but precisely because they are bad for you. They are, perhaps, the ultimate in decadent food. As a cultural item, they are the best and the worst of us.

So what if they're killing you? Sometimes you just want chips. For one thing, chips remind you of being a child, when you burned up so many calories it didn't matter. I spoke to a man who had masterminded several advertising campaigns for McCain oven chips and Microchips – chips which have been pre-cooked and whose packet-to-mouth time is three minutes. Understandably, the man didn't want to be named; he knew there was a chance I might say something bad about chips. Chips are, in a way, a controversial product. But he needn't have worried – saying something bad about chips is like saying something bad about slim, leggy models in women's magazines. It won't make a blind bit of difference. People know what they like.

We were sitting in a slick, bright conference room. The man told me about the campaigns he had participated in. As he talked, I imagined his face pixillated to anonymity. The ads were brilliant and daring. In one, a young girl, stultified with chip-lust, asks herself the question, 'Daddy or chips?' Which would she choose? Which would you choose? In another one, a couple are depicted on a sofa, stealing chips from each other's plates. In a third, black dudes force handfuls of chips into their mouths. That's more or less it – black dudes gorging on chips. It's brilliant. In a fourth, a man resembling David Ginola is, somehow, forced to choose between a chip and a gorgeous babe. It's more profound than you think – if you eat chips like some of the people in the ads, you might find yourself forgoing the pleasures of gorgeous babes.

The advertising executive told me that, according to research, chips are the biggest cause of arguments in restaurants. Couples in restaurants argue more about stolen chips than about their partner ogling members of the opposite sex. 'The thing about chips,' said the man, 'is they taste better if they're not yours. You have to nick a chip off someone's plate'.

People, said the man, want chips to taste fried. Even so, they do not, on the whole, want to fry them themselves. For most chip-eaters, chips must be something fried for you by someone else. Chips, it seems to me, are the ultimate leisure food. Chips are food as play. Chips are, in a way, a sort of holiday. And, like a holidaymaker, a chip-eater wants to engage his baser qualities – laziness as well as greed. This might be why the oven chip is gaining ground over the home-fried chip. Out of every 100 chips eaten in the home, 74 are cooked in the oven, and six come out of the microwave. As a result, the incidence of chip-pan fires is dropping. McCain's Home Fries, said the man, taste like chips which have been fried at home. They taste like they have emerged from a sexy fryer, rather than a much more prosaic oven. 'That sounds like bollocks,' said the man, 'but it's true.'

Imagine yourself holding a chip. You don't hold them for very long, do you? But if you hold a chip which you have not prepared yourself, do you ever wonder where it came from? Probably not. How much time do cocaine addicts really spend gazing down at their next white line wondering about its provenance? But wait. That chip you are about to thrust into your mouth has been on a long journey. Chances are it has been processed by McCain, the world's largest producer of chipped potatoes.

One in three of chips everywhere has been through a McCain factory. If you eat a McDonald's French fry, McCain employees, or contractors, have grown it, harvested it, trucked it, mechanically peeled it, skinned it, trimmed it, brushed it, blanched it, dried it, fried it, de-fatted it, cooled it, frozen it, bagged it, boxed it, X-rayed the box for foreign bodies such as coins or pens, and trucked it to one of three distribution plants in Manchester, Basingstoke, and Hemel Hempstead, from where it is trucked again to the parking lot behind the golden arches in your home town, to be re-fried by youngsters in cheerful aprons.

The McCain head office, and one of three McCain chipping plants, juts out of the desolate North Yorkshire landscape, five miles south of Scarborough. It is a vast, Satanic building, like a huge aircraft hangar bedecked with turrets and chimneys. It steams. This is chip central. On an average day, 1,200 tonnes of potatoes arrive at one end of the factory, and chips – a mind-boggling amount of chips – emerge, packed and boxed, at the other. Paul Major, a cheerful man with his hair cut *en brosse*, is the factory's production manager, and he loves producing chips. He gets tremendous job satisfaction out of a good day's work, with good line rates and no 'quality issues' with the potatoes. Potatoes are checked and re-checked. They must conform to very strict parameters. 'You just get a buzz out of everything,' Major tells me.

Ernie Thompson, a chip man of 24 years' standing, is in charge of the liaison between McCain and McDonald's. He eats a lot of chips. 'What's the hardest thing about the job?' 'Keeping your weight down,' he tells me. But Ernie is lucky. He is tall and slim, with grey hair and a neat grey moustache. He exercises a great deal. Donning a hairnet, a white coat, and a protective hard hat, items which I must also wear, Thompson takes me into the factory.

It's extraordinary. I've never seen so many potatoes. I am in a vast, cold, soil-smelling space. On one side of me is 100 tonnes of potatoes. Underneath me is a river of potatoes. They have all been grown from sixth-generation seed potatoes which have themselves been transported from their nursery fields, in the north of Scotland, to farms around Britain. Standing on a metal walkway, I follow the potatoes' progress through the factory. They flow into rotating tanks where the skins are blasted off with steam. Then they are fired through 'hydro-guns', forced under high-pressure water through metal pipes. At the end of each pipe is a grid of blades. This is the point where one potato becomes 10 or more chips. To make a McDonald's fry, you arrange the blades so that they are closer together. To make a chunky Home Fry, you place the blades further apart.

And then what? The river of potatoes becomes a waterfall of chips, a Niagara of what chip insiders call 'strips'. It is awesome. The strips are whizzed along on a holed conveyor, to ensure that small ones fall through, into the vast nether world below, the Hades of failed chips, chips that didn't make the grade. Making the grade, explains Thompson, is the crucial thing. Consistency is everything. Chip eaters want the chips they eat today to be exactly the same as the chips they ate yesterday and the chips they will eat tomorrow. The chips flow past mounted cameras, which photograph any blemishes which might remain; in an awesome feat of technology, blades are programmed to pop up and slice off the blemishes.

When you're standing on a thin metal walkway at the top of a cavernous factory building, skidding on fat deposits, and looking down into a swimming pool of boiling fat, you understand what people put themselves through to arrive at the perfect chip. You have plugs in your ears to protect you from the noise of the chip-making process. 'It's a very complex job,' says Thompson. 'People think that making frozen chips is the easiest thing in the world. But it's not.' Later, the chips are tasted by a panel, some of whom are thin, and some of whom are not. In its way, eating chips, like everything else in life, is a lottery.

Major and Thompson, and Graham Finn, McCain's Potato Procurement Manager, are philosophical about their work. They are potato men through and through. Finn, a teacherly man of 51, tells me that McCain's Russet Burbank potatoes are all, every one of them, the descendants of just five seed potatoes brought over from America in the Eighties; now tens of thousands of tonnes are processed every year. 'It's a key part of the role,' says Major, 'getting the right potatoes. If there's one thing I've learnt, it's about getting the right potatoes.' Thompson says, 'you can't make a silk purse out of a sow's ear.'

Look at that chip you're holding. Is it golden? Is it the same as the chip you ate yesterday? Yes, it is. Now you want another. Chip eaters start off by picking their chips out singly; soon, they are picking up bundles of two or three. Sometimes, we eat them out of cones wrapped in newspaper. They have tabloid associations. In a recent episode of *Footballers' Wives*, one of the footballers says, of the royally tarty model Chardonnay, 'the first time I saw her she was naked, wrapped around my chips'. Chips are wonderfully grungy; this is always part of their attraction.

But it's because of this grunginess, this accepted fact that chips are a part of lowlife, that they can be served, with a touch of irony, in the poshest places. John Torode, who is the chef at Smiths of Smithfield, talks about chips in lyrical tones. 'They are essentials,' he says. 'Absolute essentials.' He is a good-looking, cheeky Australian in early middle age. One of the pleasures of chips, he says, is dipping them into things; chips are excellent carriers of sauces and gravies. The Belgians, who claim to have invented the chip, eat them with mayonnaise. Germans eat them with mustard. We favour tomato ketchup, along with the Americans. 'Just dipping a chip into the yolk of an egg,' says Torode dreamily.

In the hyped world of the celebrity chef, chips are a reminder of earthy pleasures. Gordon Ramsay told me, 'I love a bowl of chips. With rock salt and vinegar. Chefs really love chips because you're surrounded by fancy food all day'. Ramsay cuts his chips thick, in the Pont Neuf style developed in Parisian restaurants; they're about the size of a big man's little finger. Torode does the same; he serves chips, cut from large Maris Piper potatoes, along with £28 steaks in his most expensive restaurant in Smithfield.

Torode takes me into the restaurant's kitchen, where he introduces me to Ashley, a commis chef who cuts his chips. Ashley picks up a large Maris Piper, about the size of a pint glass, and places it on the slab. After six quick moves with the knife, he is left with a brick of potato, just a little bit bigger than a half-pound pat of butter. Three more cuts – the whole thing is over in a few seconds – and Ashley has six near-identical Pont Neuf chips.

'You fry them twice,' says Torode. 'Once, for four or five minutes, at 120 degrees, and then, later, for three minutes at 190 degrees.' This is the essential fact about the chip – it must be fried twice. Once to force the moisture out of the chip and seal the outside, and again to make the outside tough and the inside smooth and fluffy.

I am sitting at my table in Torode's restaurant, waiting for my chips. I am thinking about chips. I am chip-fixated. I am thinking of the voice of Ian McCaskill, in a chip ad, saying, 'You just can't help yourself'. I am thinking of people stealing chips from each other's plates, of the Western world getting fatter, of the advertising executive who told me that, in focus groups, some chip-lovers went into what he described as a 'hypnotic chip world'. I am thinking of the chip-loving Cameron Diaz, who once described herself as 'a salty, greasy girl'. The chips arrive. I want the chips! I want to stuff them into my face, like the black dudes in the ad! I reach out, grab a chip, stuff it in. I look around the table and move the bowl protectively towards me. A hand is moving towards my bowl. 'Oy!' I say, 'get off my chips!'

The chipping news

Chips were first popularised in France, hence the name French fries.
Selling fish and chips was once licensed under the Offensive Trades Act because of the smell produced. During the war it was the only take-away food not to be rationed.
Today there are only 8,500 fish and chip shops compared with 30,000 in 1950.
Britain eats 22,000 tonnes of chips a week.
44 per cent of British households still use a traditional chip pan, while 34 per cent prefer a deep-fat fryer.

Northerners are most likely to fry their chips at home, with 28 per cent claiming to cook them from fresh every week. Sixty-one per cent of Southerners say they never cook chips from scratch.

In 2000 over 277 million fish and chip shop meals were sold throughout the UK, and in a new UK survey 41 per cent voted cod and chips their favourite takeaway making it the nation's top hot takeaway.

One in four of all British potatoes consumed in Britain are eaten as chips.

The British Nutrition Foundation found that an average portion of fish and chips contains 20.6 per cent of fat – almost three times less fat than a chicken tikka masala and pilau rice, which has 59.9g of fat.

In the Eighties the industry took the decision not to wrap chips in newspaper because of a suggested link between black printing ink and cancer.

McCain are king of the frozen chip industry, claiming the UK's top three favourite products. First Home Fries, then McCain Oven Chips, followed by McCain Micro Chips.

William Leith
The Observer, 10 February 2002

Find It

The art of **finding something** pinned up on the world's biggest scrapboard is, without doubt, **the most valuable skill** you can glean from your time online. If you know how to use the Net to find an answer to almost anything quickly and comprehensively, you'd have to consider yourself not only useful, but pretty saleable too. Most people, including many Net veterans, simply **bumble their way around**. Yet, it's a remarkably basic skill to master. So read this section, then get online and start investigating. Within an hour or two you'll be milking the Net for what it's worth. It might turn out to be the best investment you'll ever make!

How it works

The Net is massive. Just the Web alone houses well over two billion pages of text, and many millions more are added daily. So you'll need some serious help if you want to find something. Thankfully, there's a wide selection of search tools to make the task relatively painless. The job usually entails keying your **search terms** into a form on a Web page and waiting a few seconds for the results.

Over the next few pages, we'll introduce you to **search tools** that can locate almost anything: on the Web; linked to from the Web; or archived into an online Web database, such as email addresses, phone numbers, program locations, newsgroup articles, and news clippings. Of course, first it has to be put online, and granted public access. So just because you can access US government servers doesn't mean you'll find a file on DEA Operative Presley's whereabouts.

Your weapons

There are three main types of Web search tools: **search engines, hand-built subject directories** and **search agents**. Apart from the odd newspaper archive, they're usually free. Because they're so useful and popular, there was a trend towards tacking other services onto the side and building themselves into so-called **portals, communities,** and **hubs**. More recently that trend has begun to reverse with the launch of several skeletal search tools free of fancy overheads. Irrespective of which you use, ignore the quantity of froufrou and concentrate on the quality of the results. The next few pages discuss each category in detail, and show you how to torture them for answers.

Search engines

The best way to find just about anything online is to start with a **search engine.** The good thing about search engines is they can search through the **actual contents** of Web pages (and file servers), and not just descriptions. The better search engines can rifle through **billions of Web pages** in a fraction of a second. You simply go to the search engine's Web site and submit **keyword**s, or search terms, into a simple form. It will query its database and, almost instantly, return a list of results or '**hits**'. For example, if you were to search on the expression 'Rough Guide to the Internet', here's what might come up on top:

1. Welcome to the Rough Guide to the Internet
The Rough Guide to the Internet is the ultimate guide to the Web, complete with a 2500+ site directory
www.roughguides.com/internet/index.html

In this case the top line tells us the name of the page or site. Followed by a description excerpted from the page, and then the page's address. If it suits, click on the link to visit the site.

> Tip: Don't just click on a result, and then hit the Back button if it's no good. Instead, run down the list and open the most promising candidates in new browser windows. It will save you tons of time. Do this by holding down the **Shift key** as you click.

The reason it's so quick is **you're not searching the Web live. You're merely searching a database** of Web page extracts stored on the search engine's server. This database is compiled by a program that periodically 'crawls' around the Web looking for new or changed pages. Because of the sheer size of the Net, and a few factors relating to site design, it's not possible for the crawlers to find every site, let alone every word on every page. Nor is it possible to keep the database completely up to date. That means you can't literally 'search the Web', you can only search a snapshot taken by a search engine. So naturally, different search engines will give you different results depending on how much of the Web they've found, how often they update, how much text they extract from each page and how well they actually work.

So, which search engine?

There are dozens of search engines, but only a few worth trying. In fact, you'll rarely need more than one. But since you'll be using it often, make sure it's up to speed. You'll want the **biggest, freshest, database**. You'll want to **fine-tune your search** with extra commands. And you'll want the most hits you can get on one page with the most **relevant results on top**. Right now, that's **Google**: http://www.google.com

This completely free service has an uncanny knack of getting it in the first few hits, both from within its search engine database and its association with the **Open Directory**. It also provides local cache access to pages that have disappeared since its crawl, or are otherwise unavailable. Click on 'cached' to see how this works. Use it when you can't get a link to load.

If Google falls short, try **All the Web** and **AltaVista**. They're also big, fast, clutter free, and can deliver a long page of relevant hits. Next up, **Northern Light** is worth a shot. It's also big, but not so fast or user-friendly despite its curious system of organizing hits into folders.

All the Web http://www.alltheweb.com
AltaVista http://www.av.com
Northern Light http://www.nlsearch.com

As for the rest? Just because an engine isn't the biggest or best, doesn't mean it's worthless. Even the smallest engines can find unique hits. Still, unless you're after extra hits, you're unlikely to need them. Of course, they might improve:

Excite http://www.excite.com
HotBot http://www.hotbot.com
Lycos http://www.lycos.com

If you notice some engines give identical, or very similar, results it might be because they share technologies. **AOL, HotBot,** and **MSN,** for example, currently use the **Inktomi** system.

But if you seriously need **more results**, rather than visit several engines in turn, query them simultaneously using an agent such as **Copernic**. You can tell how each engine ranks from the results. For more detailed analysis, see:

Search Engine Watch http://www.searchenginewatch.com
Search Engine World http://www.searchenginewortd.com
Search Engine Showdown http://www.searchenginesshowdown.com
Search Lore http://www.searchlore.org

They keep tabs on all the finer details such as who owns what, how they tick, and who's currently biggest. Essential reading for budding Webmasters.

Limitations

Search engines aren't the be all and end all of what's on the Web. **They're only as good as their most recent findings**, which might be just a small proportion of what's actually there and, possibly, months old. So just because you can't find it through a Web search doesn't mean it's not there. If you're after something brand new, they're not always the best choice. You might be better off searching **Usenet** or a news service.

How to use a search engine

Okay, get this right and you'll find anything. The trick is to think up a **search term** that's unique enough to get rid of junk results, but broad enough not to miss anything useful. It will depend entirely on the subject, so be prepared to think laterally!

One search won't fit all – read the instructions

Although most search forms look alike, the mechanisms behind them differ. That means you might have to adjust your search terms slightly, depending on the engine, to get the best results. The same applies to online stores, encyclopedias, newspaper archives, and anything else you can search. It also means some engines work better than others.

While the easiest way to learn is to dive straight in, at some point, pause and read the instructions. You should find a link to an FAQ, Search Tips, or Help section on the front page. The main things to glean are how to **create a phrase**, how to **search on multiple phrases**, and how to **exclude certain words**. A few minutes' study could save hours of weeding through poor results.

A typical search

Let's start with a complex example. Suppose we want to search for something on the esteemed author, Angus Kennedy. Let's see how you'd do it in **All the Web**.

If you were to enter: angus kennedy it would return all pages that contain 'angus' **or** 'kennedy' **or both**. That means there'd be lots of pages about Angus cattle and JFK. We don't want to sift through those so let's make sure the pages contain **both words**. In Raging Search, and most other search engines, you can use a **plus sign** (+) to state that the page **must contain a word**. So let's try: +angus +kennedy.

That's better. All the pages now contain both words. Unfortunately, though, there's no guarantee that they'll be next to each other. What we really want is to **treat them as a phrase**. A simple way to do this is to enclose the words within quotes, like this: 'angus kennedy'

Now we've captured all instances of Angus Kennedy as a phrase, but since it's a **person's name**, we should look for Kennedy, Angus as well. So let's try: 'angus kennedy' 'kennedy, angus'

As with the first example we now catch pages with **either or both phrases**. Now suppose we want to narrow it down further and exclude some irrelevant results, for example, others with the same name. Our target writes books about French literature, so let's start by getting rid of that pesky *Rough Guide* author. To **exclude a term**, place a minus sign (-) in front. So let's ditch him: 'angus kennedy' 'kennedy, angus' -'rough guide'

That's about all you need to know in most instances. These rules should work in most engines, as well as the search forms on individual sites. However, there are exceptions.

Variations – such as Google

Google makes searching easier by including all the search terms. Which means you don't have to add the + sign. So searching on: 'angus kennedy' would search for pages containing 'angus' **AND** 'kennedy.' If you want to search for pages containing either, do two separate searches or use the Boolean operator 'OR': angus OR kennedy

Many engines also have a **drop down menu** with the options of 'any of the words', 'all the words', or 'the exact phrase'. If the meaning of that isn't instantly obvious, try it.

To tune your searches further, look for an 'advanced search option', or refer to the instructions. Observe how the engine interprets **capitals**, dashes between words, brackets, wild cards, truncations, and the **Boolean** operators such as AND, OR, NEAR, and NOT.

In particular, watch out for '**stop words**'. These are words that are normally ignored. In Google, for example, single letters are ignored unless you place a '+' sign in front of them. So to search for Angus J Kennedy, you'd enter: 'angus +j kennedy'.

Angus J. Kennedy
The Rough Guide to the Internet, 2002

Interrogation

Gathering information is the meat and potatoes of detective work. Information generates evidence. There are two basic types of evidence: physical evidence and verbal evidence. We've looked briefly at physical evidence; now we turn our attention to verbal evidence.

As I stated before, physical evidence is generally considered to be the most important type of evidence. One reason for this is that physical evidence, while open to interpretation, is inanimate. It's just stuff. It doesn't have motives; it can't intend to deceive. A fingerprint is a fingerprint is a fingerprint. We can debate who the print belongs to, or how it got there, or even whether it was properly collected, but the fingerprint itself is just a thing.

Collecting physical evidence certainly requires some skill, but it's technical skill. Almost anybody can be trained to collect physical evidence. Collecting a fingerprint from a body that's been in the water for a week requires a different set of skills than collecting one from a living person, but once you've learned a new technique it's only a matter of practice.

Collecting verbal evidence is a lot trickier because people are more complex. People mislead, obfuscate, make mistakes, get confused. Sometimes they just flat-out lie through their teeth. There are two primary methods of obtaining verbal evidence: interrogation and interviewing. They share a common goal: getting the subject to reveal information. Sometimes it's information the subject has and is reluctant to reveal. Sometimes it's information the subject has and isn't aware of it. Sometimes it's information the subject has and is just waiting for the opportunity to deliver. Interrogation and interviewing are generally used under different circumstances. In addition, they are grounded in radically different psychologies.

In general, people suspected of a crime are interrogated; witnesses (and potential witnesses) are interviewed. Interrogation relies on power and authority; interviewing is a form of verbal seduction. Interrogation is often high intensity; interviewing is usually more laid back. Interrogation is New York; interviewing is Los Angeles.

Interrogation

Most of what the general public knows about interrogation is based on what they've seen on television and in the movies. That's about like getting your information on cosmetics and makeup by watching circus clowns. The underlying concept is there, but it's not portrayed very accurately.

In general, interrogation is a style of obtaining information based on the authority of the questioner to compel the subject to cooperate. This is why interrogation is generally the province of police detectives. They have the inherent authority of the badge, an authority that's derived from their monopoly on the power to use lethal force and to detain and arrest (although only the latter plays a part in interrogation).

This is not to suggest that interrogation can't be subtle. It most definitely can. A good interrogator is a master of manipulation and a wonder to behold. A good interrogator could get the Archbishop of Canterbury to admit he used to drop slugs into the offering plate when he was a boy.

At the heel of the hunt, interrogation is about control – control of the setting of the interrogation, control of information, control of access to the subject by other people and control of the subject himself.

The Truth About Lying

Let's spend just a brief moment on lying. Lying is an equal opportunity activity. Guilty people lie. Innocent people lie. Crooks lie. Police lie. Presidents lie. Rock singers lie. Parents lie. Children most definitely lie. Movie stars lie. Priests and nuns and ministers and rabbis and mullahs lie. If Santa tells you he was at the North Pole when the crime was committed, you'd better put a detective in a parka and send him to check the alibi. Among the universal truths of detective work is this:
Everybody lies.
Guilty people lie because they have reason not to tell the truth. Innocent people lie because they're embarrassed, or because they think the police won't believe the truth, or to protect a friend, or for any of a thousand other reasons.

Control of the setting

All police stations have at least one interrogation room. It usually has a nickname – the box, the bowl, the shack (all cops seem to have a penchant for nicknames, though I haven't a clue why that's so). Most interrogation rooms look essentially alike: stark, bleak, bare rooms furnished with purely functional institutional-style furniture – a table and a few uncomfortable chairs. There may be other incidental features – a two-way mirror, a videotape recorder, a voice tape recorder – but the heart and soul of an interrogation room is that it looks heartless and soulless.

This is no accident. Interrogation rooms aren't spartan and austere merely because of budgetary constraints. By controlling the setting the detective sets the mood, and the proper mood for an interrogation is isolation and despair. A good interrogation room is designed to eliminate even the slightest hint that the subject has any connection to an outside world. Preferably no windows, no intercom and certainly no telephone. The table is usually set as far from the door as possible, and the subject usually sits at the farthest end of the table, as far from freedom as possible. Even the light switch and thermostat are often controlled by keys, so if a subject is left alone in the room he has no control over the environment.

The more isolated the subject feels, the more vulnerable and exposed he feels; the more uncomfortable he is, the more likely it is that he'll talk. And that's the point.

Control of information

Not only do police detectives isolate the subject physically, they also control his access to information. This includes information about what is going on outside the interrogation room, who else is present in the police station (other witnesses, other suspects, friends or family of the subject) and, most importantly, the nature of the evidence in the case. The reason for this is to deprive the subject of any source of emotional strength and to keep him off balance.

As a rule, only the information that may induce a subject to talk is allowed. There are, of course, a few legal exceptions. For example, the police are required to inform a subject if his lawyer arrived.

The control of information also includes the control of *mis*information. The courts have given police detectives a great deal of latitude with the truth when interrogating a subject. The police can, and do, lie: 'We have a witness who saw you do the shooting.' 'Your picture was taken by a surveillance camera.' 'The lab found blood on your sneakers.' 'We found where you stashed the gun.' Again, the reason for this is obvious. If the subject believes the evidence is going to show he did it, he's more likely to talk.

But lying to a subject is risky. The risk isn't that the courts might overturn any conviction that comes from the lie; the risk is that the subject will discover the lie. If you tell the subject you know where he stashed the gun, but the subject knows he didn't stash it at all but that he sold it to a buddy, then your credibility is shot. He knows you don't know what you're talking about. And he's far more likely to keep silent.

Verbal Evidence Versus Testimony

It's important not to confuse verbal evidence with testimony. Verbal evidence is what an investigator gathers during the investigation. It's what people say. Testimony is what is said under oath. Testimony is a person's sworn word.

An interesting sidenote: The term 'testimony' comes from the Latin word *testis*, the same word that forms the root of 'testicle'. When Roman soldiers swore an oath to tell the truth, they placed their hands not over their hearts but over their testicles. Needless to say, women were neither allowed nor capable of giving testimony.

Control of access to other people

One of the biggest impediments to a successful interrogation is other people, such as additional suspects, friends, family or a lawyer. Especially a lawyer. The reason for this is obvious: An outsider is likely to give the subject good advice, such as, 'Keep quiet.'

As always, there are exceptions. Detectives may allow the subject to catch a glimpse of another suspect, hinting that the other person is in the process of giving a statement incriminating the subject. This may convince the subject that he should try to cut as good a deal for himself as possible. Similarly, the detective may allow the subject to see a minister. Ministers are almost as good at getting people to confess as detectives.

Control of the subject

Above all a good interrogator controls the subject physically. By this I mean the detective controls the subject's body and his ability to meet his bodily needs. The subject's movement is restricted: He sits, while the detectives stand and move around and tower menacingly over him. The subject's speech is controlled: the interrogators can shout, whisper, bellow, murmur, even sing, but the subject is generally only allowed to speak politely or to cry. Anything the subject wants – a cigarette, a cup of coffee, an aspirin, a sandwich – must come from the interrogator. All of the subject's physical needs – to go to the bathroom, to sleep, to eat – are granted or denied by the interrogator at the interrogator's wish. The subject is dependent on and under the control of the interrogator. This fact is impressed on the subject both overtly and subtly (see the box on confessions on page 201).

Once control is established, it can be relaxed – at the discretion of the detective. Small considerations normally taken for granted, such as going to the toilet or smoking a cigarette, suddenly seem like gifts, like acts of kindness and thoughtfulness. For which the subject is very grateful. How can he express his gratitude? By talking, by giving the interrogator the information she wants to hear.

We all know the good cop/bad cop routine. It's become such a universal part of popular culture that young people in Iran and Indonesia know the routine. It's become something of a cliché. Because it works. It worked fifty years ago; it works today. And it will continue to work in the future.

In the end, an interrogation is a poker game between the subject and the interrogator. A good interrogator stacks the deck as best she can. But the subject always has access to a wild card, a joker that, played properly, will bring any interrogation to a crashing halt. The subject can refuse to answer any questions and demand a lawyer.

Sounds simple, doesn't it. Certainly we all know our Miranda rights* by now. We've heard them in the movies and on television often enough. We know we have the right to remain silent and that anything we say can be used against us in court. We know we have the right to a lawyer and that if we can't afford a lawyer one will be appointed to us. For free. We know that if we've committed a crime the very last thing we ought to do is talk about it with the police. We all *know* this.

That's why much of what the detective does in an interrogation – controlling the setting, the information and the access to others – is done in an attempt to keep the subject from playing that wild card. And hey, it usually works. Research shows that nearly 85 percent of people suspected of a crime waive their right to counsel and they answer the questions of the police.

Why? Because the police are clever. They know they must stop questioning a suspect as soon as he demands they stop and requests they fetch him a lawyer. But they also know that unless a suspect makes that demand and requests it in just the right way, they can get around it. A subject who says, 'I think I ought to talk to a lawyer,' is, according to the law, not actually asking for a lawyer. Similarly a subject who says, 'Maybe I shouldn't answer any questions until I talk to a lawyer,' isn't specifically refusing to answer questions or asking for a lawyer. He's just making comments and observations, which can legally be ignored. In fact, they can be used against the subject.

'You want a lawyer? OK, it's up to you. But once the lawyers get involved I can't do anything to help you. Go ahead, get yourself some young public defender right out of law school. But I'm telling you, the DA is looking at First Degree here. Myself, I don't think you meant to kill the guy, but hey, if you don't want to give me your side of the story ...'

This is where good interrogators become diabolically clever. Once the subject is isolated and controlled, a good interrogator offers the subject the thinnest possibility of hope. Salvation. Or at least a way out of the mess he's in. And all the subject needs to do to find this salvation is talk.

It's a cold business, interrogation.

* The form of words used with suspects to explain their rights.

Voluntary Confessions?

 How far can an interrogator legally go to get a confession? Pretty far. A confession, in order to be admissible in court, must be voluntary. But what does 'voluntary' mean? There is no single, clear answer. According to the law (People v. Breidenbach, 875 P.2d 879 Cob. 1994), a court should consider the 'totality of the circumstances' under which the confession was given. This includes:
• whether the suspect was in custody or was free to leave – and was aware of his situation
• whether the suspect had been given the Miranda warnings *prior* to any interrogation, and whether the defendant *understood* and waived his rights
• whether the suspect had the chance to talk to a lawyer or anyone else prior to the interrogation
• whether the suspect was subjected to any overt or implied threat or promise
• the method and/or style used by the interrogator to question the suspect, and the length of time and place of the interrogation
• the suspect's mental and physical condition immediately prior to and during the interrogation, as well as his educational background, employment status and prior experience with law enforcement and the criminal justice system.

That's the law. In practice, it's not quite so clear. Consider the case of Wisconsin v. Konshak. Konshak, a single male parent with two children, was suspected of being involved in a crime. One afternoon while his children were at a park with a neighbor, the police came to Konshak's home and asked him to accompany them to the police station. He agreed. He wrote a note to the neighbor asking her to care for the children until he returned. At the police station Konshak was read his rights, then interrogated – from 3.30pm until nearly 10.30pm. During that time he was not allowed to contact his children; the detectives merely informed him that the kids were being 'cared for.' Konshak later claimed the interrogating officer told him she would try to get him home to his children, but only if he told her what she wanted to hear and confessed. The detective denied this claim. The police later acknowledged Konshak had been previously diagnosed as suffering from depression. Konshak confessed.

The court later declared Konshak's confession had been voluntary. He had, after all, been given his Miranda warnings. According to the detectives in the case, Konshak had not complained of being tired (despite the seven-hour interrogation). He had been offered and had accepted coffee and cigarettes. He was allowed to use the rest room. Nor did the court believe his assertion that the interrogating detective had coerced him with promises that she would try to get him home to his children if he confessed. According to the court, the 'totality of the circumstances' did not support Konshak's argument that his confession was involuntary.

Greg Fallis
Just the Facts Ma'am, 1998

Black Holes

O f all the odd creatures in the astronomical zoo, the 'black hole' is the oddest. To understand it, concentrate on gravity.

Every piece of matter produces a gravitational field. The larger the piece, the larger the field. What's more, the field grows more intense the closer you move to its center. If a large object is squeezed into a smaller volume, its surface is nearer its center and the gravitational pull on that surface is stronger.

Anything on the surface of a large body is in the grip of its gravity, and in order to escape it must move rapidly. If it moves rapidly enough, then even though gravitational pull slows it down continually it can move sufficiently far away from the body so that the gravitational pull, weakened by distance, can never quite slow its motion to zero.

The minimum speed for this is the 'escape velocity'. From the surface of the earth, the escape velocity is 7.0 miles per second. From Jupiter, which is larger, the escape velocity is 37.6 miles per second. From the sun, which is still larger, the escape velocity is 383.4 miles per second.

Imagine all the matter of the sun (which is a ball of hot gas 864,000 miles across) compressed tight together. Imagine it compressed so tightly that its atoms smash and it becomes a ball of atomic nuclei and loose electrons, 30,000 miles across. The sun would then be a 'white dwarf'. Its surface would be nearer its center, the gravitational pull on that surface would be stronger, and escape velocity would now be 2,100 miles per second.

Compress the sun still more to the point where the electrons melt into the nuclei. There would then be nothing left but tiny neutrons, and they will move together till they touch. The sun would then be only 9 miles across, and it would be a 'neutron star'. Escape velocity would be 120,000 miles per second.

Few things material could get away from a neutron star, but light could, of course, since light moves at 186,282 miles per second.

Imagine the sun shrinking past the neutron-star stage, with the neutrons smashing and collapsing. By the time the sun is 3.6 miles across, escape velocity has passed the speed of light, and light can no longer escape. Since nothing can go faster than light, *nothing* can escape.

Into such a shrunken sun anything might fall, but nothing can come out. It would be like an endlessly deep hole in space. Since not even light can come out, it is utterly dark – it is a 'black hole'.

In 1939, J. Robert Oppenheimer first worked out the nature of black holes in the light of the laws of modern physics, and ever since astronomers have wondered if black holes exist in fact as well as in theory.

How would they form? Stars would collapse under their own enormous gravity were it not for the enormous heat they develop, which keeps them expanded. The heat is formed by the fusion of hydrogen nuclei, however, and when the hydrogen is used up the star collapses.

A star like our sun will eventually collapse fairly quietly to a white dwarf. A more massive star will explode before it collapses, losing some of its mass in the process. If the portion that survives the explosion and collapses is more than 1.4 times the mass of the sun, it will surely collapse into a neutron star. If it is more than 3.2. times the mass of the sun, it must collapse into a black hole.

Since there are indeed massive stars, some of them have collapsed by now and formed black holes. But how can we detect one? Black holes are only a few miles across after all, give off no radiation, and are trillions of miles away.

There's one way out. If matter falls into a black hole, it gives off X-rays in the process. If a black hole is collecting a great deal of matter, enough X-rays may be given off for us to detect them.

Suppose two massive stars are circling each other in close proximity. One explodes and collapses into a black hole. The two objects continue to circle each other, but as the second star approaches explosion it expands. As it expands, some of its matter spirals into the black hole, and there is an intense radiation of X-rays as a result.

In 1965, an X-ray source was discovered in the constellation Cygnus and was named 'Cygnus X-1'. Eventually, the source was pinpointed to the near neighborhood of a dim star, HD-226868, which is only dim because it is 10,000 light-years away. Actually, it is a huge star, 30 times the mass of our sun.

That star is one of a pair and the two are circling each other once every 5.6 days. The X-rays are coming from the other star, the companion of HD-226868. That companion is 'Cygnus X-1'. From the motion of HD-226868, it is possible to calculate that 'Cygnus X-1' is 5 to 8 times the mass of our sun.

A star of that mass should be visible if it is an ordinary star, but no telescope can detect any star on the spot where X-rays are emerging. 'Cygnus X-1' must be a collapsed star that is too small to see. Since 'Cygnus X-1' is at least 5 times as massive as our sun, it is too massive to be a white dwarf; too massive, even, to be a neutron star.

It can be nothing other than a black hole; the first to be discovered.

Isaac Asimov
The Roving Mind, 1983

Information Activities

Finding the Tollund Man

1. Reading the archaeologist's account
• Read the description of the discovery, retrieval and preservation of the Tollund man, which is an extract from the book *The Bog People* by P.V. Glob.

2. Picturing the scene
• You're P.V. Glob. You have just arrived at the scene of the discovery and in your notebook you do a quick sketch to remind yourself of exactly what you see. Use the descriptions on the first two pages of the text to mark the exact position of the body and any other details, the direction the head is pointing in, the clothing, anything found with him and so on.

3. An archaeologist's handbook
On the second and following pages of the text, the writer gives us details about how the man was taken out of the peat bog, transported and preserved.
• Use the account to write a set of instructions for a trainee archaeologist on what to do if you find an Iron Age body in a peat bog. You could write it as a list of 'Dos and Don'ts'.

4. A factual account or the telling of a tale?
• In small groups, work on a photocopy of the text. Decide which bits of the text are giving the reader factual information and which bits are more concerned with telling a story or describing the events so as to make them come to life. Cut up the text and stick it down on a large sheet of paper, divided down the middle and headed 'Facts' and 'Story'.

• Choose one bit of 'Fact' and one bit of 'Story' to concentrate on. Look closely at the way in which language is used. Use the questions listed here to help you.

– Are the sentences different in any way (longer or shorter, with more or less clauses)?
– Are the verbs active or passive? (For example, 'a small lump of peat *was removed* from beside his head' is passive, whereas '*I removed* a small lump of peat' would be active.)
– Are the kinds of words chosen different (poetic, scientific, geological, formal, conversational etc.)?

• Choose one sentence to re-write in a style different to Glob's.

For example:
'This disclosed a rope, made of two leather thongs twisted together, which encircled the neck in a noose drawn tight into the throat and then coiled like a snake over the shoulder and down across the back.'

might be re-written as:

I saw a snake-like coil of rope, twisting around his neck, like a constrictor squeezing the life out of him, before slipping over his shoulder and sliding away down his back.

5. An entry in an encyclopaedia
• You have been asked to write 500 words on the Tollund man for a double page spread in a Children's encyclopaedia. Decide:
– which facts are essential
– what would make interesting reading for 9-11 year olds
– how you can break up the text with sub-headings, lists, information in boxes, diagrams, sketches, photographs etc.
– make sure that you keep within the word limit, so that your text will fit the space in the encyclopaedia.

6. A poem about the Tollund man
• Try writing a poem based on your feelings and thoughts, having read the account of how the Tollund man was found. If you have ideas of your own, start to write it in your own way. If not, plunder the text itself for words and phrases that you might be able to use as they stand, or adapt or link together with your own words.

Seamus Heaney wrote a poem about wanting to see the Tollund man and his thoughts about him.
• Read Heaney's poem. Talk about what aspects of the Tollund man he is most interested in. If you only had the chance to read one of these texts, the account or the poem, which would you choose? Why?

The Secret Life of Chips

1. Before reading
• The writer of 'The Secret Life of Chips' says that chips are 'the most addictive finger food known to humanity'. Do you agree? Discuss with your partner.

2. After reading
• Look at the following extracts. For each one explain how William Leith has written in an entertaining and interesting way about a very ordinary item of food, something we usually take for granted.

The only time you want to eat chips is when you're really hungry. Or when you're quite hungry. Or when somebody else is eating chips in the same room.

They (chips) are dry enough to pick up and soft enough to cram by the fistful into your mouth.

According to nutritionist Michel Montignac, chips are a 'bad carbohydrate' ... Chips are starch covered all over with fat; they are like bread which has been buttered on both sides, and around the crusts as well.

So what if they're killing you? Sometimes you just want chips.

This is chip central. On an average day 1,200 tonnes of potatoes arrive at one end of the factory and chips – a mind-boggling amount of chips – emerge, packed and boxed, at the other.

• Look back over the whole article. Find two or three other extracts that you think grab the reader's attention. Explain what techniques the writer used to keep the reader's interest.

3. A guide to informative writing
• With a partner compile your top ten tips for writing an informative newspaper article, using what you have learnt from 'The Secret Life of Chips'.

4. The Secret Life of ...
• Now, using your tips, write your own 'Secret Life of ...' You could use one of these ideas or think of one of your own: frozen peas; fish fingers; takeaway pizza; soy sauce; tomato ketchup; beef burgers; rice; tea; toothpaste; deodorant; zips; ballpoint pens.
You will need to do some research. The Internet is probably the best place to look, for example a search for 'frozen peas' yielded all sorts of sites such as information on a well known brand (with a history of the frozen pea) and instructions on how to use a bag of frozen peas as an ice pack to cure headaches. Searching for a brand name is often a good way to start but make sure your piece doesn't turn into an

advertisement for a particular product. 'Find it' on pages 190-195, has some helpful hints for finding things on the Internet.

Find it

1. Before reading

• The first step is to find your way around the text. Read only the sub-headings and the first and last paragraph of 'Find it'.

• Now look again at the first paragraph. How has the writer tried to get you interested in reading on?

2. KWL chart

A 'KWL' chart helps you record what you already **Know**, what you **Want** to find out and later what you **Learn** through your research.

• Now draw a KWL chart with three columns like the one shown here.

K (Know already)	W (Want to know)	L (Learned)

• Fill in the first column: what do you already know about finding things on the Internet? Now try to think of two or three things for the 'want to know' column. This gives you a purpose for reading that is personal to you. No-one else in the class will have filled in their 'K' and 'W' columns in exactly the same way.

3. Reading

• Now skim read the text looking only for the three things you want to know. How quickly can you find them?

• When you have found what you were looking for fill in the third column of your chart with what you have learned.

• Talk to a partner about what helped you to find the sections of text that were useful.

• Feed back to the whole class making a note of any useful strategies people came up with.

Reading in this way is very helpful, both in exams when you are reading a text in order to answer set questions and when you are reading to answer your own questions. Remember the strategies you discussed as a class and try to use them next time you read an information text.

4. In the computer room
• Think of some information you would like to find on the Internet. This might be something for your English work or another school subject or something else that interests you. You will need to think of something specific to search for.

• Use the information you got from the article to help you to search on the web.

• When you find some sites use the skim reading strategies you discussed as a class to see if the site contains the information you are looking for.

5. Evaluating the text
• In small groups discuss how helpful you found the article 'Find It'. Consider the following.

– The layout of the text – did it help you to find the information you needed quickly? – What particular features of the layout did you like or dislike?
– The tone of the text (for example, formal or informal? Chatty or patronising?) Did you think the tone was appropriate for this kind of text?
– The clarity of the information – how easy was it to follow the instructions given?
– The relevance of the text – did it tell you what you wanted to know? Any suggestions for parts of the text that need to be changed or updated?

6. Writing your own text
'Find it' is partly informing the reader and partly instructing him/her.
• Turn 'Find it' into an instruction sheet for students using the school's computer rooms. Use the features of instruction writing such as numbered steps or bullet points, imperatives (commands), present tense, temporal connectives (first, next, then, finally).

• When you have finished make a list of similarities and differences between 'Find it' and your instruction sheet. What are the advantages and disadvantages of the two styles? Which do you think is more effective? Why?

Interrogation

This is an extract from a book called *Just the Facts Ma'am* which is a 'writer's guide to investigators and investigation techniques'. It is published in the U.S., so the details of law are based on the American legal system.

1. Before reading
• As a class, brainstorm what you know about police interrogating suspects. How do the police try to get information from a suspect? How might the suspect withhold

information? What sort of language and tone might be used by the police? By the suspect?

2. Where did you get your ideas?
• Discuss where you got your ideas about the way police officers and suspects would behave in an interrogation.

Greg Fallis, an experienced private detective writes in 'Interrogation':

> Most of what the general public know about interrogation is based on what they've seen on television or in the movies. That's about like getting your information on cosmetics and makeup from circus clowns.

• Talk about what you think he means by this.

3. The structure of information texts
• Look quickly over the text. What features of information writing has Greg Fallis used (for example, sub-headings, different fonts, bullet points and so on)?

• Try reading just the headings, subheadings, first paragraph and last paragraph. You may be surprised how much you can already tell about the text.

4. Reading an information text
Information texts are not designed to be read from page one to the end like a fiction text. They are structured in a way that helps you find your way around the information so that you can dip into the sections that are relevant to your purpose for reading. When you read an information text you will find it very helpful to be clear about your purpose for reading before you start.
• Make a list of possible purposes for reading 'Interrogation'. For instance a writer might read it to make sure his crime story is accurate.

5. Role-play – everybody lies
This role-play gives you a different kind of purpose for reading 'Interrogation'.

• Work in groups of three. You are going to perform a role-play with two police officers interviewing a suspect. The person being interrogated has been involved in a burglary. They don't have an alibi but they are hoping that their girlfriend or boyfriend will lie for them. The police are convinced that the suspect is the burglar but the only hard evidence they have is that the suspect was seen trying to sell something stolen from the flat. They need the suspect to confess. You are going to use information from 'Interrogation' to make the interrogation as realistic as possible, with the officers using all the methods available within the law.
• Before you start reading, discuss what kind of information you want from the text to help make your scene realistic.

• Take a section of text each, perhaps one person reading from the beginning to the heading 'Control of the setting', the second person reading from that point to the heading 'Control of the subject' and the third person reading to the end of the extract.

• Skim read the text noting down two or three things from your section that will help your group make the role-play realistic. This means letting your eyes 'skim' over the page until you notice a part of the text that would be useful then reading just that part in more detail before moving on. Read your section as quickly as you can, remembering your purpose and only dipping into sections that will be useful for your role-play.

• Now pool the information you have with your group and use it to plan your scene.

• Try writing your role-play as a script or as a scene from a crime novel. This could form part of an original writing assignment.

Black Holes

1. Before reading
• As a class, put together everything you know about black holes. Include vague ideas and guesses, conversational uses (e.g. 'all those ideas just disappeared into a black hole') or ideas from science fiction as well as information you are sure is correct. Make a note of all your ideas on the board or a big piece of paper.

• Now read the text 'Black Holes'.

2. After reading
• Individually, write down three statements you can make about the text.

'I was interested by ...'
'I was puzzled by ...'
'I learnt that ...'

• Share your statements with other people in the class. Can you find someone who was interested by the same thing? Or someone who can explain the thing you were puzzled by?

• Now look back at the ideas your class had about black holes before reading the text. What have you learnt?

3. Why non-fiction can be difficult to read
Non-fiction, particularly information writing, is often harder to read than fiction. On the next page there are some of the reasons given by linguist Katherine Perera.

Features of Non-fiction
Text level:

1. Non-fiction texts are often more formal and more impersonal than fiction texts. They tend to be addressed to strangers, e.g. 'Dear Customer' and are not usually written in the first person ('I').

2. With fiction texts you can often guess what is going to happen next because you are used to the way stories work. Non-fiction texts rely on signpost words such as 'moreover, therefore, on the other hand' which means it is harder to understand the way they are structured.

3. There's more information to take in – more nouns. Non-fiction texts are often about things, not people, so they can be harder to relate to or find interesting.

4. Having no story to follow means there is less to hold the text together.

Sentence level:

5. Non-fiction often uses sentences that interrupt themselves such as 'In the first instance it is odd, and slightly reprehensible, that – just as the nation worries about the alcohol intake of the young – *Big Brother* should be sponsored by Southern Comfort.' (from 'Big Brother' in the Argument section)

6. In non-fiction, sentences often have subordinate clauses that start with words like 'although', 'though', 'whose' and 'whom' for example: 'We also knew, though it was too soon to wonder how or why, that the world would never be the same.' (from 'Beyond Belief' in the Reportage section.) We don't often use clauses like this in speech.

7. Non-fiction texts generally don't use the kinds of techniques that stimulate our imagination such as similes and metaphors.

Word level:

8. The verbs in non-fiction texts are often less interesting and powerful.

9. The verbs in non-fiction are often in the passive form such as 'you will be contacted ...' rather than 'we will contact you'.

About the writer

Isaac Asimov was the son of a Russian-Jewish immigrant who owned a sweet shop in New York. He started writing science fiction when he was a teenager and went on to become a best-selling science fiction author. He also became well known for being able to explain complex scientific information to ordinary people. In 'Black Holes' Asimov writes in an interesting way so that you can enjoy reading the text, even if you are finding the ideas it describes difficult to understand. We are now going to have a look at how he achieves this.

• Draw a chart like the one on page 212.

Features of non-fiction	Example from 'Black Holes'	Features unusual in non-fiction	Example from 'Black Holes'
1. Formal/impersonal		Alliteration	
2. Signpost words		A short sentence for dramatic effect	
3. About things, not people		Addressing the reader directly	
4. No story to follow		Simple sentences	
5. Sentences that interrupt themselves		Interesting verbs	
6. Subordinate clauses beginning 'although', 'whose', 'whom'			
7. Does not stimulate the imagination			
8. Boring verbs			
9. Verbs in the passive form			

• Complete the chart by adding examples from 'Black Holes'. See if you can add to the 'Features unusual for non-fiction' as you look through the text.

• When you have finished, see if you can use your chart to help you to write a paragraph in answer to the question 'How does Isaac Asimov make the difficult concept of black holes interesting for the ordinary reader?'

4. Your own writing
• Look at one of your text books for a factual subject such as science or geography. Find a chapter that explains a difficult concept. Make sure you understand it yourself first – it will be good revision for that subject too!

• Now re-write a section of the text using some of Asimov's techniques to make it a lively and interesting read whilst still getting across the facts and concepts. You could check your chart to remind yourself of the features he uses.

How to Write a Letter

We shy persons need to write a letter now and then, or else we'll dry up and blow away. It's true. And I speak as one who loves to reach for the phone, dial the number, and talk. I say, 'Big Bopper here – what's shakin', babes?' The telephone is to shyness what Hawaii is to February, it's a way out of the woods, *and yet:* a letter is better.

Such a sweet gift – a piece of handmade writing, in an envelope that is not a bill, sitting in our friend's path when she trudges home from a long day spent among wahoos and savages, a day our words will help repair. They don't need to be immortal, just sincere. She can read them twice and again tomorrow: *You're someone I care about, Corinne, and think of often and every time I do you make me smile.*

We need to write, otherwise nobody will know who we are. They will have only a vague impression of us as A Nice Person, because, frankly, we don't shine at conversation, we lack the confidence to thrust our faces forward and say, 'Hi, I'm Heather Hooten; let me tell you about my week. 'Mostly we say 'Uh-huh' and 'Oh, really.' People smile and look over our shoulder, looking for someone else to meet.

So a shy person sits down and writes a letter. To be known by another person – to meet and talk freely on the page – to be close despite distance. To escape from anonymity and be our own sweet selves and express the music of our souls.

Same thing that moves a giant rock star to sing his heart out in front of 123,000 people moves us to take ballpoint in hand and write a few lines to our dear Aunt Eleanor. *We want to be known.* We want her to know that we have fallen in love, that we quit our job, that we're moving to New York, and we want to say a few things that might not get said in casual conversation: *Thank you for what you've meant to me, I am very happy right now.*

The first step in writing letters is to get over the guilt of *not* writing. You don't 'owe' anybody a letter. Letters are a gift. The burning shame you feel when you see unanswered mail makes it harder to pick up a pen and makes for a cheerless letter when you finally do. *I feel bad about not writing, but I've been so busy,* etc. Skip this. Few letters are obligatory, and they are *Thanks for the wonderful gift* and *I am terribly sorry to hear about George's death* and *Yes, you're welcome to stay with us next month,* and not many more than that. Write those promptly if you want to keep your friends. Don't worry about the others, except love letters, of course. When your true love writes, *Dear Light of My Life, Joy of My Heart, O Lovely Pulsating Core of My Sensate Life,* some response is called for.

Some of the best letters are tossed off in a burst of inspiration, so keep your writing stuff in one place where you can sit down for a few minutes and *(Dear Roy, I am in the middle of a book entitled* We Are Still Married *but thought I'd drop you a line. Hi to your sweetie, too.)* dash off a note to a pal. Envelopes, stamps, address book, everything in a drawer so you can write fast when the pen is hot.

A blank white eight-by-eleven sheet can look as big as Montana if the pen's not so hot – try a smaller page and write boldly. Or use a note card with a piece of fine art on the front; if your letter ain't good, at least they get the Matisse. Get a pen that makes a sensuous line, get a comfortable typewriter, a friendly word processor – whichever feels easy to the hand.

Sit for a few minutes with the blank sheet in front of you, and meditate on the person you will write to, let your friend come to mind until you can almost see her or him in the room with you. Remember the last time you saw each other and how your friend looked and what you said and what perhaps was unsaid between you, and when your friend becomes real to you, start to write.

Write the salutation – *Dear* You – and take a deep breath and plunge in. A simple declarative sentence will do, followed by another and another and another. Tell us what you're doing and tell it like you were talking to us. Don't think about grammar, don't think about lit'ry style, don't try to write dramatically, just give us your news. Where did you go, who did you see, what did they say, what do you think?

If you don't know where to begin, start with the present moment: *I'm sitting at the kitchen table on a rainy Saturday morning. Everyone is gone and the house is quiet.* Let your simple description of the present moment lead to something else, let the letter drift gently along.

The toughest letter to crank out is one that is meant to impress, as we all know from writing job applications; if it's hard work to slip off a letter to a friend, maybe you're trying too hard to be terrific. A letter is only a report to someone who already likes you for reasons other than your brilliance. Take it easy.

Don't worry about form. It's not a term paper. When you come to the end of one episode, just start a new paragraph. You can go from a few lines about the sad state of pro football to the fight with your mother to your fond memories of Mexico to your cat's urinary-tract infection to a few thoughts on personal indebtedness and on to the kitchen sink and what's in it. The more you write, the easier it gets, and when you have a True True Friend to write to, a *compadre,* a soul sibling, then it's like driving a car down a country road, you just get behind the keyboard and press on the gas.

Don't tear up the page and start over when you write a bad line – try to write your way out of it. Make mistakes and plunge on. Let the letter cook along and let yourself be bold. Outrage, confusion, love – whatever is in your mind, let it find a way to the page. Writing is a means of discovery, always, and when you come to the end and write *Yours ever* or *Hugs and kisses,* you'll know something you didn't when you wrote *Dear Pal.*

Probably your friend will put your letter away, and it'll be read again a few years from now – and it will improve with age. And forty years from now, your friend's grandkids will dig it out of the attic and read it, a sweet and precious relic of the ancient eighties that gives them a sudden clear glimpse of you and her and the world we old-timers knew. You will then have created an object of art. Your simple lines about where you went, who you saw, what they said, will speak to those children and they will feel in their hearts the humanity of our times.

You can't pick up a phone and call the future and tell them about our times. You have to pick up a piece of paper.

Garrison Keillor
We Are Still Married, 1989

The Last Post

In these days of text messaging, email and answering machines, the traditional love letter seems doomed.

Among the possessions brought home by my mother following my grandmother's death was a pile of love letters that had been preserved in a shortbread biscuit tin. As love letters go they were rather prosaic; details of meals and social encounters figured large. My grandfather was, after all, a man not given to flights of fancy. But the black ink, margined with precision on pieces of thin blue paper was a record of the early days of their courtship. In my mind, my grandparents were transformed. No longer prey to illness and peevishness, they became lovers who drank gin and tonic and flirted shamelessly at tennis parties.

Not many of us will leave a written record of our love affairs. There will be no parcel tied with faded ribbon for my grandchildren to discover. The odd fervent answering machine message and scraps of paper secured to the fridge by jovial magnets is the sum of my romantic correspondence. Passion is seldom transmitted these days on Basildon Bond.

'I look back, and in every one point, every word and gesture, every letter, every silence, you have been entirely perfect to me. I would not change one word, one look,' wrote Robert Browning to Elizabeth Barrett. 'And now listen to me in turn. You have touched me more profoundly than I thought even you could have touched me. My heart was full when you came here today. Henceforward I am yours for everything,' she wrote back to him in one of 574 letters the pair exchanged in a 20-month period.

Love letters probably come more easily to poets than they do to the rest of us, and Browning and Barrett had no other way of communicating. She was prevented from being with the man she loved by a repressive father, and as everyone knows, nothing is more conducive to passion than a parental spanner in the works. Nevertheless, it seems that these days we are unwilling to woo with words. Letter writing takes too darned long. Why bother with stamps and post boxes when at the press of a button you can cut to the chase? Why wrestle with complicated sentence structure when WT RU UP 2? FNCY MTING UP? will achieve the desired objective?

Most of us wouldn't know where to begin if we had to write a love letter. A guide to correct writing by a certain Thomas E. Hill published in 1882 is enough to strike terror in even the most fervent breast. Love letters, he said 'should be written with the utmost regard for perfection. An ungrammatical expression, or word improperly spelled, may seriously interfere with the writer's prospect, by being turned to ridicule.'

The death of the love letter is a real loss. Whereas modern methods of communication are necessarily undeveloped, hasty and lacking in romance, a letter has real substance. The writer has thought about the words, has struggled to express a particular quality of feeling. And letter writing is a sensual exchange. Technology hasn't intervened with its cold logic and standard formats. The paper has been pressed down upon by hand and pen, with handwriting that cannot be replicated. It has been touched and folded into the licked envelope. A written correspondence lends intimacy to a relationship. The gap between posting and receipt heightens longing, delays gratification. Above all, a love letter can be re-read, pondered over, and held in a tin box.

Madeleine Reiss
The Guardian, 24 August 2002

How to ... Use Email

The little ping that announces the arrival of an email is the most important sound in modern life, and takes precedence over any other activity, including sex, birth and death. Email pings are our heartbeat monitor in slow motion, and the fewer of them we hear, the less we think we're alive. Checking for email is the modern equivalent of going to your front gate to see whether the postman's coming, except you do it 47 times an hour.

The Man Who Refuses To Check His Email would be a great modern circus act. Email is so popular because it's much faster than the post and you don't have to lick anything. It's also much better than the phone because you don't have to wait until someone is in and, better still, you don't have to speak to them even if they are.

You can start an email in three ways. There's the traditional 'Dear Sir/Madam' routine, which some people still insist on doing. Then there is 'Hi', which is better than 'Good morning', because by the time people read it it'll probably be midnight. Or you can just continue your subject line – 'Why are you such a' – into the body of the text – 'super person'.

Some people write emails all in lower case with no punctuation. This is intended to give the impression that they're incredibly busy, but in fact makes people think they're the sort of person who drools when they talk.

Junk email comes in three categories: offers of baldness treatment, offers of debt relief and offers of a sexual nature. All work by offering you more of what you haven't got – i.e. hair, money and sex. If you try to remove yourself from a debt-relief mailing list by clicking on the unsubscribe button, it generally links straight through to a baldness site.

Many people think it's vital to acknowledge receipt of an email and always send you a note saying 'Thank you'. The trouble then is that you then have to acknowledge their email with a 'Think nothing of it' reply, and you can end up online for days.

There's one command in email that everyone has looked for but no one has ever found: a retrieve key, which gets the email you instantly regret sending so that the recipient doesn't read it and see you for the evil, two-faced little scrote you really are. This would be an especially useful key after you've made the most common email mistake: returning a message with a bitchy note to the sender, instead of forwarding it to a friend for a laugh.

Guy Browning
The Guardian, 27 July 2002

A Last Letter

Y ou shall receave, deare wief, my last words in these my last lynes. My love I send you, that you may keepe it when I am dead; and my councell, that you may remember it when I am noe more. I would not, with my last Will, present you with sorrowes, deare Besse. Lett them goe to the grave with me, and be buried in the dust. And, seeing it is not the will of God that ever I shall see you in this lief, beare my destruccion gentlie and with a hart like yourself.

First I send you all the thanks my hart cann conceive, or my penn expresse, for your many troubles and cares taken for me, which – though they have not taken effect as you wished – yet my debt is to you never the lesse; but pay it I never shall in this world.

Secondlie, I beseich you, for the love you bare me living, that you doe not hide yourself many dayes, but by your travell seeke to helpe your miserable fortunes, and the right of your poore childe. Your mourning cannot avayle me that am but dust.

You shall understand that my lands were conveyed to my child, bona fide. The wrightings were drawn at Midsummer was twelvemonethes, as divers can wittnesse. My honest cosen Brett can testifie so much, and Dalberie, too, cann remember somewhat therein. And I trust my bloud will quench their malice that desire my slaughter; and that they will not alsoe seeke to kill you and yours with extreame poverty. To what frind to direct thee I knowe not, for all mine have left mee in the true tyme of triall: and I plainly perceive that my death was determyned from the first day. Most sorry I am (as God knoweth) that, being thus surprised with death, I can leave you noe better estate. I meant you all myne office of wynes, or that I could purchase by selling it; half my stuffe, the jewells, but some few, for my boy. But God hath prevented all my determinations; the great God that worketh all in all. If you can live free from want, care for no more; for the rest is but vanity. Love God, and beginne betymes to repose yourself on Him; therein shall you find true and lastinge ritches, and endles comfort. For the rest, when you have travelled and wearied your thoughts on all sorts of worldly cogitations, you shall sit downe by Sorrow in the end. Teach your sonne alsoe to serve and feare God, while he is young;

that the feare of God may grow upp in him. Then will God be a husband unto you, and a father unto him; a husband and a father which can never be taken from you.

Bayly oweth me two hundred pounds and Adrion six hundred pounds. In Gersey, alsoe, I have much owinge me. The arrearages of the wynes will pay my debts. And, howsoever, for my soul's healthe, I beseech you pay all poore men. When I am gonne, no doubt you shalbe sought unto by many, for the world thinks that I was very ritch; but take heed of the pretences of men and of their affections; for they laste but in honest and worthy men. And no greater misery cann befall you in this life then to become a pray, and after to be despised. I speak it (God knowes) not to disswad you from marriage – for that will be best for you – both in respect of God and the world. As for me, I am no more your's, nor you myne. Death hath cutt us asunder; and God hath devided me from the world, and you from me.

Remember your poore childe for his father's sake, that comforted you and loved you in his happiest tymes.

Gett those letters (if it bee possible) which I writt to the Lords, wherein I sued for my lief, but God knoweth that itt was for you and yours that I desired it, but itt is true that I disdaine myself for begging itt. And know itt (deare wief) that your sonne is the childe of a true man, and who, in his own respect, despiseth Death, and all his misshapen and ouglie formes.

I cannot wright much. God knowes howe hardlie I stole this tyme, when all sleep; and it is tyme to separate my thoughts from the world. Begg my dead body, which living was denyed you; and either lay itt att Sherborne if the land continue, or in Exiter church, by my father and mother. I can wright noe more. Tyme and Death call me awaye.

The everlasting, infinite powerfull, and inscrutable God, that Almightie God that is goodnes itself, mercy itself, the true lief and light, keep and yours, and have mercy on me, and teach me to forgeve my persecutors and false accusers; and send us to meete in His glorious kingdome. My true wief, farewell. Blesse my poore boye; pray for me. My true God hold you both in His armes.

Written with the dyeing hand of sometyme thy husband, but now (alasse!) overthrowne.

Your's that was; but nowe not my owne,

W. Ralegh

Sir Walter Ralegh
December 1603

A Prison Letter

A YEAR has gone by since I was rudely roused from my bed and clamped into detention. Sixty-five days in chains, weeks of starvation, months of mental torture and, recently, the rides in a steaming, airless Black Maria to appear before a kangaroo court, dubbed a special military tribunal, where the proceedings leave no doubt that the judgment has been written in advance. And a sentence of death against which there is no appeal is a certainty.

Fearful odds? Hardly. The men who ordain and supervise this show of shame, this tragic charade, are frightened by the word, the power of ideas, the power of the pen; by the demands of social justice and the rights of man. Nor do they have a sense of history. They are so scared of the power of the word, that they do not read. And that is their funeral.

When, after years of writing, I decided to take the word to the streets to mobilize the Ogoni people, and empower them to protest against the devastation of their environment by Shell, and their denigration and dehumanization by Nigeria's military dictators, I had no doubt where it could end. This knowledge has given me strength, courage and cheer – and psychological advantage over my tormentors.

Only yesterday, the Spirit of Ogoni magicked into my cell a lovely poem by Jack Mapanje, the veteran of Kamuzu Banda's jails: four years without charge. I had met Jack in Potsdam in person in 1992 and wondered how he had survived it all.

Writing from Leeds University, his poem urged me to wear the armour of humour. The note at the end was also signed by Chengerai Hove, the award-winning Zimbabwean novelist. How wonderful to know how many fine men, the best brains, care for one's distress.

Ultimately the fault lies at the door of the British government. It is the British government which supplies arms and credit to the military dictators of Nigeria, knowing full well that all such arms will only be used against innocent, unarmed citizens.

It is the British government which makes noises about democracy in Nigeria and Africa but supports military dictators to the hilt. It is the British government which supports the rape and devastation of the environment by a valued, tax-paying, labour-employing organisation like Shell. I lay my travails, the destruction of the Ogoni and other peoples in the Niger Delta, at the door of the British government.

Ultimately, the decision is for the British people, the electorate, to stop this grand deceit, this double standard, which has lengthened the African nightmare and denigrates humanity.

Whether I live or die is immaterial. It is enough to know that there are people who commit time, money and energy to fight this one evil among so many others predominating worldwide. If they do not succeed today, they will succeed tomorrow. We must keep on striving to make the world a better place for all of mankind – each one contributing his bit, in his or her own way.

I salute you all.

Ken Saro-Wiwa, Military Hospital, Port Harcourt, Nigeria

Ken Saro-Wiwa
Written in prison, published in *The Mail & Guardian* (South Africa), May 1995.

A Sister to a Brother

I trust my dearest Love, that this is the last letter we shall have to send to you further than Kendal, for at Kendal we will meet you with one – God be thanked we are all well. Mary looks better today, and seems pretty strong and dear Sara for these two days has had no tickling cough and is in other respects without cause of complaint. But we have been, and the whole vale – since Monday afternoon in the greatest consternation. If you did not leave before Saturday you must have heard the cause of it from Coleridge for I have recounted to him the melancholy history. George Green and his wife, our Sally's Father and Mother, went to Langdale on Saturday to a Sale, the morning was very cold and about noon it began to snow, though not heavily but enough to cover the ground. They left Langdale between 5 and 6 o'clock in the evening and made their way right up the Fells, intending to drop down just above their own cottage, in Easedale – (Blenkrigg Gill under Miles Holmes's Intack). They came to the highest ridge of the hill that can be seen from Langdale in good time, for they were seen there by some people in Langdale: but alas! they never reached home. They were probably bewildered by a mist before daylight was gone, and may have either fallen down a precipice or perished with cold – six children had been left in the house, all younger than Sally, and the youngest an infant at the breast. Poor things they sate up till 11 o'clock on Saturday night, expecting their parents, and then went to bed, satisfied that they had stopped all night in Langdale on account of the bad weather; the next day they felt no alarm; but stayed in the house quietly and saw none of the neighbours, therefore it was not known that their Father and Mother had not come back till Monday noon, when that pretty little Girl, the eldest of the household (whom you will remember, having admired the exquisite simplicity and beauty of her Figure one day when you were walking with Mary in Easedale) – this Girl went to George Rowlandson's to borrow a cloak. They asked why, and she told them she was going to lait their folk who were not come home. George Rowlandson immediately concluded that they were lost and many men went out to search upon the Fells. Yesterday between 50 and 60 were out, and to-day almost as many, but all in vain. It is very unfortunate that there should be so much snow on the Fells. Mary and I have been up at the house this morning, two of the elder daughters are come home, and all wait with trembling and fear, yet with most earnest wishes, the time when the poor creatures may be brought home and carried to their graves. It is a heart-rending sight – so many little, *little* creatures. The Infant was sleeping in the cradle, a delicate creature the image of Sara Coleridge. Poor Sally is in great distress. We have told her that we will keep her till we can find a nice place for her, and in the mean time instruct her in reading, sewing etc. We hope she will continue to be a good girl.

We do not intend her to have anything to do with the children after our new servant comes. We have hired little Mary, the young woman who lived at Mrs Havill's and who has been so long desirous to come to us. This very moment three, nay four of the poor orphans (for Sally was with them) have left the room. The three had been at Mrs North's who has sent them home with a basket of provisions, and will visit them herself with clothes for all the younger, being very ragged. That sweet Girl looks so interesting, has such an intelligent, yet so innocent a countenance that she would win any heart. She is a far nicer Girl than Sally and one that we could not but have more pleasure from; but poor Sally has fallen to us, and we cannot cast her off for her Sister; but we hope that Mrs North will take *her,* or a least send her to school.

Old Molly's legs are much swoln and she grows daily weaker. I hope her sufferings will soon be at an end. She talks with chearfulness of dying except when she turns to poor John's desolate condition. I really think I have nothing more to say for I have not heart to talk of our own little concerns, all being well with us. We have been strangely unsettled for these three days. Pray bring Sally a new Testament – you can buy it at Kendal. The children are at School. I hope you will think Thomas looks better than when you went away – he is very healthy.

Remember me affectionately to Mr de Quincey and tell him that we hope to hear that he intends coming into the North this summer. We had a letter from Coleridge on Monday, written just after you set off for Dunmow. We were much disappointed that there was no letter from you. We hope for one from Dunmow tonight.

God bless thee my dearest William and grant that we may see thee again in good health and soon – thine evermore.

Dorothy Wordsworth

I open my letter to tell you that we are at ease – the poor lost creatures are found. John Fisher has called at the window to tell us – he says they had rolled a great way – and were found just above Benson's. Where that is I cannot tell; but it must have been low down. She was near a wall – and he lying a little above her.

Dorothy Wordsworth
To William Wordsworth
Grasmere, Wednesday March 23 1808

Mira's Letters Home

18 October 1960

Respected Ma,

I realize I let two weeks pass before writing you. Hope you are not too worried. I sent a post-card to baba *[Mira's father]* from London which you must have received. It took me a while to get settled. I already started my classes and I am finding out that life here is going to be quite busy. Imagine my spending all my day and even evenings doing either studies or housework. I shop twice a week, but I may have to do it only once. Fortunately the fridge is big enough. Yes, three of us girls share an apartment, and so far I like my house-mates. They are both American and around my age ... The university campus is just beautiful. I enjoy walking everyday from building to building and hear students chat or birds make funny noises. People here are very friendly and open. They even smile before they know you! I have already been invited by two students (both girls) and I enjoyed meeting their parents. But, ma, food here is really tasteless. I miss your cooking and grandma's mango pickle and Choto mashi's special spinach. Oh, well, I guess I shall get used to it all. I cook for myself only over the week-ends. There is hardly any time during the week ... Classes have been very interesting so far and I am getting used to the American system bit by bit. I like the way the professors treat the students ... There is so much I could tell you but I must make it brief and perhaps write another letter next week. Please do not worry about me. I am taking care of myself and I feel very well. The cool air of autumn seems to suit me well, after the heat in Calcutta. Please show this to baba and tell him that I would write him separately telling him all about my courses and the professors, etc., later ... Please, please do not worry if my letters take a while to arrive. Remember, I am a big girl now and if I could travel around half of the world to be here I can also take care of myself.

How is your health, and baba's? Please give my respect to grandma, mashimas and pishimas. How is Uma? I think of you all and wonder how you all are. Ma, the life here is so different that sometimes I have to talk to myself in Bengali to think about Calcutta and you all. I miss you a lot. But, time seems to fly very quickly here. With respect and love,

Yours,
Miru

10 December 1960

My affectionate Miru,

You must have received all my letters by now. We have had only three letters from you in the last month and a half. I know you are busy, but I worry if I do not hear from you. Have you received the parcel I sent by sea-mail? I put some pickles and other 'goodies' together and requested your uncle next door to mail it for me. I did not want to let your baba know about this. You know how much fuss he makes over food parcels. He always gives me big lectures that food in America is a thousand times better and more nutritious. As if that is enough! ... Uma's wedding date is now firmed up and it would be some time in February. Please plan to be here and do not tell your father that I suggested it. Everyone would be very upset if you miss this first wedding of the family. The future groom seems like a good boy and Uma and he met a couple of times when the two families went to the movies together. I think she liked him ... Your Ghosh mashima asked me the other day if I was expecting an American son-in-law. Imagine her guts! I retorted, 'Of course not. Our Miru is as she was before and she would not do such a thing. She went to America to study, not to catch a husband.' ... Have you made some friends? How do you spend your week-ends and evenings? Surely, you do not study all the time.

I have to end this letter and get back to the invitation lists. Mejo mashi and I have been digging out all the names of relatives to make a good list and not to leave out anyone. Most of our shoppings is complete except the jewelry. We do not want to pick them up until just before the wedding. It's not safe. Oh, Mira, you should have seen the diamond and ruby necklace! It is just beautiful! Write soon and remember the wedding date.

Your mother

This is the letter which Mira wished she could write to her mother in reply:

My dear ma,

With every letter from you I have an increasing feeling of a distance between us. I cannot explain it even to myself. On the one hand, I know why you are worried about my health, about my life and about my safety. Yet, I thought I had gone ten thousand miles to get away from this protective love which makes me feel suffocated sometimes. It breaks my heart to tell you this and I can never bring myself to say so. What a strange dilemma! I read between the lines of your letters and sometimes I feel like screaming with frustration and anger. What are you fantasizing about my life here? In case I fall in love with an American or whoever, be sure I will do what I wish to do. If you think that you can dictate my life from such a distance, you are under some illusions. But, you know that it's not so easy for me to act the way I would like to. I do not know why. Even when some young men ask me out, your face and the rest (aunts, neighbours, all) appear in front of my eyes. What is this inner restriction? I cannot talk about it to anyone here and I cannot talk about it, least of all, with you. It's not just being free to mix with American men, in different things I feel a tug from behind. I wish I had some power to tear away from this tug and pull ... I also wish I could do everything a good daughter is supposed to do, the way you brought me up. Believe me, it would be so very satisfying to be your good daughter who does not tarnish the name of the family or the wish of her parents, especially her mother. While I am in this interminable conflict, I seem to have no choice but to remain in this tension and confusion. I shall continue to try to please you as much as I can until some part of me gives way. I like my life here and yet I miss India, the family and most of all *you* so intensely sometimes. Sometimes, I feel I am walking in my sleep and this is a big dream after all. Is it really possible for me to close my eyes and finish my studies and be back exactly the way I came and everything would be just fine for ever. Oh, God, I wish I had some idea how to deal with these problems ... I must sleep; there is a 8.30 class tomorrow. I am so tired.

Your loving and confused daughter

This is the letter Mira really wrote:

January 1961

Respected Ma,

It was nice to hear from you and get all the news. I am happy to know that Uma's wedding date is firmed. February is a difficult month for me. The classes would be in full session and it would be a loss of nearly three to four weeks of my work here. This break will really be hard for me and I am not so sure I really want to be there only for a wedding between two people who do not even know each other well. No, don't worry. I am not talking about my choosing my own husband or anything like that. But, it seems strange to me when I tell my American friends the way marriages take place in our families. I seem to feel a bit embarrassed about it all. Perhaps I am not making myself very clear. There are things I feel more and more strange about our customs and it's no point telling you all this. I know you will begin to see mountains out of mole hills. Perhaps, baba and I could talk about these things a bit better. At any rate, I shall try.

Thanks so much for sending the food parcel. No, I won't tell baba a word. I am waiting eagerly for it. The pickles! Even the idea makes my mouth water! By the way, please tell Ghosh mashima that Miru has not changed that much yet. And, suppose I do marry an American, is it really the end of the world, ma? I thought you liked fair-skinned tall men! (Well, I am joking.) Is Uma really happy about this match? I guess I should not say things like this at this point. Forgive me. This letter has been a bit confused and please don't read between lines now. I must stop and shall write a longer one perhaps, this week-end. I must rush. *Pranam* to you and baba and greetings to all.

Your Miru

A week later:

January 1961

Ma,

This is a quick note to tell you that I am making plans to come in February. If I can finish some of my term-ending papers beforehand I may be able to come without feeling too guilty. It would be wonderful to see you all again. It would be good for me to be back in the family and taste all the good cookings of a wedding. Do you think I should bring a separate gift for Uma from here? Something she might like? Do ask her and let me know. I am terribly busy, but well. I take a glass of milk every night and feel wonderful every morning! The parcel is not here yet. How are you and baba? I wrote him a long letter giving all the details of our university and life here. Has he received it yet? Please take care of yourself and don't go out everyday on errands. How is everyone? My *pranam* and love,

Miru

A year later:

4 January 1962

My respected ma and baba,

I am writing this very important letter to ask your permission to marry John – John Cohn whom I met nearly 6 months ago. John is two years senior to me and already has a part-position in his department which is biology. He comes from a good family; his father is a professor of biochemistry and he has one sister who is in music school. I met his family over the last Christmas and we got along very well. John is very interested in India and would like to come and visit you all as soon as the summer vacation begins. But I would like to come as his wife. It would be easier. We talked and discussed the matter over many hours, and this seems like the best way to do it. Please send your blessings. We would have a civil marriage and, perhaps, a Hindu one when we come, if you so wish. I know how disappointed ma would be otherwise ... Please ma, try to understand that time has changed and perhaps I have changed too. I love John and it is important that I marry him and it would be easier and more convenient for both of us to continue our studies when we are married. It's also less expensive to share the same living space ... I am sorry that I had to break the news like this. I did not know how to do it any other way. Both of you gave me enough independence to allow me to think for myself for my life and this is a very important decision for me to make. Ma, I realize this is going to shock you. But, as I said, you do try to understand and I know that neither you nor baba would stand in the way of my happiness. Please write soon and let me know if you want to know anything more about John ... We do not plan to get married until April or May just before the summer holidays.

Please accept my *pranam* and love.

Yours,
Miru

This was the reply from her mother after a week:

Mira,

Both your father and I are astounded by your letter. So Ghosh mashima was not so wrong after all! How can you do such a thing to us? We suggest that you come home as soon as you can and we will discuss the matter face to face. Your baba is sending you enough money for your trip. If marriage is what is in your mind, I don't see any point of your remaining in America. We could arrange a marriage for you here in no time. It's pity that all the effort and expenses for your trip abroad came to this. At any rate, I always told your baba that a woman's higher education comes to little. But, who listens to me? Now, he could learn some lessons. Please drop a line as soon as you get the money and get your air-ticket.

Affectionately yours,

ma

My respected parents,

John and I got married last week-end and used the money you sent me for a small reception we gave. I felt good that something arrived from my family for this important occasion of my life. I have to get married without your verbal blessings, but I considered the token money as your blessings. We still hope to visit you in summer and I would like to know if you so wish. My address will change from next week and I give it below. Hope your health is good and everyone in the house is fine.

With *pranam,*

Miru

This is the letter which Mira wished she had written:

Dear baba and ma,

I am even more astounded by your lack of understanding. I know you have feelings and hopes for me. How can you not be flexible enough to realize that I am not in your generation? You show no sympathy for my inner struggle before I decided to take this step. Perhaps, in your time it was not important to love a man or woman to marry. You loved later and loved slowly (or did not love, perhaps). I am in America, not India, and I am influenced by the atmosphere here. I take the responsibility of my marriage. If I make a mistake (I know it is always possible), at least *I* make it, not you. Marriage now-a-days does not have to be for ever. I love John and I am happy with him. If I have occasional doubts, these are my own. The security I lost when I made the step to come here is not going to offer me the security you had to protect your marriage. There are many others around you. I am alone here, so is John and many others. Unfortunately this is true and this situation makes us bold and perhaps, even, daring. I don't believe I could ever make you see this. Sometimes, I feel as if I am split in the middle. Please let me live the other half, at least now. My life and learning here go well with this step. I know many other Indian girls would not do this. Their love and concern for their parents and families would be paramount and they will sacrifice their desire to live a new life, to experiment perhaps. Even if it turns out to be nothing but only an experiment, let me go through it myself. I am a big girl now ... Oh, God, I wish I could be freer to be happy right now. Yet the same nagging tag continues. Maybe, I should stay here for ever to erase this nagging pull from behind. Perhaps, John can help me do so. But he is so eager to go to India. I suppose I am alone after all, in this. Please try to understand the struggle within me and be with me. I need you for myself.

Love,

Your daughter

Twenty years later Mira's own daughter wrote to Mira:

June 1981

Dear Mummy,

This last trip to India with you has brought home to me a few hard facts – facts that I wanted to avoid seeing for some time. As you well know, you and I have had a few arguments and several days of tensions during the trip. As I approach my seventeenth year I suddenly ask myself where do I belong. I know this is the usual teen-age identity crisis, etc., etc. You came to this country when you were slightly older than I am now and married my father and admired the American lifestyle and tried to be an American as much as you could. I am born of you who is Indian and my father who is American. Of course, I am American. Except for a few trips to India I have little to do with India outwardly. But, I feel how much you would like me to become Indian sometimes. I cannot explain it with examples. But I feel it in my bones. The India that you never quite shook off your system comes back to you now and you want to see your daughter live it, at least partly.

Yes, mummy I know I am wrapped up in many superficial things, things my friends and peers indulge in and I can understand your need to protect me. But, I am part of them and in order for me to be accepted by my friends sometimes I do things which do not always please me either. I need their approval and I want to be like them sometimes. But, your good intentions to teach me those good Indian things then clash. Although I dislike the superficiality of my friends, I cannot move back to your life-style just because it is better (for you) or more ancient or deep. Let me live the life I am

231

surrounded by and reject and suffer as I wish and as many of my friends are going through ... While I understand your point, I must admit sometimes I really do not know how to communicate to you what I really feel. Words seem to fail on both sides. That's why I am writing this letter. Perhaps it will be a bit easier. Dad does not seem to be the problem in this regard. When I argue with him or reject something he wants me to do, I do not feel such ambivalence as I do when the same thing happens with you. Isn't it strange! Perhaps, I am a bit Indian under my skin after all. Although every time I visit India after the first two weeks of love and food, I begin to weary of all the slow sloth and all the rest. I ache to come back to my superficial friends with whom I do not always need to use even language. It's the communication that I feel is at stake between you and me and between India and me. Mummy, you did not have to grow up in America; you grew up in India and could keep a lot of nostalgia and good memories when you decided to reject India. When you criticize me, you never think that we were born in two different worlds and that makes a big difference between us even though I am your flesh and blood as you often point out, rightly.

My dearest mother, I cannot be protected by you. Forgive me if I remind you of something you related to me many times. You could not be protected by my grandparents (your parents) when you decided to embrace this culture along with my father. Nor can you protect me despite the fact that we are not separated by physical distance. Perhaps, we are separated by something else and I suspect, that is India.

I have never written a letter like this before in my short life. I feel good about writing this and I would like to hear what you have to say. Ma, perhaps, you and I still can be friends in this way that you and your mother could not be. Let's try. I love you.

Yours,

Rita

from *Between Ourselves, Letters between Mothers and Daughters,* 1994

Letters Activities

How to Write a Letter

1. Before reading – the title
• Talk about the title 'How to Write a Letter'. What does it lead you to expect the piece will be about?

2. Advice on letter writing
• In pairs, write your own list of advice to letter writers, then compare your list with that of another pair.

• Now read Garrison Keillor's piece.

3. Keillor's advice
• Go through the text carefully, finding at least two different things that Keillor says under each of the headings listed here.

– Why letters need to be written
– Why letters are better than telephone calls or conversations
– Getting ready to write
– Getting going
– What to do once you're writing

• Talk about anything which surprises you or which contradicts what you have been told in the past about writing letters. For example, you might think it would be better to plan out what you want to write before you begin.

You might also find it interesting to read 'The Last Post' by Madeleine Reiss and 'How to ... Use Email' by Guy Browning. These articles explore the rise of email culture and the 'death' of the letter.

4. Writing a letter of your own
Garrison Keillor suggests that it can be exciting to find even the most ordinary letter written sometime in the past.
• What letter would you like to find from the past and why? For instance, would you be interested to read a letter from an ordinary soldier in the trenches of the First World War to his wife? Or perhaps you'd like to read a letter from a servant of Anne Boleyn to her friend, describing events at the court of Henry VIII? Or maybe you'd

prefer to read a letter from someone who was your age in the 1960s describing their everyday life?

• Follow Keillor's instructions yourself and write a letter which captures something about your everyday life. You could begin in the way he suggests by writing about what you are doing at this very moment and just see what follows! For example:

I'm sitting at my desk at the back of the English classroom on a miserable Tuesday afternoon. Everyone is busy writing letters so it is quiet except for the small sounds of pens scraping over paper and people scratching their heads ...

Some of the things you might go on to write about include:
– your normal school day routine
– what you wish would happen
– your hopes for the future
– the place where you live
– your friends and what you like to do on the weekend.

The Last Post

1. The title
• Talk briefly about what this title might mean.

• Read the article and talk about your first response to it.

In his article 'How to Write a Letter' (pages 213-215) Garrison Keillor writes about the advantages of a letter over a phone call. Madeleine Reiss is more concerned that the rise of emails and text messages are making letter writing a dying art.
• Identify three reasons she identifies for people no longer writing letters. Now choose three quotations which show why she thinks this is something to regret. Do you agree with what she says? Is there something special about the letter as a form?

• What do you think Madeleine Reiss would make of the following attitude?

For many, email has given the opportunity to keep in touch with dozens of far-flung, otherwise unreachable acquaintances on a daily basis. 'Email is no less personal than using the telephone or writing letters,' argues new media strategist, James Green. 'The Internet actually reduces barriers that exist with other forms of communication. Writing a letter is seen by many as a time consuming hassle, whereas an email can be dispatched as quickly as you can type the message and email actually allows you far more freedom of expression in some senses than the telephone.'

Precious Williams, *The Independent on Sunday*

---

2. A love email?

In 'The Last Post' Madeleine Reiss suggests that, unlike the poets Elizabeth Barrett Browning and Robert Browning who exchanged nearly 600 letters in just 20 months, 'Most of us wouldn't know where to begin if we had to write a love letter'.

• Talk about what would have been lost or gained if instead of writing a letter these people had phoned or emailed each other. You should think about the difference it would have made to the following:

– what they said
– how they said it
– their relationship with each other.

• Do you think it is important that we can read the collected letters of writers, politicians, actors and so on? If so, why? What about ordinary people? What, if anything, do you think would have been lost by not having this correspondence?

3. Your own writing

• Think back to an email or phone conversation you have had recently and re-write it as a letter.

• Discuss what difference it makes to what you say and how you say it.

How to ... Use Email

1. Before reading – the etiquette of emailing

Friends, family and businesses all take email for granted as a way of keeping in touch. What advice would you give someone who has never used email before? Would it be the same as for writing a letter?

• Write a short set of instructions on how to use email. You should comment on:
– how to address the person you are writing to
– possible problems and issues, for instance emailing when you are angry with someone, times when it is not appropriate to email and so on
– the differences between writing an email and writing a letter.

You could also look at 'How to Write a Letter' on pages 213-215. What do you think Garrison Keillor would say about email? Does email fulfil the same role as a letter?

2. Serious or silly?

• Read the article 'How to ... Use Email' and pull out quotations which you think:
– show the writer offering serious advice or a sensible comment about email
– show the writer being silly
– could be taken as either serious or silly.

• Talk about your discoveries. How does Guy Browning manage to make serious comments and offer sensible information in an amusing way?

• Go back to your own email instructions from Activity 1: 'Before reading – the etiquette of emailing' and redraft them using some of Browning's techniques.

Letters Activities

3. Letters v. emails

• Which do you prefer to write – an email, letter or text message? Or do you prefer to speak to someone on the telephone? Which do you prefer to receive? Are there times when it would be more appropriate to use email, the phone or write a letter?

• In pairs, draw up a list, then share your thoughts as a class. You could organise your ideas in a grid like the one shown here.

	Email	Letter	Telephone call
Advantages			
Disadvantages			
When it would be appropriate			
When it would not be appropriate			

• If you haven't read them already, read 'How to Write a Letter' by Garrison Keillor (pages 213-215) and 'The Last Post' by Madeleine Reiss (page 216).

• Imagine a conversation between Garrison Keillor, Guy Browning and Madeleine Reiss in which they debate the advantages and disadvantages of letters and emails.

A Last Letter and A Prison Letter

1. The end of the letters

The final paragraphs of two letters written almost four hundred years apart are printed on page 237.
• Read both paragraphs and for each one think about the following:
– who it seems to be written to
– he sort of letter it is
– the purpose of the letter
– the type of person who wrote it
– what the rest of the letter might be about.

• Share your ideas and talk about any similarities you notice about the two paragraphs, for example style, tone, subject and so on.

236

The everlasting, infinite, powerfull, and inscrutable God, that Almightie God that is goodnes itself, the true lief and light, keep and yours, and have mercy on me, and teach me to forgeve my persecutors and false accusers; and send us to meete in His glorious kingdome. My true wief, farewell. Blesse my poore boye; pray for me. My true God hold you both in His armes.
Written with the dyeing hand of sometyme thy husband, but now (alasse!) overthrowne.
Your's that was; but now not my owne.

Whether I live or die is immaterial. It is enough to know that there are people who commit time, money and energy to fight this one evil among so many others predominating worldwide. If they do not succeed today, they will succeed tomorrow. We must keep on striving to make the world a better place for all of mankind – each one contributing his bit, in his or her own way.
I salute you all.

2. Looking for clues about the context
• Read 'A Last Letter' and 'A Prison Letter' aloud.

• Work in small groups. For each one ask yourselves these questions, to see how much you can discover about the context of these letters just by reading closely and finding clues in the text.

- Who?
- What?
- When?
- Where?
- Why?

• Share your findings as a whole group, then listen to the brief account of the stories behind the two letters (pages 239-40).

3. 'A Last Letter' – charting Ralegh's concerns
Ralegh's letter is a man's last testament, written in dangerous times, and wanting to express the last things he will ever be able to say to his wife. Perhaps it is also his last statement, for himself, about feelings and ideas he holds dear.

• Make a chart for yourself and find examples from the letter of the writer showing each of the concerns listed.

- Practical arrangements
- Feelings about his death
- Feelings about his family
- Concern about his family's future
- Thoughts about God
- Thoughts about his enemies

• What thoughts do you have about what concerns him most? Are you surprised by the emphasis he gives to any of them? What do his concerns tell you about life for a man like him in those times?

4. Charting the emotional temperature of the letter

• Give each of the paragraphs a number. For each paragraph, choose which of these descriptions seems to best match the emotional state of the writer.

Matter of fact
Full of grief
Cracking up
Concerned
Afraid
Angry
Regretful
Calm
Purposeful
Self-pitying
Confessional

5. Who is the letter for?

You could say that the letter was written to Ralegh's wife Elizabeth. But you could also make a case for saying that it was written for Ralegh himself, that it was written to God, that it was written to be seen by his jailors and those close to the King, to make them more sympathetic to him, or even that it was written to let people in the future know what had happened to him.

• Go back to the letter, looking for evidence of the different possible audiences for the letter. Decide which you think is most important, then share your conclusions with another group, or with the class as a whole.

6. Letters, responses and replies

• Write one of these letters, responses or replies to Sir Walter Ralegh's letter.

– Elizabeth (or her son) writes a letter to the King, begging for a reprieve for Ralegh.
– The jailor reads the letter before passing it on to Elizabeth. He writes a report for the King on the state of mind of the prisoner.
– The King, having seen the letter, discusses with a trusted companion what he should do about Ralegh.
– On 11 December, after his reprieve, Ralegh writes another letter to Elizabeth and his son.

7. 'A Prison Letter' from Ken Saro-Wiwa

• Read the letter from Ken Saro-Wiwa again and talk about your response to this letter, the circumstances in which it was written and the eventual death of the writer (see page 240).

Ralegh's last letter was written to his wife. Ken Saro-Wiwa's letter is not addressed to any one person in particular.

• Who do you think it is written for and why do you think he wrote it? Read the suggestions listed below and add any more you can think of.

---

1. To let the world know what has happened to him.
2. To continue the fight/argument.
3. To thank his supporters.
4. To accuse the British Government of supporting Shell.
5. To let people in the future know what he was trying to do and what has happened to him.
6. To let his enemies know he has not been defeated, even if he has been imprisoned.

• Look through the letter and choose a short quotation to illustrate each of the reasons you think Ken Saro-Wiwa had for writing the letter.

• In pairs choose the three reasons you think would have been of most importance to Ken Saro-Wiwa. Be prepared to explain your choices in whole class feedback.

Background information on Sir Walter Ralegh and Ken Saro-Wiwa

---

The story of Sir Walter Ralegh

Ralegh lived from 1554-1618. He was a poet, historian, colonialist, soldier and courtier. He became the favourite of Queen Elizabeth I and was rewarded with estates in Ireland and England, positions of power and importance and a knighthood. He secretly married Elizabeth Throckmorton, one of the Queen's attendants. When the marriage became public in 1592 because of the birth of their son, Ralegh was briefly imprisoned in the Tower of London. In 1595 he led an expedition up the Orinoco and in 1596 took part in a raid on Cadiz with the Earl of Essex. As the Queen's favourite Ralegh had not been popular and he gained many enemies who accused him of pride and extravagance.

When James I came to the throne in 1603, Ralegh fell out of favour and was arrested on suspicion of plotting to dethrone the king. He was sentenced to be executed on 11 December. He was reprieved on 10 December, after having written this letter of farewell to his wife. He lived imprisoned in the Tower with his wife until 1616 when he was released to undertake an expedition to the Orinoco in search of gold. The expedition failed and on his return he was arrested again and finally executed in 1618.

The story of Ken Saro-Wiwa

Ken Saro-Wiwa was the eldest son of a leader of the Ogoni tribe.

In 1958, Shell discovered oil in Ogoniland. Shell's drilling operations in Ogoniland divided Ogoni communities and damaged Ogoni forests and water supplies. Despite this they were supported in their operations by the Nigerian government.

Until the events which led to his death Saro-Wiwa was best known as a Nobel Prize winning writer. However, ever since his university days he had used writing to protest about the environmental and economic state of the Ogoni. By 1989, he had realized that it wasn't enough to protest about the Nigerian government and Shell Oil as an individual. He had to do something on a much bigger scale. With other Ogoni leaders he formed MOSOP (Movement for the Survival of the Ogoni People), a movement which protested at a national and international level.

These protests led to his arrest on several occasions during 1993 and 1994. In May 1994, Ken Saro-Wiwa and eight others were arrested and charged with the murder of four Ogoni chiefs who supported the government, though this was never proved to the satisfaction of outside observers. Throughout his imprisonment many people wrote letters to newspapers protesting his innocence and drawing attention to the conditions under which he was tried. Despite such international outrage, Ken Saro-Wiwa was executed on November 10, 1995.

This is what Thilo Bode, Executive Director of Greenpeace International said about his execution: 'Ken Saro-Wiwa was hanged today for speaking out against the environmental damage to the Niger Delta caused by Shell Oil through its 37 years of drilling in the region. Ken Saro Wiwa was campaigning for what Greenpeace considers the most basic of human rights: the right for clean air, land and water. His only crime was his success in bringing his cause to international attention.'

8. Writing letters, taking action

As Ken Saro-Wiwa knew, letters can be a powerful way both of informing people and of bringing about change. Amnesty International, the organisation which campaigns against human rights abuses across the globe knows just what a powerful weapon a letter can be. This is what they say on their website:

An appeal from you to the authorities can help the victims of human rights violations whose stories are told here. You can help free a prisoner of conscience or stop torture. You can bring liberty to a victim of 'disappearance'. You may prevent an execution. Every appeal counts.

Find out what has happened to the subjects of previous Worldwide Appeals. Many have been released; many have had their sentences commuted or quashed; many of those who had 'disappeared' have been freed. Many more still need your help.

Amnesty International has put together a letter writing guide to help people voice their concerns about these human rights violations. These are reproduced here.

Letter writing guide

There are a few simple rules:

1. Always be polite. This rule is essential and invariable. Your aim is to help a prisoner, not to relieve your own feelings. Governments don't respond to abusive or condemnatory letters (however well deserved).
2. Always write your letters on the basis that the government concerned is open to reason and discussion.
3. It is important where possible to stress a country's reputation for moderation and justice, to show respect for its constitution and judicial procedures, and to demonstrate an understanding of current difficulties. This will give more scope to point out ways in which the human rights situation can be improved.
4. Follow strictly the instructions given by Amnesty International in the case in question. For instance if the World Wide Appeal asks you to appeal for medical treatment for a prisoner, make sure that you request this, and not a speedy trial or release which might be appropriate in another case.
5. Never use political jargon. Don't give the impression that you are writing because you are ideologically or politically opposed to the government in question. It is far more effective to stress the fact that your concern for human rights is not politically based in any way, but in keeping with basic principles of international law.
6. If appropriate, please explain who you are and what you do. This indicates that the letter is genuine, and also shows that people from varying walks of life are following events in the country concerned.
7. If you have any special interest or link with the country, it is a good idea to mention this in your letter. For instance, you may have visited it or studied its history.

BE BRIEF. A simple, one-line letter is adequate and is certainly better than no letter at all. A good rule is not to write more than one page (i.e. one side).

You can read sample letters by visiting the following section of the website: http://www.amnesty.org/actnow/wwa/letguide.htm#sample.

• Follow the guidelines set down by Amnesty International to write the letter you would have sent to protest about Ken Saro-Wiwa's imprisonment if you had had the opportunity.

• Each month new Worldwide Appeals are listed on Amnesty International's website. You might prefer to write your letter in support of one of these. Visit http://www.web.amnesty.org/web/wwa.nsf for further details.

A Sister to a Brother

1. Reading it aloud
• Working in pairs, first read the letter aloud to each other, sharing the reading.

• Now read it aloud again, choosing a tone of voice from the list below.

– Sad but able to cope
– Full of grief and uncertainty about what to do for the best
– Matter of fact, given that, living in the early nineteenth century, death is something that occurs quite frequently
– Perfectly cheerful

• Which tone seemed to you to suit the text best?

2. Emails and phone calls
Dorothy Wordsworth was writing at a time when there were no telephones, fax machines or email. How differently might she have communicated her thoughts, feelings and news if this modern technology had been available to her?

• Write an email from Dorothy to William. Decide what kinds of things might be left out. For instance, would she give her feelings? Would she describe things in as much detail? Would any bits of news or information be more important than others? Would the style be any different? (Before you begin writing, you might find it interesting to read 'The Last Post' by Madeleine Reiss and 'How to ... Use Email' by Guy Browning on pages 216-219.)

• Role-play a telephone conversation between Dorothy and William, in which Dorothy conveys her news and William responds. If possible tape record it so that you can listen back to it.

• Listen back to your tape, then look at the text again. Look at what kinds of things were left out of your telephone conversation (for example, feelings, or descriptions, or details of the main events)? What difference did it make to have someone responding?

3. Telling a story
Dorothy Wordsworth's letter tells the story of what has happened to the parents of her servant girl, Sally.
• Look closely at the telling of the story. It is told not as a story to excite or entertain the reader but rather as a series of events that the reader (William) will want to know about, given that he knows all the people involved.

• Try re-writing the story of Sally's family as a ballad, to be handed down to future generations as a tragic tale.

4. The social historian's view

Letters are a very good source of information about the past and are often used by historians researching a particular period or event. Letters can give insights into people's lives, their housing, work, standard of living, health and social relationships. Social historians are particularly interested in how society was organised and the details of life for ordinary people.

• If a social historian were reading Dorothy Wordsworth's letter, what would there be to interest him/her? Look through the letter and pick out any phrases which give you information or ideas about any of these areas of life.

Health and life expectancy
The poor and what support was provided for them
Media and communications
Work and employment rights
Childhood
Life in the countryside
Transport
Religion
Sense of community
Gender roles
Families and family life

Mira's Letters Home

1. Mira's first letter

• Read Mira's letter written on 18 October 1960, then try writing the first paragraph of Ma's reply to her. Now read Ma's actual reply.

2. What Mira wanted to say

• Read what Mira would have liked to write to her mother, in response to her letter of 10 December 1960.

• Imagine what Mira actually wrote to her mother, then read what she did write in reply. Does anything surprise you about what she actually wrote?

3. Changing attitudes

• Read Mira's next letter written in January 1961.

• Mira wrote again on 4th January 1962. Predict what kinds of things she might say to her parents in this letter.

4. Conflict of identity

• Read all of the other letters, except the last one.

• Look closely at the letter Mira wished she had written. Talk about the conflicts experienced by Mira. Is she entirely happy? What does she feel about India, America and her parents?

5. Mira's daughter

Mira and her American husband stay in America and have a daughter. At seventeen. she writes a letter to her mother. Talk about what Mira's daughter might write to her.

• Now read Mira's daughter's letter.

6. Ma and Babu

• Choose one of Mira's letters. Role-play the conversation between Ma and Babu, as they receive the letter.

7. Other voices

• Choose one of the people mentioned in the letters whose voice is not heard, for example Babu, John Cohn or Uma. Write a letter from that person to Mira, or the letter they would like to send to her.

8. A story told in letters

Mira's letters and her parents' replies tell the story of a girl's journey to a new country, the clash of cultures she experiences, her marriage and relationship with her daughter. It is not fiction. These are actual letters written by real people. In fiction, writers sometimes use the letter form to tell stories. Alice Walker's novel *The Color Purple*, for instance, is written entirely in letters.

• Try writing a story of your own, in which the characters, plot and issues are entirely revealed through letters. The titles below give some suggestions for the kinds of storylines or subject matter that might lend themselves to being told in letters.

The Old Man's Will
The Evacuee
The Prisoner
The Holiday Romance

Legalising Drugs – Letters to the Paper

See pages 61-63 in the 'Argument' section of this anthology for examples of and activities on letters written to a newspaper.

CITY AND ISLINGTON
SIXTH FORM COLLEGE
283-309 GOSWELL ROAD
LONDON EC1V 7LA
TEL 020 7520 0652

Sources

Klondyke Kate, Liza Cody, *The Independent*, 25 July 1992, reprinted in *Heroes and Villains*, Victor Gollancz, 1994

Boring, Boring Arsenal, Nick Hornby, from *Fever Pitch*, Victor Gollancz, 1992

Hating Football, Andrew O'Hagan, *London Review of Books*, 27 June 2002

Stud U-Like, Diane Taylor, *The Guardian*, 3 October 2000

Tattoos, Amalie Finlayson, *The Guardian*, 22 March 2002

How to be a Celebrity?, Rosemarie Jarski, from *How to be a Celebrity*, Ebury Press, 2002

On a Train, Paul Theroux, from *The Great Railway Bazaar*, Hamish Hamilton, 1977

Des Moines, Bill Bryson, from *The Lost Continent*, Abacus, 1992

Tokyo Pastoral, Angela Carter, *New Society*, reprinted in *Nothing Sacred*, Virago, 1992.

Travelling in Ireland, Pete McCarthy, from *McCarthy's Bar*, Sceptre 2000

The Toughest Trip, Don George, The Lonely Planet website (www.lonelyplanet.com) 8 May 2002

Legalising Drugs, Fulton Gillespie, *The Guardian*, 28 March 2002

Letters to the Paper, *The Daily Telegraph*, 24th-31st May 2002

Big Brother – a Boring Showcase for Exhibitionists, David Aaronovitch, *The Independent*, 9 August 2000

The Man With No Name, John Pilger, *New Statesman*, 1991, reprinted in *Distant Voices*, Vintage, 1992

Beggars of Britain, Tony Parsons, *Arena*, September/October 1991, reprinted in *Dispatches From the Front Line of Popular Culture*, Virgin, 1994

Gather Together in My Name, Maya Angelou, from *Gather Together in My Name*, Virago, 1974

And When Did You Last See Your Father?, Blake Morrison, from *And When Did You Last See Your Father?* Granta, 1993

Black Boy, Richard Wright, from *Black Boy*, Longman Imprint Books, 1970

A Passage to Africa, George Alagiah, from *A Passage to Africa*, Time Warner Books, 2001

Saroeun's Story, Saroeun Ing, from *More Lives*, English and Media Centre, 1987

Don't Let's Go to the Dogs Tonight, Alexandra Fuller, from *Don't Let's Go to the Dogs Tonight*, Picador, 2002

Bad Blood, Lorna Sage, from *Bad Blood*, 4th Estate, 2000

Arithmetic Town, Todd McEwen, from *Granta 55: Childhood*, Autumn 1996

The Eruption of Vesuvius, Pliny the Younger, from *Letters*, translated by Betty Radice, reprinted in *The Faber Book of Reportage*, Ed. John Carey, 1987

Beyond Belief, Ian McEwan, *The Guardian*, 12 September 2001

My Beating by Refugees, Robert Fisk, *The Independent*, 10 December 2001

On the Bottom, Primo Levi, from *If This is A Man*, and *The Truce*, translated by Stuart Woolf, Abacus by Sphere Books, 1987

Down and Out in Paris and London, George Orwell, from *Down and Out in Paris and London* (1933), this edition Penguin, 1993

Night Cleaner at the Savoy, Fran Abrams, *The Guardian*, 20 January 2002

Finding the Tollund Man, PV Glob, from *The Bog People*, Faber and Faber Ltd, 1969

The Tollund Man, Seamus Heaney, *Wintering Out*, Faber and Faber Ltd, 1972

The Secret Life of Chips, William Leith, *The Observer*, 10 February 2002

Find It, A.J. Kennedy, from *The Rough Guide to the Internet*, 2002

Interrogation, Greg Fallis, from *Just the Facts Ma'am*, Writer's Digest Books, 1998

Black Holes, Isaac Asimov, from *The Roving Mind*, Prometheus Books, 1983, reprinted in *The Faber Book of Science*, Ed. John Carey, 1996

How to Write a Letter, Garrison Keillor, from *We Are Still Married*, Faber and Faber, 1989

The Last Post, Madeleine Reiss, *The Guardian*, 24 August 2002

How to ... Use Email, Guy Browning, *The Guardian*, 27 July 2002

A Last Letter, Sir Walter Ralegh, from *The Faber Book of Letters*, Ed. Felix Pryor, Faber and Faber, 1990

A Prison Letter, Ken Saro-Wiwa, *The Mail and Guardian* (South Africa), May 1995

A Sister to a Brother, Dorothy Wordsworth, from *Letters*, Penguin

Mira's Letters Home, from *Between Ourselves, Letters between Mothers and Daughters*, Ed. Karen Payne, Virago, 1994